VISIBLE LEARNING
in Early Childhood

VISIBLE LEARNING
in Early Childhood

KATERI THUNDER
JOHN ALMARODE
JOHN HATTIE

FOR INFORMATION:

Corwin

A SAGE Company

2455 Teller Road

Thousand Oaks, California 91320

(800) 233–9936

www.corwin.com

SAGE Publications Ltd.

1 Oliver's Yard

55 City Road

London EC1Y 1SP

United Kingdom

SAGE Publications India Pvt. Ltd.

B 1/I 1 Mohan Cooperative Industrial Area

Mathura Road, New Delhi 110 044

India

SAGE Publications Asia-Pacific Pte. Ltd.

18 Cross Street #10–10/11/12

China Square Central

Singapore 048423

President: Mike Soules

Associate Vice President and

    Editorial Director: Monica Eckman

Publisher: Jessica Allan

Senior Content

    Development Editor: Lucas Schleicher

Associate Content

    Development Editor: Mia Rodriguez

Production Editor: Tori Mirsadjadi

Copy Editor: Christina West

Typesetter: C&M Digitals (P) Ltd.

Cover Designer: Rose Storey

Marketing Manager: Olivia Bartlett

Library of Congress Cataloging-in-Publication Data

Names: Thunder, Kateri, author. | Almarode, John, author. | Hattie, John, author.

Title: Visible learning in early childhood / Kateri Thunder, John Almarode, John Hattie.

Description: Thousand Oaks, California : Corwin, [2022] | Includes bibliographical references and index.

Identifiers: LCCN 2021029975 | ISBN 9781071825686 (paperback) | ISBN 9781071825716 (epub) | ISBN 9781071825709 (epub) | ISBN 9781071825693 (pdf)

Subjects: LCSH: Visual learning. | Early childhood education.

Classification: LCC LB1067.5 .T58 2022 | DDC 372.21—dc23

LC record available at https://lccn.loc.gov/2021029975

Printed in the United States of America

This book is printed on acid-free paper.

21 22 23 24 25 10 9 8 7 6 5 4 3 2

Contents

Visit the companion website at
resources.corwin.com/VLforEarlyChildhood
for downloadable resources.

Note From the Publisher: The authors have provided video and web content throughout the book that is available to you through QR (quick response) codes. To read a QR code, you must have a smartphone or tablet with a camera. We recommend that you download a QR code reader app that is made specifically for your phone or tablet brand.

Videos may also be accessed at **resources.corwin.com/VLforEarlyChildhood**

List of Videos

This library of videos captures a vision for Visible Learning® in early childhood classrooms (ages 3–6) as well as a vertical view of Visible Learning through Grade 12. Through the video footage, you are welcomed into classrooms across the United States where educators are striving to implement Visible Learning research in their actual classrooms with their actual learners. As you know, no two days are the same in the classroom. These videos are simply snapshots of teachers' interactions with learners and their reflections as they engage in intentional teaching and learning. We hope they give you an "in-the-moment" perspective for what Visible Learning can look like and sound like.

This video library is also available online at **resources.corwin.com/VLforEarlyChildhood**. As we gather additional footage from early childhood classrooms across the globe, we will share these on the website.

The videos in Table V.1 capture big ideas about Visible Learning in the early childhood classroom and beyond. As you read, watch these videos to further unpack and make sense of the big ideas within the practical context of classrooms.

TABLE V.1

QR CODE	VIDEO TITLE	VIDEO DESCRIPTION
From *Teaching Literacy in the Visible Learning Classroom, Grades K–5*, Video 5	Visible Learners: "What I Learned Today"	Let's begin with a clear picture of visible learners. When teaching is intentional and learning is purposeful, children can take ownership over their learning journeys. What do visible learners sound like?
From *Teaching Mathematics in the Visible Learning Classroom, Grades K–2*, Video 2	Creating Assessment-Capable Visible Learners	Our goal is to grow visible learners. Visible learners demonstrate six characteristics. To reach our goal, our focus must be on learning.

To read a QR code, you must have a smartphone or tablet with a camera. We recommend that you download a QR code reader app that is made specifically for your phone or tablet brand.

QR CODE	VIDEO TITLE	VIDEO DESCRIPTION
From *Teaching Mathematics in the Visible Learning Classroom, Grades K–2*, Video 3	What Does Teacher Clarity Mean in K–2 Mathematics?	Teacher clarity is communicating the what, why, and how of learning. Through teacher clarity, educators partner with young learners to intentionally communicate and make sense of learning intentions and success criteria.
From *Visible Learning for Science, Grades K–12*, Video 1.2	Balancing Surface, Deep, and Transfer Learning	As learners progress toward mastery, they go through three phases of learning: surface, deep, and transfer learning. We need to select the right instructional strategy at the right time to meet each learner where they are and help move them forward through the phases.
From *Visible Learning for Literacy, Grades K–12*, Video 2.2	Surface, Deep, and Transfer Learning: Kindergarten	Step into a kindergarten (5-year-old) classroom to see children engaged in surface, deep, and transfer learning through a read-aloud.
From *Teaching Mathematics in the Visible Learning Classroom, Grades K–2*, Video 8	Student Modeling Through a Think-Aloud	Watch a 4-year-old learner teach his class by modeling and thinking aloud. See learning intentions and success criteria communicated through the learner's model and think-aloud as well as visuals.
From *Visible Learning for Science, Grades K–12*, Video 1.7	Making Learning Clear for Students	See a 3-year-old classroom with success criteria displays to support both teachers and learners' intentional engagement.
From *Visible Learning for Mathematics, Grades K–12*, Video 2.1	Learning Intentions in the Elementary Classroom	Mathematics is mathematical content, practices, and dispositions. Learning intentions should reflect all three. Watch a kindergarten teacher engage children in making sense of learning intentions based on mathematical practices.

(Continued)

TABLE V.1 ● (Continued)

QR CODE	VIDEO TITLE	VIDEO DESCRIPTION
From *Visible Learning for Mathematics, Grades K–12*, Video 2.3	Achieving Teacher Clarity With Success Criteria	Communicating and making sense of learning intentions and success criteria is key for effective learning. Concrete materials, language, and collaboration can make success criteria clear.
From *Visible Learning for Science, Grades K–12*, Video 1.6	Discussion in the Science Classroom	Before we engage with children through conversation, we need to listen. This teacher values listening to her 3-year-old learners as the starting point for all of her instruction.
From *Visible Learning for Mathematics, Grades K–12*, Video 4.5 (0:00–1:53)	Vocabulary to Solidify Surface Learning	Language is the linchpin of learning in early childhood. In this kindergarten classroom, the teacher intentionally engages children in learning mathematical vocabulary in order to solidify their learning in the surface phase.
From *Visible Learning for Science, Grades K–12*, Video 2.3	Making Science Surface Learning Visible	See 3-year-olds engage in deliberate vocabulary instruction and practice in science.
From *Visible Learning for Mathematics, Grades K–12*, Video 3.2	Questioning That Guides Learning	Teacher questioning is another way to facilitate language and conversation as well as scaffold meta-cognitive strategies.
From *Visible Learning for Mathematics, Grades K–12*, Video 3.3	Student Discourse That Builds Understanding	Talk is critical in early childhood language development. When children talk with each other, they build understanding. Here is a kindergarten class engaged in mathematical discussion.

QR CODE	VIDEO TITLE	VIDEO DESCRIPTION
From *Visible Learning for Science, Grades K–12*, Video 1.4	Student Engagement Through Active Learning	Intentional learning is relevant to young learners, facilitates the making of connections, and sparks conversation. These 3-year-old scientists are active visible learners.
From *Visible Learning for Science, Grades K–12*, Video 4.3	Transferring Scientific Processes to Science Learning	Through language and learning experiences with the developmentally appropriate or right level of challenge, this teacher engages her 3-year-old learners in meaningful scientific content and processes.
From *Teaching Mathematics in the Visible Learning Classroom, Grades K–2*, Video 7	A Model for Structuring a Conceptual Lesson	Visible Learning is a method and a mindset. In this Visible Learning prekindergarten classroom, watch and listen as the teacher explains how she uses Visible Learning to create lesson structures and engage intentionally with learners in math.
From *Teaching Mathematics in the Visible Learning Classroom, Grades K–2*, Video 9	Using Guided Questions to Clarify and Extend Understanding	As 4-year-olds work on math tasks, watch their teacher ask questions aligned with the learning intentions and success criteria in order to make learning intentional.
From *Teaching Mathematics in the Visible Learning Classroom, Grades K–2*, Video 10	Feedback Without Taking Over the Thinking	Feedback is a critical piece of Visible Learning classrooms. In this 4-year-old classroom, watch the teacher interact with a learner, provide feedback, and engage her in meta-cognitive strategies.
From *Teaching Mathematics in the Visible Learning Classroom, Grades K–2*, Video 11	Building Meta-Cognition	Early childhood educators and their learners work together as evaluators of learning growth. Listen as these prekindergartners demonstrate their growth as visible learners who know their current level of understanding and can communicate what they do and do not yet know.

(Continued)

TABLE V.1 • (Continued)

QR CODE	VIDEO TITLE	VIDEO DESCRIPTION
From *Visible Learning for Science, Grades K–12*, Video 3.3	Effective Feedback	Watch 3-year-olds engage with feedback through discourse and practice meta-cognitive skills.
From *Visible Learning for Mathematics, Grades K–12*, Video 5.3	Grouping Strategies for Deep Learning	Formative evaluation can help drive next instruction, including identifying small groups of children who are ready for similar levels of challenge.

The videos in Table V.2 provide a picture of a whole lesson from planning to implementation to reflection and planning for the next day. Watch this series of videos to see both the method and mindset of Visible Learning in action in a kindergarten mathematics classroom. Note: All videos in Table V.2 are from *Teaching Mathematics in the Visible Learning Classroom, Grades K–2*.

TABLE V.2

QR CODE	VIDEO TITLE	VIDEO DESCRIPTION
Video 12	Choosing the Right Task for Procedural Knowledge	Listen as this kindergarten teacher shares her planning process, including creating learning intentions and success criteria, selecting a task, and intentionally planning each component of her lesson: mini-lesson, worktime with conferences, and sharing.
Video 13	Setting the Stage for Procedural Learning	See the mini-lesson.
Video 14	Supporting Procedural Learning and Checking for Understanding	Follow the teacher as she interacts with the children while they work.

QR CODE	VIDEO TITLE	VIDEO DESCRIPTION
Video 15	Differentiating Procedural Learning	Watch the teacher adjust the task so that each learner engages at the right level of challenge at the right time.
Video 16	Assessing Student Progress and Planning Next Steps	Sit in on a planning conversation after the lesson as the teacher analyzes student work and uses her conference notes for formative evaluation and planning the next day's lesson.

The videos in Table V.3 offer a unique opportunity to watch peer tutoring in action within an early childhood classroom. Peer tutoring is effective when

- The program is structured,
- The tutors receive training, and
- The tutor and the tutee are different ages.

When these three conditions are met, the effect of learning through peer tutoring is as high on the tutor (the learner tutoring) as it is on the tutee (the learner being tutored) (Hattie et al., 2017). Watch a class of fourth-grade learners engage in training before working with a class of 4-year-olds. See the mini-lesson, work time, and sharing structure of the program. Hear the teachers of each class discuss how they collaborate to plan learning intentions and success criteria that are just right for each class. Note: All videos in Table V.3 are from *Teaching Mathematics in the Visible Learning Classroom, Grades 3–5.*

TABLE V.3

QR CODE	VIDEO TITLE	VIDEO DESCRIPTION
Video 16	Setting the Stage for Transfer	See the fourth-grade mini-lesson— the tutors' training session.
Video 17	Scaffolding Learning in a Transfer Lesson	Watch the fourth-grade tutors engage intentionally with the prekindergarten tutees.

Acknowledgments

Each day, the challenging and complicated, messy and miraculous, hilarious and busy work of teaching young learners is met with passion, kindness, and brilliance by early childhood educators around the world. We are thankful for their daily work to make an impact in the lives of young learners.

Educators in Charlottesville and Orange, Virginia, and in Auburn, Alabama, graciously opened their classroom doors to us. Spending time in the classroom spaces of these educators is inspiring. Being welcomed into conversations about their decision-making processes is an honor. Their interactions with young learners provide a vision for the complexity and possibility of early childhood education. The openness of these educators allowed us to make Visible Learning in early childhood visible to readers:

- Ms. Alisha Demchak, Kindergarten Teacher, Charlottesville City Schools, Virginia

- Ms. Cheryl Lamb, Head Start Teacher, Orange County Public Schools, Virginia

- Ms. Calder McLellan, Mathematics Specialist, Charlottesville City Schools, Virginia

- Ms. Katie Witthauer Murrah, Owner and Director of Auburn Day School, Alabama

It is a privilege to strive toward making learning visible alongside exceptional early childhood educators. Ms. Robyn Davis and Ms. Kelly Bullock are phenomenal early childhood teachers in Charlottesville City Schools in Virginia. Dr. Charlie Heaton is an extraordinary principal of Aspire Inskeep Academy in Los Angeles, California. We are forever thankful for these educators' willingness to make their practice visible to us so that we can envision the Visible Learning early childhood classroom and share that vision with you.

We are extremely grateful to Drs. Tricia Eadie and Nicola Yelland, professors at the University of Melbourne, for their insights and feedback to make our work international and accessible.

About the Authors

Kateri Thunder, PhD, served as an inclusive, early childhood educator, an Upward Bound educator, a mathematics specialist, an assistant professor of mathematics education at James Madison University, and Site Director for the Central Virginia Writing Project (a National Writing Project site at the University of Virginia). Kateri is an author for Corwin's *Visible Learning for Mathematics* series, a member of the National Council of Teachers of Mathematics' Research Committee and of the Writing Across the Curriculum Research Team with Dr. Jane Hansen, co-author of *The Promise of Qualitative Metasynthesis for Mathematics Education* with Dr. Robert Berry, and co-creator of *The Math Diet*. Currently, Kateri has followed her passion back to the classroom. She teaches prekindergarten, serves as the PreK–4 Math Lead for Charlottesville City Schools, and works as an educational consultant. Kateri is happiest exploring the world with her best friend and husband, Adam, their daughter, Anna Rixey, and family. Kateri can be reached at www.mathplusliteracy.com.

John Almarode, PhD, has worked with schools, classrooms, and teachers all over the world. John began his career teaching mathematics and science in Augusta County to a wide range of students. Since then, he has presented locally, nationally, and internationally on the application of the science of learning to the classroom, school, and home environments. He has worked with hundreds of school districts and thousands of teachers. In addition to his time in PreK–12 schools and classrooms, he is an Associate Professor and Executive Director of Teaching and Learning in the College of Education at

James Madison University. At JMU, he works with preservice teachers and actively pursues his research interests, including the science of learning and the design and measurement of classroom environments that promote student engagement and learning. John and his colleagues have presented their work to the United States Congress, the United States Department of Education, as well as the Office of Science and Technology Policy at The White House. John has authored multiple articles, reports, book chapters, and over a dozen books on effective teaching and learning in today's schools and classrooms. However, what really sustains John and is his greatest accomplishment is his family. John lives in Waynesboro, Virginia, with his wife Danielle, a fellow educator, their two children, Tessa and Jackson, and Labrador retrievers, Bella and Dukes. John can be reached at www.johnalmarode.com.

John Hattie, PhD, is an award-winning education researcher and best-selling author with nearly 30 years of experience examining what works best in student learning and achievement. His research, better known as Visible Learning, is a culmination of nearly 30 years synthesizing more than 1,500 meta-analyses comprising more than 90,000 studies involving over 300 million students around the world. He has presented and keynoted in over 350 international conferences and has received numerous recognitions for his contributions to education. His notable publications include *Visible Learning, Visible Learning for Teachers, Visible Learning and the Science of How We Learn, Visible Learning for Mathematics, Grades K–12,* and, most recently, *10 Mindframes for Visible Learning.*

Introduction

Early childhood education is a place where we have the opportunity to begin teaching and learning on the right path from the very start. We can grow independent learners who value their identities and the funds of knowledge they bring to learning (Hammond, 2015; Vélez-Ibáñez & Greenberg, 1992). We can create spaces where young learners understand where they are going, have confidence to take on challenges, and recognize that they are also teachers themselves (Frey et al., 2018). We can interact with young learners in ways that expand and deepen their thinking and language while sharing with them the ownership of their learning journeys. We can form partnerships and community among all children and their families. To get it right from the very start, we have to appreciate and understand the developmental stage of early childhood and the complexity of effective teaching in early childhood education. And then, we have to strive toward that vision.

We hold the utmost respect for educators of young learners. Kateri has worked as an early childhood, elementary, and high school educator as well as a mathematics specialist, an interventionist, an education professor, and an education consultant. Kateri then followed her passion back into the classroom to spend every day working out the puzzle of learning with her 4-year-olds. John Almarode, drawing from his work with schools and classrooms across the globe, teaches methods courses in the Inclusive Early Childhood and Elementary Education Programs at James Madison University. This allows him the opportunity to bridge the gap between theory and practice for the next generation of early childhood educators. And John Hattie has devoted over 30 years to understanding and capturing *what works best in education* and how to leverage that research through implementation in the classroom. Through this book, we want to dig in deep and stretch high with you. Teaching young learners is challenging and complicated, messy and miraculous, hilarious and busy. In this book, we want to celebrate the complexities and unpack the decision points. We want to make learning about effective early childhood education visible so that together we can create Visible Learning classrooms. Let's explore more of our vision for early childhood education in Visible Learning classrooms.

Each developmental stage presents unique qualities to capitalize on within instruction. Early childhood is a developmental stage uniquely sensitive to development across multiple domains, including language, literacy, mathematics, executive functioning, social and emotional skills, reasoning, problem solving, and fine and gross motor skills. Development across these domains is interwoven and concurrent. Our instructional decisions can maximize this development when we foster integrated and meaningful connections across domains and tap into the brain's plasticity for growth. Integration remains an important piece of meaningful and engaging learning throughout our lives. In early childhood, we can use integration to communicate the value of children's experiences and the cognitive routine of always building upon what children already know.

At every developmental stage, we have the opportunity to engage students as lifelong learners. Early childhood is particularly poised to lay this foundation of wonder and ownership over the learning journey. Young learners, ages 3–6 years, are just beginning to explore who they are in relationship to school and learning. Our instructional decisions can reflect back to children a vision of themselves as confident, capable, and meta-cognitive learners.

And so, just like every other grade and subject, our decisions as educators matter in early childhood. We need to know what works best when, and we need to make instructional decisions that align with this research. When we do, we maximize learning.

WHAT WORKS BEST

As early childhood educators, we make myriad decisions each day about what content, skills, and understandings we want our young students to learn. In addition, we have to design and implement learning experiences that engage learners in the content, skills, and understandings. We make decisions about how much time to spend on specific topics and how frequently to engage learners in those topics. We assess learners' progress and decide when to intervene, on what, and at what level of intensity. We have intuitive ideas from decades of working with young children, experiential ideas from our own learning and from observing other educators, and a trove of traditional early childhood experiences from which to draw on. However, it is also our responsibility as educators to leverage our professional expertise through the identification and implementation of evidence-based approaches and then to continually seek evidence of the impact of our decisions on student learning (Hattie et al., 2021). This responsibility requires that we make learning visible.

The Visible Learning research reaches beyond our experiences, traditions, and observations to examine and consider variances across learners and contexts. How should we spend our precious time with these young learners? Within a unit of study and a learner's progress toward mastery, which instructional approach or strategy should we use and when should we use it? The Visible Learning research helps us answer these questions and make these decisions—decisions based on *what works best*.

VISIBLE LEARNING

Enter Visible Learning. The *Visible Learning* database is composed of more than 1,800 meta-analyses, with more than 100,000 studies and 300 million students.

Visible Learning database

The *Visible Learning* database is a synthesis of meta-analyses. A meta-analysis is a statistical tool for combining findings from different studies with the goal of identifying patterns that can inform the collective work of teachers and leaders. In other words, meta-analyses are studies of studies. Take, for example, the role of discovery learning in moving learning forward. Administrators and teachers could easily find a study that suggests discovery learning has a positive influence on young children's learning. Tomorrow, they may find a study that presents an opposite finding. Remember, the challenging and complicated, messy and miraculous, hilarious and busy nature of teaching in the early childhood classroom leaves little time to referee disputes in academic journals. So, what is an educator to do? A synthesis of meta-analyses analyzes the collective findings from the studies on discovery learning to unpack the overall trends in these findings. In other words, what does the combined research say, in this case, about discovery learning?

However, the story behind the findings is not solely based on whether the findings were positive or negative or found no influence on learning. Instead, meta-analyses look at the magnitude of the influence as well (e.g., how positive, how negative, and compared to what). The tool that is used to aggregate the information from these combined studies and calculate magnitude is known as an effect size. An effect size is the magnitude, or size, of a given effect. Effect size information helps readers understand the impact in more measurable terms. For example, imagine a study in which teaching young children while having them sit on an exercise ball resulted in statistically significant findings ($p < 0.01$, for example). People might remodel all of their early childhood classrooms to include exercise balls, and stock in companies that sell these to schools or centers would skyrocket. It might even become common and accepted educational practice for all early childhood classrooms to be supplied with exercise balls.

But then suppose, upon deeper reading, you learned that the exercise balls had a 0.01-month gain over the control group, an effect size pretty close to zero. You also learn that the sample size was very large, and the results were statistically significant because of this large sample size, even though the impact was not very valuable. Would you still limit seating in your early childhood classroom or center to exercise balls? Probably not (and we made this example up, anyway). The meta-research seeks out those factors we may need to consider that lead to higher or lower effects on young children's learning. The takeaway message is that this approach to research helps administrators and teachers make better decisions in their schools and classrooms by focusing on both the impact and the magnitude of that impact.

> To have the biggest impact on student learning in the early childhood classroom, we must build our professional knowledge around those things that have the potential for the greatest impact on our students' learning.

Understanding the concept of an effect size lets us know how potentially powerful a given influence is in changing achievement, or said another way, the return on investment for a particular approach. Some things are hard to implement in our schools and classrooms and have very little impact. Other things are easy to implement and still have limited impact. To have the biggest impact on student learning in the early childhood classroom, we must build our professional knowledge around those things that have the potential for the greatest impact on our students' learning. Some of these will be harder to implement and some will be easier to implement with 3-year-olds up to 6-year-olds. Knowing the effect size would allow you to decide if a particular influence, strategy, or action has the potential to accelerate student learning.

But what is the threshold for "worth it" and "not worth it"? At what point does an effect size indicate a large impact and at what point does an effect size indicate a limited impact? We use the average of all effects as a first guide: an effect size of 0.40 or greater. The average growth in learning resulting from 1 year's worth of formal school was found to be 0.40. Thus, influences, approaches, strategies, and actions with an effect size greater than 0.40 indicate the potential to learn at a rate greater than that expected from 1 year's worth of formal schooling. We need to be a little cautious, as many of the effects are based on data not only from early childhood but also across school years, and the more important consideration is to find patterns among those effects higher and lower than the 0.40 hinge point. This hinge point or threshold provides the basis for the Barometer of Influence shown in Figure 0.1.

Before this level was established, educators and researchers did not have a way to determine an acceptable threshold; thus, weak practices, often with studies that were statistically significant, continued. In other words, educators and researchers advocated for practices that showed a positive and statistically significant relationship with learning but did not equate to a year of growth for a year in school. Yes, sometimes these lower effects may lead us to raise our eyebrows—and maybe, if they are lower than we expect, we should be asking, "Why are they so low?" Answering this question can then help us modify our implementation of a practice aiming to raise the effect on student learning. An effect that is less than 0.40 does not mean we "throw it away" but it should make us pause and ask, "Why would this be so low?" Caution then is the name of the game for such low influences.

FIGURE 0.1 ● Barometer of Influence

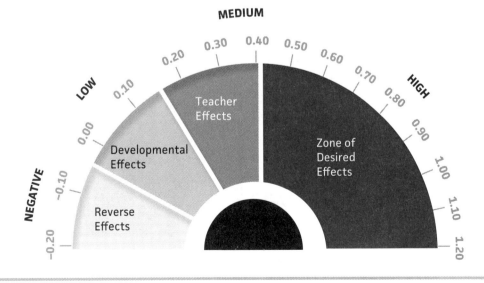

Let's take two real examples. There have been countless numbers of conversations in schools about reading instruction and whether whole-language or phonics instruction curricula are best. First, let's consider a whole-language approach to reading. The barometer reading for the whole-language approach to reading can be found in Figure 0.2.

As you can see, the effect size is 0.09, well below the hinge point or threshold of 0.40. This is based on five meta-analyses, with 81 studies that examined 288 effects (Visible Learning Meta[x], 2021). While some studies show a positive effect, Jeynes and Littell (2000) found a negative effect size (–0.65) for learners with low socioeconomic status. Thus, whole-language reading is likely to have minimal to no impact on the growth and achievement of readers in our early childhood classroom, and for some learners it is quite detrimental. In fact, the 0.09 effect size is within the range of growth and development effects, meaning that this small effect size is likely due to development and not the intervention of whole-language reading.

Second, let's consider phonics instruction—often viewed as the other side of the argument in reading instruction. Phonics instruction stresses the acquisition of letter-sound correspondences in reading and spelling. Specifically, phonics instruction involves teaching children the sounds made by individual letters or letter groups (for example, the letter "c" makes a /k/

FIGURE 0.2 ● Barometer of Influence for Whole-Language Reading

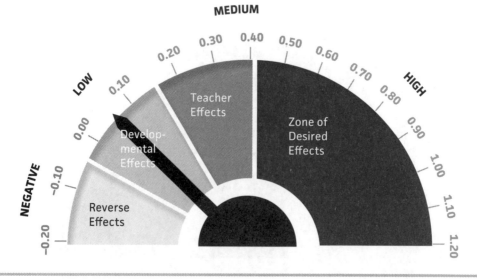

FIGURE 0.3 ● Barometer of Influence for Phonics Instruction

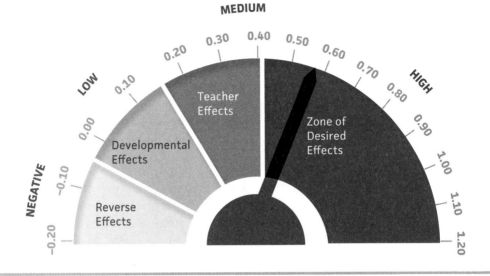

sound) and teaching children how to merge separate sounds together to make one word (for example, blending the sounds /k/, /a/, /t/ makes CAT). As can be seen in the barometer in Figure 0.3, the effect size is 0.57, well above the hinge point or threshold, and has the potential to accelerate reading in our early childhood classroom.

This finding is generated from 536 studies that examined 2,090 effect sizes from 13 meta-analyses (Visible Learning Meta[x], 2021). Thus, as early childhood educators, we would be wise to focus our energy on this approach given its potential to have a high impact on our young children's reading growth and achievement. (We will look more deeply at literacy in the Visible Learning early childhood classroom in Chapter 4.)

THE POTENTIAL FOR IMPACT

The *Visible Learning* database has been useful in identifying what has the potential to work best in our early childhood classrooms. A lot of things work. But some things work better than others. The good news is that 95% of the influences, approaches, strategies, or actions early childhood educators use work when our threshold is zero and we simply ask, "Can we improve young children's learning?" In this case, we are only looking for an influence, approach, strategy, or action that yields a positive outcome. However, this sets the bar low. We should not simply be striving for a positive impact. We should purposefully, deliberately, and intentionally strive to accelerate our students' learning, across all domains, to at least 1 year's worth of growth for 1 year's input. What we set out to do over the next several chapters is focus on what works best. This requires us to move beyond a list of influences and simply checking the ones with an effect size greater than 0.40. Instead, we must build a story to make sense of the many underlying and overlapping, high-impact influences.

> We should purposefully, deliberately, and intentionally strive to accelerate our students' learning, across all domains, to at least 1 year's worth of growth for 1 year's input.

You may have noticed that we use the word *potential* when referring to effect sizes and the interpretation of the magnitude of those effect sizes (e.g., potential to have a high impact, potential to accelerate, etc.). *Visible Learning in Early Childhood* requires not just knowing what works best but also ensuring high-quality implementation in the local context of our early childhood settings. We have to make the necessary adaptions based on the local context and then continually monitor our impact on student learning. The greatest effects on children's learning come from the expertise of the early childhood educator. The most powerful influence on our young learners comes from the dispositions and skills to implement what works best and evaluate our impact on students. This means we do not subscribe to favorite influences, approaches, strategies, or actions. We must use the list as we design learning experiences that implement what works best in teaching and learning. However, this implementation requires these learning experiences to be designed with purpose and intention, driven by where learners begin in their learning and where they need to go next in their learning. In the subsequent chapters of this book, we engage in thinking about teaching and learning that reflects the following seven big ideas:

> The greatest effects on children's learning come from the expertise of the early childhood educator.

1. Early childhood educators and their learners work together as evaluators of learning growth. (Effect Size = 1.32)

2. Early childhood educators and learners have high expectations for learning. (Effect Size = 0.90)

3. Learning experiences move learning toward explicit success criteria. (Effect Size = 0.77)

4. Learning experiences and tasks have the developmentally appropriate level or right level of challenge. (Effect Size = 0.74)

5. Trust is established so that errors and mistakes are viewed as opportunities for new learning. (Effect Size = 0.72)

6. Early childhood educators are continually seeking feedback about their impact on their students' learning. (Effect Size = 0.72)

7. There is the right balance of surface and deep learning in the early childhood classroom. (Effect Size = 0.69) (Rickards et al., 2021)

These seven big ideas help us navigate some of the most compelling questions about early childhood education. Should early childhood instruction emphasize social-emotional learning or academic learning? Meta-cognitive strategies (0.60), self-regulation strategies (0.54), and effort management (0.77) each have effect sizes with the potential to considerably accelerate student achievement. Teaching specific skills mathematics (0.58), science (0.55), phonics (0.57), and vocabulary (0.63) also have effect sizes that hold high potential for improving student achievement. Rather than asking either-or questions, the Visible Learning research redirects us to consider our decisions about integrating social-emotional learning with academic content and then collaboratively evaluate learning growth with our young learners. Both are important and can be taught with high expectations, the right level of challenge, and a focus on explicit success criteria in a learning environment that welcomes mistakes and strikes the ideal balance between surface and deep learning. We will unpack this symbiotic relationship in Chapters 2–7.

Another compelling question in early childhood teaching and learning is about the role of play. Should play be the central focus of early childhood learning? We argue that the pivotal component of early childhood learning is language (Lillard et al., 2013). Interactions and language embedded in play and in all learning tasks maximize learners' growth. Play is both motivating and engaging, but the conversation, the discussion, and the use of language (classroom discussion, 0.82) are uniquely important for children's development. Without language and interaction, play loses its power. We will examine the role of play and playful learning more closely in Chapter 2.

Should early childhood be treated as unique and separate from primary and secondary school learning? While early childhood presents unique qualities, we also know that the benefits of early childhood learning can fade with time (Cooper et al., 2010; Gilliam & Zigler, 2000). By themselves, Head Start programs (0.33) and preschool programs (0.38) are not enough. Rather than creating a divide between early childhood and primary school to protect its uniqueness, we need to intentionally align early childhood instruction with primary instruction to create a continuous, seamless, and strong foundation that sustains the gains made and leads to better long-term learning outcomes (Stipek et al., 2017). Coherent practices (classroom cohesion, 0.53) can counter the fade of effects by implementing common instructional frameworks, common curricula, common assessment systems, common professional learning, opportunities for cross-grade teacher collaboration, and administrator knowledge, support, and communication across grade levels (Stipek et al., 2017). We will examine this developmentally appropriate alignment moving from early childhood to primary school in each chapter through the lens of two educators (Ms. Demchak and Ms. Murrah) as they collaborate in a vertical professional learning community.

Should early childhood instruction take place in family childcare programs or in day-care centers? Should young learners attend half-day or full-day kindergarten? Should early childhood instruction take place face-to-face or through distance learning? The Visible Learning research shows that it hardly matters (family childcare program or day-care center, 0.10; half- vs. full-day kindergarten, 0.18; face-to-face or distance learning, 0.17). This means there is not a significant difference in impact on learners' achievement whether instruction takes place in family childcare or day-care centers, during half-day or full-day kindergarten, or face-to-face or at a distance. It is what you do within the learning setting and with the time you have that becomes more important. While the format may not be in our control as educators, so many much more important factors are within our control, such as teacher clarity (0.84), teacher expectations (0.42), and teacher–student relationships (0.47). In other words, the time or setting does not matter as much. What does matter are the teaching and learning strategies we choose to use in those contexts.

WHAT WORKS BEST WHEN

As learners progress toward mastery, some teaching and learning strategies are more effective than others. Children need different types of support and engagement to maximize learning at each step. The Visible Learning research can answer the question: What works best when?

For example, often we debate whether to engage young learners in deliberate instruction or inquiry-based instruction. Instead, we should ask: *When* should we engage learners in deliberate and inquiry-based instruction? Let's take a moment and look at how the Visible Learning research can help us answer this question.

When learners are initially making sense of new concepts, we should use deliberate instruction to explicitly teach important vocabulary, ask guiding questions, and model concrete manipulatives. These instructional strategies build the foundational language and ideas learners need to begin talking about and making sense of new concepts. If we wait to use deliberate instruction, learners may flounder because they lack familiarity with the language and the physical models that support making sense of concepts deeply. Using the right instructional strategy at the right time creates opportunities for these initial ideas to be deepened and broadened.

When learners are ready to apply their deep understanding of a concept to new contexts, we should use inquiry-based instruction to support this transfer. Learners can rely on the many connections among ideas that they have built to explore similarities and differences, to problem solve, to think meta-cognitively, and to collaborate with peers. If we use these strategies too early, learners may not have the understanding, tools, and language to meaningfully engage in the openness of inquiry. Using the right instructional strategy at the right time places learners in the "just-right" space with the "just-right" challenge where they can use what they know to move toward mastery.

Recognizing where our learners are along their learning path and selecting instructional strategies to match can help us foster independent learners. In Chapters 2–7, we will see early childhood educators make decisions about using the right instructional strategies at the right time as their learners work—again, continually monitoring their impact.

 ## HOW THIS BOOK WORKS

Early childhood is defined as birth through 8 years of age. Within early childhood, children's experiences with learning programs vary. For the sake of this book, we focus on the learning experiences of children ages 3–6 years. When we use the term "early childhood," we are specifically targeting this pre-compulsory schooling phase. There are a wide variety of early childhood settings, including early learning centers, nursery schools, preschools, day-care centers, family care programs, primary schools, and elementary schools, where children can be grouped by age and grade or they can be in multiage

> Recognizing where our learners are along their learning path and selecting instructional strategies to match can help us foster independent learners.

classrooms. The settings featured in this book represent children's learning across these early childhood contexts, and we refer to them all as classrooms.

Regardless of the setting, inclusivity has a significant role in early childhood. Early childhood classrooms are spaces where all children are included with strengths to share and countless opportunities to learn with and from each other. Each classroom we enter into over the next several chapters will be filled with children from diverse experiences and backgrounds, with and without special needs, and who speak a variety of first, second, and even third languages.

The importance of inclusivity extends to another vital feature of early childhood classrooms: the family. Partnerships, relationships, and community are pivotal to including families in classroom life and including schools in family life. The classrooms featured in this book interweave family interactions intentionally into their daily work.

Much work has been done on the developmental stages of young children. Whether cognitive, social, emotional, behavioral, psychomotor, or language development, researchers have provided amazing insight into what this development looks like across the span of early childhood. This book does not focus on this research, but instead leverages these seminal findings and translates them into what works best in supporting this development in the early childhood learning environment.

In Chapter 1, we share our vision for intentional teaching, or teaching with clarity, in early childhood and establish a common language for talking about what this looks like and sounds like in practice. When teaching is intentional and learning is purposeful, children can take ownership over their learning journeys. When we make learning visible, children can describe what they are learning, why they are learning it, and how they will know when they are successful. We examine the ways educators partner with young learners to intentionally communicate and make sense of learning intentions and success criteria. We explore the three phases of learning (surface, deep, and transfer) and the ways we can support learners' movement through the phases of learning by selecting the right strategy at the right time. We also introduce the five early childhood educators we will follow throughout the book.

In Chapter 2, we unpack the research on play in early childhood education. We examine the significant qualities of playful learning and the resounding importance of language in play and in every aspect of early childhood learning. Children know intuitively what they are trying and testing, why, and what they envision success will look like. Through interactions and language, this intuitive knowledge becomes explicit: young children can describe what they are learning, why they are learning it, and how they will know when they are successful. We will follow educators into their classrooms to see and hear how young learners engage in units of study as the educators intentionally capitalize on their playful learning.

In Chapters 3–7, we take a similar approach of unpacking what the research tells us is critical for early childhood learning in mathematics, literacy, understanding the world, social and emotional development, the arts, and motor skills. Then we experience this research in action inside early childhood classrooms. When teaching is intentional and learning is purposeful, children can take ownership over their learning journeys. Educators make learning visible through the contexts they create. We will unpack the intentional decisions educators make as they create contexts that facilitate mastery learning, including the tools and materials as well as the language and interactions. We will refer to the vignettes to highlight examples of these decision points. Each content area is highlighted within a unique chapter in order to elucidate content-specific research and instructional decisions as well as the intersection of Visible Learning research with early childhood education research; however, the intentional interdisciplinary qualities of the units will also be explored.

In the final chapter, we return to the vision of visible learners in early childhood. Using the vignettes as references, we highlight the ways educators engage in formative assessment and use these data to drive instructional decisions about selecting the right strategy at the right time, orchestrating classroom discourse, leveraging learners' interests and experiences, and differentiating based on the developmentally appropriate level or right level of challenge. Educators can also make learning visible through the feedback they provide learners and families. This can be in-the-moment feedback through language and interactions while engaging in playful learning and tasks. This can also be at significant learning junctures throughout the year where the educator must decide what formative assessment data and feedback to share, when to share them, and how to share them. Again, we will refer back to the vignettes to highlight examples of these in-the-moment feedback decisions. Finally, we will share a new vignette of student-led family conferences in early childhood to highlight examples of these decision points from learner–teacher–family conferences at the beginning, middle, and end of the year.

Throughout the book, we highlight the specific influences, approaches, strategies, and actions with an effect size greater than the hinge point of 0.40. These influences have the potential to positively impact children's learning across school years. We hope that by pointing these out, you will see examples of the strategies in action in early childhood classrooms so that you can see patterns among them and make sense of what they could look like and sound like in your setting. In the list of videos for this book, there is footage of additional early childhood classrooms striving to make learning visible. All of the educators on the pages and in the videos are doing just that: striving. Their stories are snapshots along their journeys to create Visible Learning classrooms. Together, we hope to be companions along your learning path. As you peek into their classrooms, we hope you see aspects of your own classroom reflected as well as glimpses of possibility.

CHAPTER 1

Teaching With Clarity in Early Childhood

Of the seven big ideas from the Visible Learning research, four focus specifically on the role of clarity in the early childhood classroom (Rickards et al., 2021):

1. Early childhood educators and learners have high expectations for learning.

2. Learning experiences move learning toward explicit success criteria.

3. Learning experiences and tasks have the developmentally appropriate level or right level of challenge.

4. There is the right balance of surface and deep learning in the early childhood classroom.

EFFECT SIZE FOR TEACHER AND STUDENT EXPECTATIONS = **0.90**

EFFECT SIZE FOR SUCCESS CRITERIA = **0.77**

EFFECT SIZE FOR GOAL DIFFICULTY = **0.74**

EFFECT SIZE FOR DEEP MOTIVATION AND APPROACH = **0.69**

These four guiding principles lay the foundation for clarity, which is the driving force behind implementing evidence-based practices or high effect size practices in the local context of our classrooms. Clarity about learning, shared between us and our learners, paves the way for all of our instructional decisions: how we organize our instruction, the nature of our explanations about concepts, skills, and understandings, the examples we use in our teaching, and the assessments that provide evidence of learning (Fendick, 1990). Our ultimate goal is to grow visible learners who have the efficacy to be active decision makers about their learning journeys. Visible learners demonstrate the following characteristics:

• Know their current level of understanding; they can communicate what they do and do not yet know,

- Know where they are going next in their learning and are ready to take on the challenge,

- Select tools to move their learning forward,

- Seek feedback about their learning and recognize errors as opportunities to learn,

- Monitor their learning and make adjustments when necessary, and

- Recognize when they have learned something and serve as a teacher to others. (Frey et al., 2018).

These six characteristics set up our young learners for sustained success beyond our early childhood classrooms. We can meet this goal by ensuring that both educators and learners clearly and intentionally make sense of what they are learning, why they are learning it, and how they will know they are successful. We can support our class as a whole and each individual learner in reaching this goal by using the right instructional strategy at the right time. Let's look at what this means in an early childhood classroom.

FOUR-YEAR-OLDS AT WORK

"What do you want to be when you grow up?" "What are you making?" What are you trying?" We ask young children these kinds of questions all the time. And they have answers, sometimes unexpected answers, that reflect their curiosity and drive. Children are natural goal setters. They see someone do something and they want to try it too. They mimic and repeat. They demand to do it themselves even on the first try. Their work starts and stops, changes and continues, deepening and extending with each iteration. They are aware of what they do not know or cannot do yet, and they want to try what they see the children and adults around them doing.

Robyn Davis sees this often in her prekindergarten classroom filled with eighteen 4-year-olds. As Ms. Davis looks around during centers, she sees Anissa reenacting "Five Little Monkeys Swinging From a Tree," Ava and William pretending to work in a hair salon, and DeAndre and Malayah building taller and taller towers to knock down.

Anissa counts the wooden monkeys hanging from a balance that looks like a tree. She sings, "Eight little monkeys swinging from a tree, teasing Mr. Alligator 'Can't catch me! Can't catch me!' Along comes Mr. Alligator quiet as can be aaaaaaaand SNAPS that monkey right out of that tree!" She grabs a monkey off the balance (Figure 1.1) and, as it tilts to one side, she stops and says aloud, "How many monkeys now?"

Ms. Davis asks, "How could we figure it out?"

Anissa says, "I can count them." She points to each monkey and counts, "1, 2, 3, 4, 5, 6, 7. There are 7 monkeys left." Anissa sings the next verse; after taking off another monkey, she pauses, unsure of the number of remaining monkeys.

Ms. Davis says, "This song has a pattern in it. What pattern do you notice?"

Anissa replies, "When we sing, we go 5, 4, 3, 2, 1, 0, but I want 8 monkeys."

"You're changing the numbers to try a new version of the pattern and you're representing the pattern with our monkeys and tree. Let's describe the pattern. What happens to the number of monkeys each time?" Ms. Davis asks.

"Mr. Alligator eats one. Like when we count 5, 4, 3, 2, 1 . . . blast-off!" Anissa connects.

"That's a shrinking pattern. You take off one monkey each time. You're counting backward by 1. I wonder what the same shrinking pattern will be if you start at 8," Ms. Davis ponders aloud. Anissa slowly thinks back to the numbers she has already said, "8, 7 ..." She silently counts the monkeys and says, "6."

Ms. Davis echoes her, "8, 7, 6 ..."

"5, 4, 3, 2, 1, 0!" Anissa shouts.

"You extended the shrinking pattern by describing the pattern first: one monkey gets eaten each time. Then you used the pattern to solve your problem. You are counting backward by 1. Now, you can finish the song."

Anissa sings, "Six little monkeys swinging from a tree ..."

Ava and William are leaning against cushions, twisting their dolls' hair. Ava is talking aloud to coach William as he twists: "Keep switching hands. Switch, switch, switch, switch. And pull tight." She tells her doll, "Your hair twists are done! Now the hair ties." She returns

FIGURE 1.1

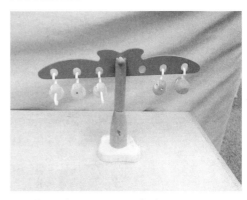

Monkeys hanging on a balance

to talking to her fellow beautician, William, "I want to make a pattern with hair ties. Her favorite colors are pink, purple, and gold." Ava starts putting on hair ties—pink, purple, pink, purple.

"What about gold?" William asks.

"I don't know how to make the pattern with gold," responds Ava dejectedly.

Ms. Davis asks, "What kind of pattern do you want to make—repeating, growing, or shrinking?"

"Repeating," Ava responds.

"How could you create a repeating pattern with three colors?" Ms. Davis asks.

"You could go pink, purple, gold, over and over," William offers. "Just put a gold hair tie there and there," adds William as he points to places in the doll's hair to adjust Ava's pattern.

Ava revises her pattern by adding two gold hair ties—pink, purple, *gold*, pink, purple, *gold*—and then extends the pattern, "Now a pink, a purple, and a gold!"

Ms. Davis says, "You worked as a team to create a repeating pattern with three colors in the core!"

Ava turns to William and asks, "What color hair ties does your doll want? Let's make another pattern!"

DeAndre and Malayah are building towers with wooden blocks. They work side-by-side comparing each other's towers and then squealing with joy as they fall or get knocked over. Malayah notes, "You always build a taller one."

"Let's look at DeAndre's tower," Ms. Davis directs. "What's different about it? Why can it get so tall without falling over?"

DeAndre notices, "I put a lot of blocks on the bottom and then make it littler and littler to the top." DeAndre points and counts from the top of his tower down, showing how the base gets wider and wider with blocks. "See? 1, 2, 3, 4, 5 . . . like a pyramid," he says

"Malayah, where do you use the *most* blocks in your towers?" Ms. Davis inserts new, quantitative language in her question.

Malayah thinks for a moment and says, "I don't know. I just try to pile as high as possible." Ms. Davis furthers their analysis, "Why might it help the tower stay tall to put the *most* blocks on the bottom and the *least* on top?"

DeAndre points to a block near the middle of Malayah's tower with two blocks teetering on top, "If you put just one block, it gets wobbly when you put more on top."

"Yeah, watch!" Malayah gives a gentle push to the single block and the blocks above it wobble and start to fall. They cheer.

"DeAndre, I noticed you used a growing pattern to describe your tower: 1, 2, 3, 4, 5. I think your pattern could help Malayah with her design," Ms. Davis connects their work to patterns to help Malayah and DeAndre generalize their structural patterns. "What pattern do you think about as you build your tower?"

"I go 5, 4, 3, 2, 1," DeAndre reflects.

"That's interesting. You have a growing pattern 1, 2, 3, 4, 5 and a shrinking pattern 5, 4, 3, 2, 1. It just depends on how you look at it."

"I'm going to start with 10 blocks on the bottom so my tower is stronger. My tower is going to be taller than yours!" Malayah starts building again.

"I wonder how many blocks you'll put on next," Ms. Davis thinks aloud.

"9, 8, 7, 6, 5, 4, 3, 2, 1!" shouts Malayah as she gathers more blocks.

It is a typical day of center work and these 4-year-olds exhibit the characteristics of visible learners.

VISIBLE LEARNERS

As we introduced at the beginning of this chapter, growing learners who own their learning journeys is our ultimate goal as educators. Visible Learning is about seeing learning through the eyes of our young learners and our learners seeing themselves as their own teachers. The path to visible learners begins with young children and lays a foundation that fosters, nurtures, and sustains learning growth through compulsory schooling. As discussed earlier, Frey et al. (2018) describe six characteristics of visible learners:

- Know their current level of understanding; they can communicate what they do and do not yet know,

- Know where they are going next in their learning and are ready to take on the challenge,

- Select tools to move their learning forward,

- Seek feedback about their learning and recognize errors as opportunities to learn,

- Monitor their learning and make adjustments when necessary, and

- Recognize when they have learned something and serve as a teacher to others.

EFFECT SIZE FOR SELF-JUDGMENT AND REFLECTION = 0.75

In the earlier snapshot of Ms. Davis's classroom during centers, each of her learners demonstrates these six characteristics. Through their interactions with the teacher and peers, the children are aware of what they currently understand and can do.

They know what they are working toward and have confidence to take on that challenge.

EFFECT SIZE FOR CONCENTRATION/PERSISTENCE/ENGAGEMENT = 0.54

Anissa knows she can retell and build the monkey song starting with five monkeys. Ava knows she can make two repeating patterns, an A pattern with hair twists and an AB pattern with pink and purple hair ties, but she is not sure how to make a repeating pattern with three colors. Malayah knows she can build a tower, but it falls down easily and is not as tall as DeAndre's tower. Note also how these children are learning the language of learning—a critical precursor for taking on more challenging learning and when working and listening to others, and the basis of becoming a lifelong learner.

EFFECT SIZE FOR STRATEGY MONITORING = 0.58

EFFECT SIZE FOR META-COGNITIVE STRATEGIES = 0.60

As they work, the children monitor their learning and make decisions about what tools to use to help them reach their goals.

They seek feedback from their peers and teacher and recognize mistakes as opportunities to learn.

EFFECT SIZE FOR FEEDBACK = 0.62

They also recognize their own learning and teach their peers.

EFFECT SIZE FOR SEEKING HELP FROM PEERS = 0.72

Anissa knows to take one monkey off each time, she can count the remaining monkeys with one-to-one correspondence, and she can count backward from 5; using the monkey manipulatives, she combines this knowledge to count backward from 8. Ava helps William make the A hair twist pattern by modeling and describing aloud and uses what she knows about AB repeating patterns to make a color pattern with hair ties. William shows Ava how to revise her AB repeating pattern into an ABC repeating pattern. Malayah and DeAndre analyze their tower-making processes with Ms. Davis. They use their many toppled towers and their knowledge of patterns as opportunities to determine what makes a strong structure.

Starting with our youngest learners, growing visible learners is vital. In fact, being a visible learner is a hallmark of early childhood education. Often in early childhood education, child-centered or child-directed learning, where the child's interests, discoveries, and wonderings lead the learning, is highly valued and celebrated. Developing children's autonomy and agency is a common emphasis.

Growing visible learners takes this concept a step further and deeper by making explicit young children's awareness of their learning journey. Ms. Davis intentionally immersed at each center to make the learning process visible to them. selves. She asked questions, encouraged feedback and coaching, and summarized their progress. By making their children's natural curiosity and goal setting, working making their learning processes explicit, Anissa, Malayah became active decision makers. Visible learners partner with their teachers to make sense of what they know, where they will get there. One foundational way teachers can make learning visible is through teacher clarity.

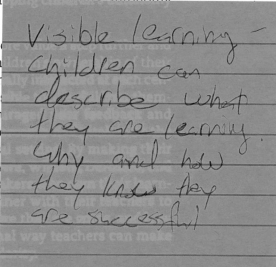

Visible learning — children can describe what they are learning. Why and how they know they are successful

 TEACHER CLARITY

When teaching is intentional and learning is purposeful, children can take ownership over their learning journeys. This is the heart of Visible Learning. When we make learning visible, children can describe what they are learning, why they are learning it, and how they will know when they are successful. In other words, they become visible learners.

To meet this goal, we must communicate the what, why, and how of learning. This is teacher clarity. With an effect size of 0.84 (Visible Learning Meta[X], 2021), teacher clarity is significant at all levels of learning and in all settings for learning, whether in person or distance (Fisher et al., 2020).

Communicating clarity in the early childhood classroom must occur in a variety of learning contexts, using a variety of modes, and through a variety of intentional, language-based interactions (Thunder et al., 2021). Through teacher clarity, educators can partner with young learners to intentionally communicate and make sense of learning intentions and success criteria.

Learning intentions (0.51) communicate what is being learned and why.

Success criteria (0.88) communicate what successful learning will look like and sound like.

Learning intentions and success criteria are aligned with grade-level standards or learning goals. In the example from

> When we make learning visible, children can describe what they are learning, why they are learning it, and how they will know when they are successful.

EFFECT SIZE FOR TEACHER CLARITY = 0.84

EFFECT SIZE FOR LEARNING INTENTIONS = 0.51

EFFECT SIZE FOR SUCCESS CRITERIA = 0.88

Ms. Davis's classroom, she first identified the following standards from multiple domains for her patterns unit from Virginia's Early Learning and Development Standards (ELDS): Birth–Five Learning Guidelines:

> **Sorting, Classifying, and Patterning:** Identifies, duplicates, extends, and creates simple repeating patterns
>
> **Comparing Numbers, Counting, and Recognizing Quantities:** Counts forward to 20 by memory. Counts backward from 5. Answers the question "How many?" for up to 10 objects.
>
> **Learning and Engaging in Conversational Interactions:** Engages in multiple back-and-forth conversations with adults in ways that can be goal-directed.
>
> **Persisting and Problem-Solving:** Figures out more than one solution to a problem. (Virginia Department of Education, 2021)

Next, Ms. Davis created a content-focused learning intention and integrated social and language learning intentions to ensure that she intentionally supported learners' development across multiple domains. These additional learning intentions reflect what learners are focusing on in the language domain (language learning intention) and how they are expected to interact within the classroom community (social learning intention). Ms. Davis created the aligned success criteria by analyzing the learning intentions and describing an accessible pathway to successful mastery of the learning intentions:

> **Content Learning Intention:** We are learning patterns can grow, shrink, and repeat.
>
> **Language Learning Intention:** We are learning ways to talk about patterns.
>
> **Social Learning Intention:** We are learning to use what we know to solve problems.
>
> ### Success Criteria
>
> - We can describe, extend, and represent patterns.
> - We can use patterns to solve problems.

However, Ms. Davis did not post these on the board and read them to her learners. Instead, she communicated the learning intentions and success criteria throughout the three parts of her lesson: mini-lesson, work time, and sharing and closure. She wants her learners to understand and be able to talk about what success looks like. Then, they are more receptive to receiving feedback and working with others, and they will learn more as they attain success.

During her mini-lesson at the beginning of center time, Ms. Davis explained the learning intention: "As you work today, look for growing, shrinking, and repeating patterns. We've found so many patterns already!" To illustrate the success criteria, Ms. Davis pointed to the class anchor chart about patterns and paused. There were three columns labeled "Growing," "Shrinking," and "Repeating" with photos and sketches of patterns as well as anecdotes with pictures listed ("Zimir used a repeating pattern to teach shoe tying."). As she pointed to corresponding examples, Ms. Davis explained the success criteria:

> Maybe you'll create patterns. Maybe you'll notice patterns in your work. When you create or notice patterns, use words to talk about the patterns, words like growing, shrinking, repeating, core, and next. When there's a pattern, we can predict what is next. When you have a problem, talk about how you could use a pattern to solve the problem. After cleanup, we'll share the patterns you found and made.

Ms. Davis continued her communication of the learning intentions and success criteria while children worked in centers by intentionally engaging in language-based interactions. She asked Anissa to describe the pattern in the song and to use that pattern in order to extend her translation of the pattern. When William noticed a problem with Ava's pattern, Ms. Davis asked Ava which type of pattern she wanted to make and then engaged Ava and William in using language to describe the core of the pattern. With DeAndre and Malayah, Ms. Davis asked reflective questions to engage them in analyzing their towers and naming the structural pattern that helped create the tallest, strongest tower. In this way, each learner was able to engage with the learning intentions and success criteria; they described, extended, and represented repeating, growing, and shrinking patterns as well as used the patterns to problem solve.

At the end of center time, the class gathered as a community once again to make sense of the learning intentions and success criteria. Ms. Davis began sharing time by reminding them, "When we share our work today, think about when you noticed a pattern, created a pattern, or used a pattern to solve a problem." From her interactions with learners during work time, she knew many of the patterns and problems the children would share so she could facilitate their explanation and reflection. For example, when Malayah and DeAndre shared their tower patterns, Ms. Davis asked under which column to place their advice, and they decided to put it in the middle of "Shrinking" and "Growing" with an arrow pointing down the tower under "Growing" and an arrow pointing up under "Shrinking." As learners shared their work, she added photos, drawings, and anecdotes to the anchor chart, carefully sorting the children's sharing based on the type of pattern.

Throughout her lesson, Ms. Davis used the essentials of communicating clarity in the early childhood classroom (Thunder et al., 2021):

1. Use visuals alongside academic vocabulary in the context of learning. Have learners articulate what they are learning and connect multiple representations with academic vocabulary.

2. Demonstrate the higher-order thinking skills and processes by modeling (i.e., thinking aloud) the connections between what they are learning and why.

3. Explicitly teach meta-cognitive skills through listening and questioning so that learners are guided to think about their own learning.

4. Fina   lars, and
   mo   itor their
   lear   ike.

Ms. Da   nd success
criteria   models. Her
questio   ern vocabulary a   ons on the
lesson's   y communicating   rns at the
forefron   k and talk.
She was   ns to meet
each lea   deeper in
their un

✎ SURFACE, DEEP, AND TRANSFER LEARNING

While we have and communicate high expectations for learning through learning intentions and success criteria, we also know children bring a variety of rich experiential knowledge and varying levels of language for describing and connecting these experiences to school-based experiences. Our role is to facilitate their connections, grow their language, and deepen their knowledge and understanding. This facilitation occurs when learning experiences and tasks have the developmentally appropriate level or right level of challenge and strike the right balance of surface and deep learning. One way we can accomplish this is by selecting the right instructional strategy at the right time. We can do this by recognizing and supporting learners' movement through the three phases of learning: surface, deep, and transfer learning

The surface learning phase is when learners are initially using their prior knowledge to build understanding of a new concept. This phase is not superficial or unimportant. It is foundational to mastery of the content. Surface learning marks the beginning. It is the "knowing that" part of learning. In the surface learning phase, learners benefit the most from instructional strategies, such as deliberate instruction (0.59), vocabulary instruction (0.63), guided questioning (0.48), imagery (0.51), and manipulatives (0.39).

The deep learning phase is when learners are making conceptual connections and relations among ideas. They use their initial understanding from surface learning to dive deeper into making meaning and forming connections among concepts. Deep learning is the "knowing how" phase. In the deep learning phase, learners benefit the most from instructional strategies, such as concept mapping (0.64), self-questioning (0.59), and classroom discussion (0.82).

The transfer learning phase is when learners are applying their understanding to new contexts. They use their conceptual connections from deep learning to make sense of and make adjustments in a new situation. In the transfer learning phase, learners benefit the most from instructional strategies, such as cooperative learning (0.46), meta-cognitive strategies (0.60), strategy monitoring (0.58), transfer strategies (0.86), and problem-solving teaching (0.67).

Language-based interactions are the way Ms. Davis learns where her children are along the three phases of learning. Every day, she talks with her learners as they work and she takes notes about their interactions. Across days and weeks, Ms. Davis notices patterns across her class and individual children. During this third week of their patterns unit, she noticed that most of her class is in the deep phase of learning—actively making connections among patterns and their day-to-day work creating and exploring. Her whole group instruction focused on adding to a concept map (the anchor chart) connecting multiple

> Our role is to facilitate their connections, grow their language, and deepen their knowledge and understanding.

EFFECT SIZE FOR DELIBERATE INSTRUCTION = 0.59

EFFECT SIZE FOR VOCABULARY INSTRUCTION = 0.63

EFFECT SIZE FOR QUESTIONING = 0.48

EFFECT SIZE FOR IMAGERY = 0.51

EFFECT SIZE FOR MANIPULATIVES = 0.39

EFFECT SIZE FOR CONCEPT MAPPING = 0.64

EFFECT SIZE FOR SELF-QUESTIONING = 0.59

EFFECT SIZE FOR CLASSROOM DISCUSSION = 0.82

EFFECT SIZE FOR COOPERATIVE LEARNING = 0.46

EFFECT SIZE
FOR META-
COGNITIVE
STRATEGIES
= 0.60

EFFECT
SIZE FOR
STRATEGY
MONITORING
= 0.58

EFFECT
SIZE FOR
TRANSFER
STRATEGIES
= 0.86

EFFECT
SIZE FOR
PROBLEM-
SOLVING
TEACHING
= 0.67

representations of patterns and class discussions sharing their ideas and experiences. As Ms. Davis conferred with the children, she engaged them in self-questioning by making statements and asking questions like these: "I wonder what the same shrinking pattern will be if you start with 8." "How could you create a repeating pattern with three colors?" "How could we figure it out?" These instructional strategies provided just the right support to deepen their conceptual understanding of patterns.

At the same time, DeAndre was ready to move into the transfer phase of learning. Ms. Davis asked him and Malayah to identify similarities and differences between their towers: "What's different about it? Why can it get so tall without falling over?" She specifically asked DeAndre to meta-cognitively reflect on how he thought about patterns while building: "What pattern do you think about as you build your tower?" These instructional strategies provided just the right support to foster DeAndre's generalization of patterns for problem solving.

Moments earlier, Ms. Davis supported Ava, who was in the surface phase of learning, by asking a guiding question that deliberately connected Ava's plan with the new pattern vocabulary: "What kind of pattern do you want to make—repeating, growing, or shrinking?" She allowed William to provide the deliberate instruction of how to make a repeating pattern with three colors, and then she summarized their work together, "You worked as a team to create a repeating pattern with three colors in the core!" These instructional strategies provided just the right support to help Ava practice using the language and concepts of patterns in her work.

With each topic and concept, learners may move at different paces through the three learning phases. At any given moment, learners can be at different places with different needs. At the center of each of these phases is language. Through language-based interactions, we can discover where our learners are along the three learning phases and we can support them with the right instructional strategy at the right time in order to maximize the effect of our interaction.

In the subsequent chapters, we will see more classroom communities where educators, learners, and families collaborate to grow visible learners, where both educators and learners understand what they are learning, why they are learning it, and how they will know they are successful, and where educators use the right instructional strategies at the right time to support each individual learner and the class as a whole. We will see what this looks like and sounds like in the early childhood classrooms of five educators. Let's meet them.

PROFILES OF FIVE EDUCATORS

KELLY BULLOCK

Kelly Bullock works with 3-year-olds in a neighborhood day-care center in the United States (Illinois). She earned dual certification in special education and early childhood education, teaching 5-year-olds in kindergarten for 15 years before deciding to move to a neighborhood day-care center. Ms. Bullock decided to move grades in order to help create high quality and better alignment in children's experiences from preschool to kindergarten to primary school. The local school divisions have been under added scrutiny due to the significant "achievement gaps" between racial, ethnic, socioeconomic status, home language, and ability groups. Yes, this diversity is reflected in both classrooms and day-care centers across the community, and Ms. Bullock's classroom is no exception. There are multiple languages spoken in her classroom and there is a lot of diversity given that the school division is classified as a rural school division. Ms. Bullock is fluent in Spanish. Her classroom has seven typically developing children and five children with special needs. She is both their classroom teacher and their special education case manager given that she is credentialed in both special education and early childhood education.

In the United States, each state creates its own standards of learning for early childhood education, typically delineating separate standards for birth through age 2 years, ages 3–6 years, kindergarten, and primary Grades 1–3. While primary grades are nationally compulsory, kindergarten (at age 5) is compulsory in some states but not others. Ms. Bullock relies on the Illinois ELDS to guide her intentional teaching with her 3-year-olds (Illinois State Board of Education, 2013).

Two paraprofessionals work with Ms. Bullock each and every day. Together, they believe that the "achievement gaps" that persist across the school divisions are actually opportunity gaps that exist because of low expectations, a lack of balancing surface and deep learning, and not finding the right challenge that moves learning forward in each child. Their daily schedule kicks off at 7:50 a.m. with a morning meeting that shares the learning intentions and success criteria for the day. Then, significant time is committed to building and supporting classroom cohesion (0.53).

EFFECT SIZE FOR CLASSROOM COHESION = 0.53

From greeting classmates to singing songs, Ms. Bullock and her paraprofessionals strive to allow learners to make meaning through the what, why, and how of the day's experiences.

CHARLES HEATON

Charles Heaton teaches 3- and 4-year-olds at a nursery school in the United Kingdom (Nottingham, England). The nursery serves families working for a nearby corporation. Nottingham is the ninth largest urban area in England, famous for being the hometown of the heroic outlaw Robin Hood. This alone makes teaching young children in Nottingham fun! Mr. Heaton has taught at the school for 8 years as the key teacher. Mr. Heaton is adamant in his belief that his learners grow, develop, and learn best through their interactions. Thus, his nursery is abuzz with activity. Learners are provided with multiple opportunities that leverage their interests (0.35) along with their strengths to promote and support self-regulation in learning (0.54). Student-centered teaching, alone, does not amplify our impact unless we focus on building the assessment capability of learners.

EFFECT SIZE FOR STUDENT-CENTERED TEACHING = 0.35

EFFECT SIZE FOR SELF-REGULATION STRATEGIES = 0.54

However, the day in Mr. Heaton's nursery is not a free-for-all. Instead, he deliberately, intentionally, and purposefully weaves learning intentions and success criteria into carefully orchestrated experiences and tasks that promote engagement through centers, tasks, words, and guided inquiry to find the right level of challenge for his learners. Mr. Heaton uses learners' interests and curiosity as a springboard to their development in all areas, such as problem solving, memory, and information processing. Regardless of their backgrounds and prior experiences, he and his colleagues meet learners where they are and focus on each child's emerging needs and interests, guiding their development through warm, positive student–teacher interactions.

In the United Kingdom, the national curriculum is organized into key stages with ages birth through 5 years defined as the Early Years Foundation Stage (EYFS). Children who turn 5 years old before the end of August enter Year 1 Stage and are required to attend school. Schools and early years providers in England must follow the EYFS. Within the learning and development section of the EYFS there are seven categories of standards, which Mr. Heaton and his colleagues use to shape the educational programs in this nursery. At Mr. Heaton's nursery, various classrooms are dedicated to working with babies through preschool, but each emphasizes trauma-informed supports.

With extended hours from 7:30 a.m. to 6 p.m. each day, Mr. Heaton's class shifts over the course of the day. He leads a mixed-age class of 14 children with a paraprofessional in the morning and a class of four children, all 4-year-olds, without a paraprofessional in the afternoon.

ALISHA DEMCHAK ✯

Alisha Demchak lives in Australia (New South Wales) and is a preschool educator at the local public primary school. Her class is filled with eighteen 4-year-olds. She has a bachelor's degree in primary education and is qualified to teach early childhood education. This is Ms. Demchak's third year teaching and she is currently working toward her full teacher registration.

Ms. Demchak's primary school is a growing, diverse inner-city school. In fact, the teachers spent time developing a motto that reflected their beliefs about student learning. This new motto, "We Achieve," reflects their expectation that all learners, regardless of where they begin in learning, will experience significant growth. However, what is most inspiring about this school is that Ms. Demchak and her colleagues believe that they are the agents of change and thus believe that this growth in learning comes from best practice teaching (1.46).

EFFECT SIZE FOR TEACHER ESTIMATES OF ACHIEVEMENT = 1.46

There is a commitment to quality teaching, new technology, and the creative arts. Academic performance is highly valued and is supported by a strong visual and performing arts program.

Ms. Demchak and her colleagues also attribute learning growth to an active and committed family-based community (0.42).

EFFECT SIZE FOR FAMILY INVOLVEMENT = 0.42

She has the pleasure of working with a dynamic and energetic team who is committed to working as a team that includes multiple stakeholders in education.

As part of an urban school, Ms. Demchak's classroom is very diverse. Learners come from a multitude of racial, ethnic, and socioeconomic backgrounds. Furthermore, there is considerable variance in the background knowledge and prior knowledge of each learner. Focusing on diversity, equity, and inclusion, Ms. Demchak's classroom is a secure and safe learning environment for each one of her learners, providing an inclusive environment for all learners—an environment that actively engages all learners, welcomes and embraces every learner as an important member of the community, and provides the necessary support to each learner so that they have an equal opportunity for success (see Jimenez et al., 2012; Spooner et al., 2011).

KATHERINE MURRAH

Katherine Murrah also lives in Australia (New South Wales) and is a Foundation educator, sometimes called Prep Year or kindergarten. Ms. Murrah's class is filled with 22 children who all turned 5 years old by June 30. She teaches at the same local primary school as Alisha Demchak and collaborates with Ms. Demchak to successfully transition their learners from preschool to kindergarten. In fact, the prekindergarten classrooms are in the same hallway as the kindergarten classrooms.

In Australia, school is compulsory at age 6, when the national curriculum's Foundation Year Standards are mandated. From birth to age 5 years and through the transition to school, the Early Years Learning Framework for Australia guides learning experiences (Australian Government Department of Education and Training, 2019). Ms. Demchak and Ms. Murrah's collaboration between preschool and kindergarten ensures continuity in learning expectations and support for learners.

What makes this particular collaboration so powerful is that Ms. Murrah and Ms. Demchak are part of a vertical professional learning community with teachers across multiple grades within the primary school.

Furthermore, Ms. Murrah is also in her third year of teaching and she is also working toward her full teacher registration. Together, these two teachers collaborate, continually seeking feedback about their impact on their students' learning (0.72).

ROBYN DAVIS

Finally, you have already met Robyn Davis. This year, Ms. Davis teaches twelve 4-year-olds in a public elementary school in the United States (Virginia), where she uses Virginia's ELDS: Birth–Five Learning Guidelines to guide her instructional decisions (Virginia Department of Education, 2021). Ms. Davis worked in other industries before switching her career to become an educator. She has taught Grades 2 and 4, but she loves her current role teaching prekindergarten. This year, her class is engaged in distance learning. She meets with her children via video conferencing each morning for 2 hours for whole group and small group learning. In the afternoon, she and the paraprofessional meet one-on-one with the children for 30 minutes each. Ms. Davis is working hard to transfer what she knows about applying Visible Learning research during in-person learning to distance learning. She is also working to maximize the new opportunities that distance learning has presented. We will hear and see what her in-person instruction was like as well as her distance learning instruction.

EFFECT SIZE FOR TEACHER EXPECTATIONS = 0.42

EFFECT SIZE FOR COLLECTIVE TEACHER EFFICACY = 1.36

EFFECT SIZE FOR SEEKING FEEDBACK ABOUT IMPACT ON STUDENT LEARNING = 0.72

Inside Ms. Davis's Distance Learning Classroom

At first glance, every aspect of Ms. Davis's classroom looks different this year because the class is engaged in distance learning. But if you close your eyes and listen, it sounds similar. This distance learning classroom continues to be filled with Ms. Davis's intentional language and a lot of children talking!

The mini-lesson during centers time sounds the same. The anchor chart is a shared slide with photos and anecdotes, some taken by Ms. Davis and others taken by family members and shared with Ms. Davis via the class communication platform. Ms. Davis uses the mini-lesson time to initially communicate the learning intentions and success criteria through images, words, and models.

As work time begins, instead of choosing and moving to a center, the children choose materials from their learning supplies tub and remain working in their learning space at home. Rather than walking from center to center, Ms. Davis talks with each learner through the video conference. The other children chime in as each learner talks through what they are doing, trying, and thinking about.

"Ahmad, what are you working on today?" Ms. Davis asks.

Ahmad is making piles of playdough balls and using his finger to make indents on each. "I'm making cookies. I'm putting chips on them. One chip on this cookie. Two chips on this cookie. Three chips on this cookie."

"I notice a pattern of chips! Does anyone else notice a pattern in Ahmad's cookies? One chip, two chips, three chips." Ms. Davis asks a guiding question to help make the connection.

"I notice a pattern. 1, 2, 3, 4. Ahmad, put four chips on the next cookie!" Mercy says.

"Mercy, why should Ahmad put four chips on his next cookie?" Ms. Davis asks.

"Because 4 is next. 1, 2, 3, 4," Mercy replies.

"And then I'm putting five chips!" Ahmad says.

"And then six chips!" adds Braylen.

"It sounds like you can predict what Ahmad will do next because he's making a pattern with his chips. He's making a growing

(Continued)

(Continued)

pattern. 1, 2, 3, 4, 5, 6." Ms. Davis connects back to the learning intentions and success criteria using specific pattern vocabulary and then moves to the next learner. "Anna, what are you working on today?"

"I'm making a train on the whole table," Anna responds while snapping together Unifix cubes to make a long train.

"How are you deciding which color to put on the train next?" Ms. Davis probes.

"It's a pattern: green, yellow, pink, green, yellow, pink, green, yellow, pink," Anna holds her cubes to the camera and points as she talks.

"You're creating a repeating pattern with three colors. Julius, I notice you're making a repeating pattern train too. How many colors are you using?" Ms. Davis asks.

"My favorite—black and orange," Julius shares.

"Anna and Julius, hold up your repeating pattern trains so we can all see them. What do you notice about their repeating pattern trains?" Ms. Davis poses a question to everyone.

"They keep using the same colors." "Anna's is longer." "Julius only has two colors and Anna has three." "They're making patterns." There are many noticings to share.

Then, Malayah holds up her Unifix cubes and says, "I'm making a pattern train too but mine is different. Mine goes blue, red, red; blue, red, red; blue, red, red."

After comparing Malayah's pattern train with Anna and Julius's, Ms. Davis continues to have each learner talk about their work. She models vocabulary, asks questions, and engages the class in discussion. Each of her language-based interactions allows Ms. Davis multiple opportunities to communicate the learning intentions and success criteria in the context of their work as well as to discover which phase of learning each child is in and to use the right instructional strategy at the right time to move each one forward.

After cleanup, the whole class share also sounds similar. Children take turns sharing and reflecting on their learning as ideas are added to the digital anchor chart.

While these five early childhood educators live across the globe and work with children in different settings, they share a common set of dispositions and skills to implement what works best and to evaluate their impact on learners (Rickards et al., 2021):

1. They collaborate with their learners and work together as evaluators of learning growth.

2. They have high expectations for learning and convey those high expectations to their learners.

3. They develop and implement learning experiences that move learning toward explicit success criteria.

4. These learning experiences and tasks have the developmentally appropriate level or right level of challenge.

5. They establish trust so that errors and mistakes are viewed as opportunities for new learning.

6. They are continually seeking feedback about their impact on their students' learning.

7. They find the right balance of surface and deep learning in the early childhood classroom.

In the next chapters, we follow these early childhood educators into their classrooms to explore what these principles look like and sound like as children engage in playful learning, mathematics, literacy, understanding the world, social and emotional development, art, music, and motor development.

CHAPTER 2

Visible Learning in Early Childhood Playful Learning

Traditionally, play is described as the universal, natural learning process for children across cultures and continents. Many educators believe that if they create opportunities for children to play, then children will intuitively learn. With this belief, play becomes the ultimate goal of early childhood learning.

We cannot, however, continue to teach from this belief any longer. Lillard et al. (2013) researched the relationship between pretend play and learning, specifically creativity, problem solving, reasoning, social skills, language, literacy, and executive functioning. They could not find evidence that pretend play is critical to development; in fact, they could not find evidence that pretend play causes any significant development in children. Lillard et al. (2013) did find that language and interactions are pivotal and that many positive adult–child interactions with rich language take place in pretend play. This may explain why we have believed for so long that pretend play is significant, because it is a context for a lot of talk. Play can also be motivating, which can lead to positive engagement and interactions.

Yet the real learning takes place because of the language-based interactions. This is important for us to know as early childhood educators so that we know what to spend our time planning carefully and implementing intentionally—our language. And this focus on our language cannot exist for just one year or just the early childhood years; we need to create long-term, systematic change so that the effects of our intentional teaching and learning do not fade over time.

EFFECTIVE PLAYFUL LEARNING IN EARLY CHILDHOOD

Research on play and its many forms indicates that we need to reframe what we know about play in early childhood. As early childhood educators, we must shift to focus on intentional "playful learning" rather than creating opportunities for pretend play, open play, or free play (Hirsh-Pasek et al., 2009; Lillard et al., 2013). In playful learning, the content, the structure of problems or tasks, and the interactions with peers and adults are intentional and significant. The linchpin is language. Playful learning is rich with verbal inquiry.

LANGUAGE AND EXPLICIT, INTENTIONAL INTERACTIONS

Playful learning can be both child and adult initiated. Playful learning can include pretend play, inquiry and exploration, and deliberate instruction. In each of these settings, language makes learning explicit; by naming objects, processes, and ideas, we make them retrievable and transferable to new contexts. While there are many things children can learn nonverbally, verbal inquiry places new information in memorable chunks that can then be accessed and applied.

In fact, research tells us that significant ideas and skills are learned most effectively through language-based interactions. Through adult interaction, communication, and language, children acquire vocabulary and comprehensive language skills during playful learning (Lenhart et al, 2019; Lillard et al., 2013; Massey, 2013; Sophian, 1999; Wasik & Jacobi-Vessels, 2017). Vocabulary acquisition and comprehensive language skills, including syntax, semantics, and narrative abilities, are important across the curriculum. For example, we know young children do not have differences in their nonverbal mathematical knowledge (Tudge & Doucet, 2004); differences only exist based on socioeconomic status in young children's verbal, formal mathematical language. In order for us to prevent perceived gaps, we must explicitly teach mathematics vocabulary and phrases. We must also deliberately teach young children social and communication skills in order for them to internalize these skills (Murano et al., 2020).

EFFECT SIZE FOR VOCABULARY INSTRUCTION = 0.63

EFFECT SIZE FOR TEACHING COMMUNICATION SKILLS AND STRATEGIES = 0.35

Therefore, we must interact with children as they engage in play, and our interactions must be intentional. We must make their learning of new language explicit and focus our intentional interactions on developing vocabulary for objects, processes, and ideas as well as meanings of words and sentences, sentence organization and grammar, and narration of stories, events, and experiences.

In playful learning, we should assume both the roles of conversational partner and language facilitator. Through these roles, we can intentionally model, scaffold, and engage peers in elaborate word exposures across classroom contexts and time. Multiple experiences with the same language help children to deepen and extend their conceptual understanding of language or its multiple meanings and uses across situations (Neuman & Dwyer, 2011).

> In playful learning, we should assume both the roles of conversational partner and language facilitator.

With intentionality, we can grow our awareness of and strategies for conversing and facilitating language with young children.

LANGUAGE AND EXECUTIVE PROCESSING

One area of development where language can have a marked impact in early childhood education is executive processing. Executive processing supports the development of attention, working memory, and inhibitory control. Through adult interactions in playful learning, children's facility to hear, decode, understand, and use language is developed. High-quality interactions promote children's thinking, challenge their ideas, and enrich their language capability. We can use abstract language to model and engage children in inferencing, reasoning, predicting, and explaining. We can ask questions that invite extended responses and new questions, provide in-the-moment, meaningful feedback, define words, create opportunities for children to practice using vocabulary words, revisit and review children's ideas to allow for repetition of language and concepts, and use wait time so that children engage conversationally as well (Wasik & Jacobi-Vessels, 2017). Verbal inquiry in playful learning can be a space to intentionally encourage, teach, and practice executive processing and reasoning skills (Lillard et al., 2013), which, in turn, can develop meta-cognitive and self-regulation skills.

> EFFECT SIZE FOR META-COGNITIVE AND SELF-REGULATION STRATEGIES = 0.60

All of these skills are critical in the development of children's "theory of mind"—that is, how they develop a capacity for empathy and understanding of others and thus of the world all around them. They begin to see others as having beliefs, intents, emotions, and knowledge, and this is an important part of respect for self as well as respect for others. Intentional pretend play (to be a nurse or teacher) can also help develop these ideas, and Wellman and Liu (2004) outlined critical steps to support intentionally developing children's theory of mind:

- **Understanding "wanting"**: the realization that others have diverse desires, wants, and views about the world.

- **Understanding "thinking"**: the understanding that others also have diverse beliefs about the same thing, and that people's actions are based on what they think is going to happen. There is no such notion as "immaculate perception."

- **Understanding that "seeing leads to knowing"**: recognizing that others have different access to knowledge, and if someone hasn't seen something, they will need extra information to understand.

- **Understanding "false-beliefs"**: being aware of the fact that others may have false-beliefs that differ from reality.

- **Understanding "hidden feelings"**: being aware that other people can hide their emotions, and they can feel a different emotion from the one they display.

Each of these understandings is important in adult life, and the scene is set in these early years. Children who fail to develop these understandings often have difficulty with formal learning situations, critique, and working with others, and they develop fixed notions of their world when it is forever changing.

Specifically, literacy and mathematics learning can be increased through the intentional selection of literacy materials (Neuman & Roskos, 1992; Roskos & Neuman, 1998) and mathematics materials (Ramani & Siegler, 2008) to engage with during playful learning. By talking while using literacy and mathematics tools, children learn both concepts and language (Sarama et al., 2012). In other words, purposefully choosing materials that inspire and cultivate talk using literacy and mathematics language leads to increased learning of literacy and mathematics ideas and skills.

LANGUAGE AND HOME–SCHOOL CONNECTION

All children start school with important knowledge about the world around them. This knowledge may be nonverbal based on home contexts or it may be verbal knowledge in families' home languages. Some of our learners may be learning a second or third language at school. These are incredible strengths that we can cultivate and draw upon in our classrooms.

David Ausubel et al. (1968) proclaimed that connecting to a child's prior knowledge is the single most important factor influencing learning. In our creation of playful learning contexts, we should include home-familiar materials and experiences that will make the informal and nonverbal knowledge of learners visible to educators (Civil, 1998; Clements & Sarama, 2007; Goldstein, 2008; Sophian, 1999).

We can partner with families to learn about their routines, traditions, and celebrations, and we can then incorporate these into our classroom contexts. When children engage in play with these familiar materials and experiences, we can capitalize on their play by engaging in verbal inquiry with children; this is playful learning. We can teach vocabulary and comprehensive language skills by describing actions and emotions, naming objects, modeling language, and inviting conversational responses.

We can ask questions to challenge and extend their thinking, to make connections, and to learn about children's home language as well as their thinking.

For children learning English, we must support their growing vocabulary in their home language because this cultivates their overall language development and comprehension (August & Shanahan, 2006; Raikes et al., 2019; Riches & Genesee, 2006). We should encourage children to speak their home languages at school with peers and educators who speak the same home language. We can learn from our children by encouraging them to teach peers and educators words and phrases. And again, our partnership with families is important so that we can increase families' awareness of the importance of engaging in playful learning at home, including reading books, playing board games, and talking throughout family routines, in their home languages.

Our relationships with families can foster the connection between home and school by creating a two-way bridge.

Our relationships with families can foster the connection between home and school by creating a two-way bridge. We can learn from families and bring home-familiar contexts into school. We can also share with families the value of playful learning at home. Learning is more effective when we create continuity or stacking of interventions with home and school (Murano et al., 2020).

This is where playful learning research and Visible Learning research intersect: While play is an important part of children's learning, its power lies in the language-based interactions that take place during play. Playful learning must be rich with talk where the teacher is both a conversational partner and language facilitator. We must be intentional with our language-based interactions in playful learning to grow executive processing and to connect home and school knowledge and language. It may be hard to envision this shift from creating opportunities for play to creating playful learning interactions within your classroom. To support your vision, let's see and hear this intersection of playful learning and Visible Learning research within three early childhood classrooms.

MS. DEMCHAK AND SORTING

Ms. Demchak, Ms. Murrah, and their vertical professional learning community (PLC) have talked each year about their learners' areas of strength and need centered around language. About a third of each of the children in their classrooms are learning English as a second or third language. Their first languages include Mandarin, Cantonese, Arabic, Vietnamese, Spanish, Korean, Italian, Greek, and Dharug. There are also children in each classroom whose receptive and expressive language needs are high and who need Tier 1 vocabulary instruction. By Tier 1 vocabulary, we are referring to those words or terms that are used in everyday life and are common in spoken language. In many cases, this vocabulary is built through conversation. As a result, the PLC has been studying effective vocabulary instruction.

In previous years, the educators taught vocabulary around themes, shared experiences, and read-alouds. This year, they read research about building semantic networks (Hadley et al., 2018) and are planning their instruction around taxonomically related words or words organized into hierarchical categories. Taxonomies support the brain's desire to categorize and to notice the relationship between big ideas and details. Taxonomically related words also foster a conceptual organization of words so that learners can make inferences. As learners encounter new words, they are more likely to make sense of words related to previously learned categories and then "hook" the new words to these familiar categories for easy retrieval.

EFFECT SIZE FOR VOCABULARY INSTRUCTION = 0.63

This research resounded with what Ms. Demchak, Ms. Murrah, and their team have noticed over time—their learners struggle to sort and classify, especially resorting the same set using different attributes. In order to fluently sort and classify, learners need to notice and name categories of attributes and how categories are related to each other in a hierarchy from broad to more specific groups as well as groups nested within each other. Intentionally teaching categories and attributes of vocabulary matches this need.

Ms. Demchak and Ms. Murrah are both teaching sorting units at the same time so that they can analyze student work, make differentiation plans, and support each other's planning for playful learning. Ms. Murrah has noticed her kindergartners know a wide range of animals and enjoy learning about new animals, so they will begin with sorting animals. Most of her children already use the word "sort" and talk about sorting or grouping objects, so she could jump right in. Ms. Murrah anticipates making sense of five broad categories of animals (mammals, birds, reptiles, amphibians, and fish) and then noticing groups within those categories, such as carnivores, primates, frogs and toads, and birds of prey. Ms. Demchak has noticed that her prekindergartners love playing with and talking about vehicles, so they will sort vehicles first. Most of her children intuitively and nonverbally sort; they are at the surface level of learning. So Ms. Demchak began with explicitly sorting vehicles by easily perceived features, such as color and number of wheels. Now, she has moved onto vehicles categorized by where they travel—land, air, or water.

LEARNING INTENTIONS AND SUCCESS CRITERIA

While vehicles are not part of the 2019 Australian Early Years Learning Framework, sorting and positive interaction are important outcomes for identity and communication development. Ms. Demchak is able to center the content of sorting and interactions around her learners' interests, strengths, and needs, which change from year to year. This year, vehicles are a topic that unites her class. In previous years, she has capitalized on her class's interests in weather, animals, food, superheroes, and magical creatures. Ms. Demchak identifies three aims related to two outcomes for her sorting unit (Australian Government Department of Education and Training, 2019):

Outcome 1: Children Have a Strong Sense of Identity
- Children learn to interact in relation to others with care, empathy, and respect.

Outcome 5: Children Are Effective Communicators
- Children interact verbally and nonverbally with others for a range of purposes.
- Children begin to understand how symbols and pattern systems work.

Referring to these outcomes, Ms. Demchak creates learning intentions and success criteria to help her communicate what the class is learning, why, and how they will know when they are successful:

> **Content Learning Intention:** We are learning to notice and sort objects by attributes.
>
> **Language Learning Intention:** We are learning to name objects by attributes.
>
> **Social Learning Intention:** We are learning to actively listen.
>
> **Success Criteria**
>
> - We can sort the same objects by different attributes.
> - We can describe sorts using words.
> - We can listen to and respond to each other's sorting strategies.

These learning intentions and success criteria can be adjusted easily as the class explores other objects to sort. This repetition will help Ms. Demchak's learners become more confident in knowing the purpose of their work. The openness of the word "attributes" allows for her learners to show what they know—some may return to sorting by color and number of wheels, some may be ready to sort by where they travel, and some may notice new attributes to sort by.

ACTIVATING PRIOR KNOWLEDGE

Ms. Murrah's sorting unit takes place during her mathematics time, but Ms. Demchak's prekindergarten schedule is different from kindergarten and she does not have a "mathematics" period. Instead, Ms. Demchak has a variety of times throughout her day where she can implement her sorting unit—during their daily outdoor time, centers time, class meeting, and goal time.

EFFECT SIZE
FOR SPACED
PRACTICE
= 0.65

Today, she has put vehicles and vehicle-related materials in every center, along with the usual centers materials, and her lesson will take place during centers time. For example, in Art Area, there are vehicle stickers and stamps and vehicle play-dough cutters as well as "how-to" visual directions for drawing different vehicles. In Costumes Area, there are costumes for people who drive different vehicles—construction worker, fire-fighter, pilot, astronaut, and so on—and parts of vehicles for pre-tending, such as a steering wheel and walkie-talkies. In some areas, there are tubs of miniature vehicles. One set of vehicles can be taken apart and put together using screws, screwdrivers, and plastic drills.

With Ms. Murrah, Ms. Demchak practices her intentional language for sorting the vehicles.

Ms. Demchak knows she wants to make explicit through her language the taxonomy or category membership and non-membership of vehicles. She says, "We have sorted vehicles by color and by counting the number of wheels. Today, we're going to sort using a new attribute. We're going to sort by where the vehicle travels. Does it travel on land, in the air, or in water?" Ms. Demchak begins her mini-lesson. Each child is holding a vehicle while sitting in a circle. "Look at your vehicle and ask yourself, 'Does it travel on land, in the air, or in water?'"

FIGURE 2.1

An anchor chart for sorting vehicles

Ms. Demchak pauses and then thinks aloud, "I have an airplane. It can have wheels to drive on land—on the runway—to get ready to take off. There are airplanes that can land on the water and float too. But airplanes travel by flying through the air. So I think an airplane travels in the air. I'm going to put it right here." She places her airplane under a large picture of clouds labeled "Air" on her anchor chart (Figure 2.1).

"Let's go around the circle. When it's your turn tell us where your vehicle travels and how you know. Be listening to hear whether you agree or disagree," Ms. Demchak continues. Each child takes a turn describing their vehicle and sorting it. There is some debate about a tugboat versus a submarine.

Ruby wonders, "A tugboat floats but a submarine sinks. Maybe they don't go together."

Noah, who rarely talks in whole group discussion, is vocal and confident today. He knows a lot about submarines and explains how they travel under water but can also float at the surface, like a tugboat. The class decides to put submarine with the water vehicles, but at the bottom to show it can travel under water.

Another conversation arises when Jedda has a train, Oliver has a race car, and Zoe has a dirt bike. "These don't go on roads," Zoe points out.

"That's interesting. These three vehicles travel on land but not on roads like trucks and vans do. What do you know about where these vehicles travel?" Ms. Demchak summarizes Zoe's idea and redirects the question to the whole class to consider.

"A train goes on a track," Jedda responds.

"So does a race car. A race track," adds Oliver.

"A train track and a race track aren't the same," Isla points out.

"But both tracks tell them where they have to go. They can't go a different way," extends Coen.

"Mine goes on dirt and grass. It's a *dirt* bike," says Zoe.

EFFECT SIZE FOR CLASSROOM DISCUSSION = 0.82

"I think we're going to have to sort the vehicles that travel on land so we can be more specific with what we know. Just like with the submarine, we can make groups within the land group," Ms. Demchak says, making the hierarchical relationships and the process for forming them explicit. "How can we further sort land vehicles?" she asks. The class decides to have three groups: roads, tracks, and grass.

When it is Isaac's turn, he explains, "My tractor can go on roads or grass. But it always goes on land."

After engaging the class in discussion and deliberately practicing the vehicle sort with modeling, think-alouds, and peer feedback, Ms. Demchak connects this work to their learning intentions and success criteria.

> When you go to centers, be looking for ways to sort. You might sort vehicles by color, by number of wheels, by where they travel, or by something else you discover. You might sort something different than vehicles. See if you can sort the same things more than one way. See if you can describe your sort with words. See if your friends can help you by listening and talking about your sort. These are all ways to practice and be successful with sorting.

EFFECT SIZE FOR TEACHER CLARITY = 0.84

The class then moves into their routine of making choices and plans for their work in centers. The children move to centers and Ms. Demchak checks her notes. Both Ms. Demchak and the paraprofessional interact with the children as they work in their centers to create playful learning contexts filled with language. Today, Ms. Demchak has specific learners she plans to talk with about sorting vehicles, so she joins them first.

SCAFFOLDING, EXTENDING, AND ASSESSING THINKING AND LANGUAGE

Noah likes to work quietly either alone or parallel to peers. He rarely talks in whole group discussion and uses one- or two-word phrases while interacting with peers. His previous teacher in nursery school recommended he be evaluated for speech and language intervention because he was nearly silent at school. But Ms. Demchak knows from talking with his mom that Noah at school is vastly different from Noah at home. During her fall home visit, Ms. Demchak learned Noah is a verbose, vehicle expert; he showed her a crate of vehicles, named each one, and explained what type of work it did. He spoke in multiword sentences with enthusiasm.

EFFECT SIZE FOR FAMILY INVOLVEMENT = 0.42

Since the beginning of the sorting unit, Ms. Demchak has noticed Noah talking more in whole group discussion, often knowing the name of a vehicle when no one else does and sharing attribute details to help sort the vehicle. Ms. Demchak is excited by this change, that Noah is growing in his comfort and confidence at school and that he is seeing himself as the expert he is.

Noah is working in the Construction Zone with Jacob and Alinta who are building a race track with wooden blocks. Noah has found the submarine and is turning it over in his hands.

"What are you noticing, Noah?" Ms. Demchak asks.

"Why does it have wheels?" Noah asks puzzled.

"I don't know. Do submarines have wheels?" Ms. Demchak responds honestly.

"I don't think so. See this little exploring thing? It has wheels. It pops out the submarine. Then drives on the ocean bottom. It explores things. It gets real close. Not the submarine," Noah explains. He has so much to say and he knows so much! The context of playing with vehicles is home-familiar. Jacob and Alinta stop their work to watch as Noah pulls a lever and the submarine opens to release another small vehicle.

"Wow! I didn't know it could do that!" Jacob says in awe.

"What's the little exploring thing called?" Ms. Demchak wonders.

"I don't know. Maybe little submarine," Noah responds quietly.

"Let's research submarines. Where can we read about submarines?" Ms. Demchak prompts.

Noah walks to the crate of vehicle books in Construction Zone; there is a crate of vehicle books in each center and a special labeled shelf in the classroom library (Figure 2.2). Noah pulls out the book on submarines. He has clearly looked at these books before during centers. Together, Ms. Demchak, Noah, and now Alinta and Jacob, flip pages "reading" the photos. Ms. Demchak also reads the words. They learn that some submarines have wheels that retract and are called seafloor-crawling subs. Some submarines also have mini-subs with or without wheels to deploy. All three children repeat new words they heard with wonder: "retract," "seafloor-crawling subs," "deploy."

EFFECT SIZE FOR INQUIRY-BASED TEACHING = 0.46

"Our submarine has wheels. There's a special name for submarines like ours with wheels. Do you remember it?" Ms. Demchak circles back to Noah's noticing to allow for repetition of the new language and concepts.

EFFECT SIZE FOR DELIBERATE PRACTICE = 0.79

"Crawling subs?" Noah tries.

"Seafloor-crawling subs," Ms. Demchak adds. "They crawl on the bottom of the ocean, which is called the seafloor." Noah repeats the new word as he rolls it along the ground. "Do the wheels retract, which means they pop up inside of the sub, or do they stay out and ready to use all the time?" Ms. Demchak extends.

"They don't retract," Noah says as he tries to push them in.

"And that's a mini-sub!" Jacob says with excitement.

FIGURE 2.2

An early childhood classroom library with image and word labels to sort books

"Let's do that thing where it pops out to explore. How do you do it?" Alinta asks.

"Noah, can you explain to us how to deploy the mini-sub?" Ms. Demchak inserts another new word. Noah explains as he shows how to push the button and a side of the submarine opens for the mini-sub to roll out.

"Why would it be useful to deploy a mini-sub?" Ms. Demchak asks an inferencing question and waits so the children can think and respond.

Noah shares his prior knowledge and expands on it, "It's good for exploring close up. Like if you want to see a jellyfish but not scare it away."

"Yeah, you could be sneakier in it because you're smaller," continues Jacob.

"I bet it moves faster and turns faster. Like a race car," Alinta proposes.

"Those are some great inferences!" Ms. Demchak transitions the conversation back to sorting. "I wonder how the mini-sub would fit into our sort. Where should we put it?"

"We could make a new one. Vehicles that go inside. Like this one!" Jacob suggests as he pulls out a truck that opens and inside are cars.

"That's a car hauler," Noah shares. Noah, Jacob, and Alinta start to pull out the vehicles from the tub and sort them. Ms. Demchak notes that these learners are moving into the deep level of learning.

As Ms. Demchak transitioned from conversation partner with Noah to language facilitator with all three children, Noah moved from working parallel and silently to being an active and verbal collaborator with this peers. Ms. Demchak reiterates the learning intentions and success criteria within the context of their chosen work, "You're noticing, naming, and resorting our vehicles by a new discovery—some vehicles carry other vehicles inside. You're describing your sort with words and working as a team to listen and respond to each other's ideas. I'm excited to see how you sort the rest of the vehicles!"

Ms. Demchak records notes from her playful learning interaction with all three children and notes who she plans to interact with next.

TEACHING FOR CLARITY AT THE CLOSE

After cleanup, the class gathers in a circle to review their centers work. Ms. Demchak has joined three centers to talk with the children as they played. She asks two learners to share about their sort; they have papers and a book sitting in front of them. Illarah and Liam sorted vehicle stamps and stickers by type of vehicle: car, train, bus, truck, plane, and so on. As they share, Ms. Demchak adds this way of sorting to the class anchor chart.

EFFECT SIZE FOR CONCEPT MAPPING = 0.64

Their sort inspires many more types of vehicles shared by peers. Then she asks meta-cognitive questions to facilitate their deliberate practice of this higher-level thinking: "When we sorted vehicles by where they travel, we put planes and helicopters together because they both fly in the air. How did you decide that planes and helicopters are two different types of vehicles?"

Illarah picks up the paper with helicopter stamps and stickers and points to the propeller. "We saw helicopters have a special spinning thing," she explains. She flicks the propeller and it spins.

"Yeah, that's the propeller and helicopters have those to fly. Well, we thought only helicopters had propellers. But then we found out planes do too," Liam explains.

Illarah adds, "Planes have two on their wings. But helicopters don't have wings."

"And they both have wheels," Liam concludes.

"Wow. To sort these vehicles in a new way, you really had to notice their parts—the propellers, wings, and wheels. You noticed something that was unique or special about planes that helicopters don't have even though they fly in the air. What did you notice?" Ms. Demchak makes explicit their process and facilitates their thinking about the unique traits of each category.

"We thought it was propellers but it's wings," Illarah says.

"Planes have wings but helicopters don't," Liam summarizes.

Noah raises his hand and says, "Submarines have propellers too." Noah's voice within the classroom community is finding strength.

"Interesting. But submarines travel in the water and helicopters and planes travel in the air. How could we sort these vehicles so that submarines, helicopters, and planes go together?" Ms. Demchak waits, allowing for the children to ponder her abstract question.

Max suggests, "We could sort by parts. They all have propellers. But cars and trucks don't."

"Cars and trucks can have trailers," Mirrin adds. As learners contribute more ideas for vehicle parts, Ms. Demchak begins a list for the anchor chart. Then she brings closure to the class discussion:

> You are noticing and naming so many attributes of vehicles. We can sort the same pile of vehicles by all of them. We can describe our sorts using words. And we can listen and respond to each other's ideas as a team. I have a challenge for you that we'll talk more about tomorrow. Can you think of something that moves people or things but is *not* a vehicle? Can you think of something that travels on land, in water, or in the air but is *not* a vehicle? Be thinking about it and we'll see if we can find some things that don't fit our vehicle sort tomorrow.

MS. BULLOCK AND OCCUPATIONS

When Ms. Bullock first began the unit on community jobs, she asked families to visit the class or record themselves telling about their jobs. The class learned about the work of a police officer, nursing assistant, house cleaner, landscaper, receptionist, hairdresser, and mechanic. By inviting community members, going on field trips, and reading books, children learned about many more occupations as well as what they wear, what tools they use, what vehicles they drive, where they work, and what they do each day.

Now, most of the children are ready to transfer what they know about jobs to create extended play scenarios where they can deliberately practice the language of the jobs within playful learning.

Ms. Bullock has created a mini-community where each center is a business and between the centers are roads (Table 2.1). Each center is stocked with the clothing and tools needed to do the work. There is a post office, hospital, veterinarian's office, construction site, hair salon, garage, fire station, day care, restaurant, and grocery store. There is also a tricycle "van" ready for house cleaners or landscapers.

TABLE 2.1 ● Mini-Community "Businesses"

FIGURE 2.3

Veterinarian's Office

FIGURE 2.4

Restaurant

FIGURE 2.5

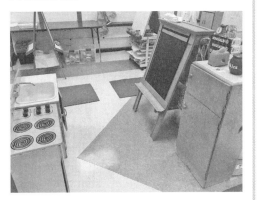

FIGURE 2.6

Day Care

FIGURE 2.7

Grocery Store

LEARNING INTENTIONS AND SUCCESS CRITERIA

The Illinois Early Learning and Development Standards include many verbs related to discussion, description, and communication (Illinois State Board of Education, 2013). Ms. Bullock intentionally selects both content and socioemotional development learning standards that focus on language as she plans her unit:

Social Studies Learning Standard 15.A.ECab: Describe some common jobs and what is needed to perform those jobs. Discuss why people work.

Social/Emotional Development Learning Standard 31.B.ECab: Interact verbally and nonverbally with other children. Engage in cooperative group play.

Next, Ms. Bullock reflects on the transfer work for which most of her learners are ready. She uses the standards to create learning intentions and success criteria that also focus on language and actively using this language to make decisions about their playful learning:

Content Learning Intention: We are learning about jobs in our community.

Language Learning Intention: We are learning the specific words needed to do the jobs in our community.

Social Learning Intention: We are learning to cooperate.

Success Criteria

- We can use the clothing, tools, vehicles, and buildings of jobs in our community to do work.
- We can work in different businesses and work together.
- We can make, do, and reflect on a work plan with friends.

Now, Ms. Bullock is ready to plan how she will communicate the learning intentions and success criteria to her 3-year-old learners. She wants to make these ideas concrete and provide her learners with a vision of success without narrowing their choices or removing their creativity.

ACTIVATING PRIOR KNOWLEDGE

Ms. Bullock finishes reading aloud *Saturday* by Oge Mora (2019) and announces, "Today is our first day of working in centers using our new mini-community!" The class is excited as they sit in a circle listening to Ms. Bullock. She has been telling them about the mini-community for several days and their anticipation is mounting.

EFFECT SIZE FOR CONCENTRATION/ PERSISTENCE/ ENGAGEMENT = 0.54

> Just like we always do, you will each make a choice and a plan for where you will start your work. When you are finished with your work there and ready to move to a new location, you need to clean up first. The centers are new! Each one is a business for you to work in just like the jobs we've been studying. I want to show you what I mean, so I'm going to make one of the businesses right here for us to practice.

Ms. Bullock has a mirror, chairs, table, cash register, phone, clipboard, and tub of hair salon supplies set up at the edge of their circle. "Here is a hair salon, just like where Zakeisha's mom works. If we want to pretend to run a hair salon business, what could we do?" she asks. The children offer ideas about roles and Ms. Bullock has three children come into the hair salon—a hairstylist (Kayvion), a receptionist (Carmen), and a customer (Kadisha).

Kayvion puts on an apron and begins to look through the tub of supplies while asking his customer, "You want haircut or hair braid?"

Kadisha sits in the chair facing the mirror and says, "Blow dry."

Carmen sits at the table with the phone and a clipboard, "Hello, what hair you want?"

Ms. Bullock narrates who they are pretending to be and what they each are doing. "Kayvion is blow drying Kadisha's hair with the hair dryer. Carmen is writing down the new person's hair appointment." This narration models the language of the hair salon work and activates the children's prior knowledge.

The class has pretended previously to create a hair salon during center time, but they only had one business available at a time in order to deliberately practice the language, tools, clothing, and work of that job. Now, Ms. Bullock wants to help the children see and hear how they could pretend to have multiple businesses interact in their mini-community. Ms. Bullock knows her children have all experienced this interaction in their home lives. At the beginning of the lesson, she read aloud the book *Saturday* to help activate these experiences. Now, her role is language facilitator to help them verbally name and describe these interactions.

EFFECT SIZE FOR DELIBERATE INSTRUCTION = 0.59

> Today, in our new mini-community, we will have many businesses open for you to work in. And just like in our neighborhood, people working in different businesses

may need to work together. Let's think about what that might look like and sound like. Think about when you are home with your family on Saturday, just like Ava in our book. Ava and her mom ride the bus to the library, the hair salon, the park, and the puppet show. What do you do? What businesses do you go to?

Ms. Bullock waits for everyone to have think time. Then, pairs of children turn toward each other, knee-to-knee and eye-to-eye, to tell about their family on Saturdays.

"Now let's think about our hair salon. Did you know there's a post office on the same road? I wonder who might work at the post office," she says. Several children volunteer, and Ms. Bullock asks Ethan to be the mailperson who delivers the mail. "How could Ethan, our mailperson, help the hair salon? Or how could the hair salon help Ethan?" Again, Ms. Bullock waits while the children ponder this open question with many possibilities.

Dayquan suggests, "Ethan can deliver mail."

Ms. Bullock extends his idea, "Ethan could deliver mail to the hair salon. Maybe they're expecting a delivery of shampoo!"

Zakeisha says, "Kayvion can cut Ethan's hair."

Ms. Bullock expands on this idea, "Ethan's a mailperson but he's also someone who needs a haircut! He could call Kadisha for an appointment and then get his hair cut by Kayvion when he's finished his work."

Then Machele says, "Carmen mail letter."

"Carmen could give Ethan a letter to mail. Maybe it's a letter to her grandma or maybe she's paying a bill," Ms. Bullock responds.

With many ideas, Ms. Bullock wants the children to make their own decision about how to interact so she says, "Let's watch and see how the mailperson decides to interact with the hair salon."

Ethan walks over, says, "Mail for you," and hands Carmen a letter.

Carmen takes it, saying, "Thanks. You want haircut?"

Ethan responds, "Yes. After work today." Ms. Bullock summarizes the action that just took place and everyone claps for the workers as they bow and return to their seats.

Finally, Ms. Bullock articulates how each of the workers exemplified the learning intentions and success criteria:

> Today when we work in the mini-community, be sure to use the clothing, tools, vehicles, and buildings of your job, just like Carmen, Kayvion, and Ethan did. Think about ways the different businesses can work together,

like Ethan delivering mail to Carmen and Carmen asking Ethan if he wanted a haircut. To work together, you'll have to make a plan with friends. After you try your plan, we'll come back together and share what we tried.

The children select the business they will start their work in and they enter the mini-community. Ms. Bullock and the paraprofessionals have planned to visit the businesses to engage the children in conversations and to facilitate the interaction between businesses. They will also check for and document evidence of the children meeting the success criteria (Figure 2.8).

FIGURE 2.8 ● Occupations Observation/Conference Checklist

Content Learning Intention: We are learning about jobs in our community.

Language Learning Intention: We are learning the specific words needed to do the jobs in our community.

Social Learning Intention: We are learning to cooperate.

Success Criteria:

- We can use the clothing, tools, vehicles, and buildings of jobs in our community to do work.
- We can work in different businesses and work together.
- We can make, do, and reflect on a work plan with friends.

Questions:

- What are you doing?
- How does the clothing/tool/vehicle help you?
- How could you help (work with) _____?
- How do you know?
- What could happen if ...?
- Where do you ...?

Name: Business:	Name: Business:	Name: Business:	Name: Business:	Name: Business:
Name: Business:	Name: Business:	Name: Business:	Name: Business:	Name: Business:
Name: Business:	Name: Business:	Name: Business:	Name: Business:	Name: Business:

Photos for sharing: 1. _____ 2. _____ 3. _____ 4. _____

Sharing Questions:

- With talking partners: *What was your plan? What did you do?*
- Analyzing photos: *What do you notice? What do you wonder?*

online resources ⟍ Available for download at **resources.corwin.com/VLforEarlyChildhood**

SCAFFOLDING, EXTENDING, AND ASSESSING THINKING AND LANGUAGE

Ms. Bullock's first stop is at the veterinarian's office. Alex is wearing a white coat and stethoscope and listening to the heartbeats of various stuffed animals. "Excuse me, Dr. Alex. My dog is sick. Will you help him feel better?" Ms. Bullock is carrying a toy dog as she engages Alex in conversation. Alex takes the dog and puts the stethoscope on him. "What are you checking, Dr. Alex?"

"His heart. I hear it go beep beep," Alex replies.

"Oh wow. I can't hear his heart. How can you hear it?" Ms. Bullock is engaging Alex in talk about his tools as he acts out being a veterinarian, requiring him through the playful learning context to practice language.

EFFECT SIZE FOR DELIBERATE PRACTICE = 0.79

"With this. It's a scope. I put it in my ears like this," Alex says as he shows how he uses the stethoscope. "A stethoscope helps you listen to his heart. What other tools do you use?" Ms. Bullock prompts.

"I can put him on here. It tells if he's heavy," Alex puts the stuffed animal on a scale and watches the arrow barely move, and then says, "Nope. Not heavy."

Ms. Bullock can see Alex knows how and why to use a scale and she wonders if he knows the words to describe this work. "How do you know he's not heavy?" she asks.

Alex is now scribbling on paper and says, "The scale didn't move. I have one in my bathroom."

Ms. Bullock models language, "When the numbers on the scale don't move, it means he's not heavy. He's light. What are you writing down?"

"Dog is not heavy. Get more food," Alex points to the scribbles on his writing as he reads it.

"You recommend getting my dog more food so he'll feel better? Okay, I need to go to the grocery store." Ms. Bullock stands up to leave as Sabina comes in with a stuffed animal cat. "Thank you, Dr. Alex, for using your veterinarian tools to help my dog!" Ms. Bullock takes a photo of Alex as he listens to the cat's heart. She records the evidence of meeting the success criteria that she observed. Next, she walks to the garage.

Alaysia is hammering a toy fire engine. She is wearing protective glasses and a tool belt. "What's the problem with your car?" she asks as she sees Ms. Bullock walk in carrying a toy car.

"I'm not sure. I was driving to school and I heard a big pop. Then the car bumped around until I stopped. What could that be, Mechanic Alaysia?"

Alaysia's dad is a mechanic and she sees him work on cars at their house too. She asks, "A big pop?"

"Yup, a big pop. Like a really big balloon. What could pop on a car?" Ms. Bullock scaffolds her inference.

EFFECT
SIZE FOR
SCAFFOLDING
= 0.58

"Your tire popped. That's called a flat tire. I give you a new tire with lots of air." Alaysia hammers a tire on the car. Then she puts the hammer back in her tool belt, gets out a wrench, and uses it to turn the tire.

"What are you doing?" Ms. Bullock prompts Alaysia to explain her tools.

"The wrench turns to put the tire on." She hands the car back to Ms. Bullock and says, "Fixed!"

"Wow, that was so quick!" Ms. Bullock also wants to scaffold the interactions between businesses so she asks, "Did you get the fire engine fixed?"

"Yeah, the ladder was cracked but I taped it," Alaysia shows Ms. Bullock the tape on the ladder rungs.

"I bet the firefighters will be so glad to get their fire engine back. Will you deliver it or do you want them to pick it up?" Ms. Bullock poses.

"Them pick it up," Alaysia responds.

"I can give them your message. I'll drive there now that you've replaced my flat tire. How much do I owe you?" Ms. Bullock pays Alaysia and walks to the fire station to tell them to go pick up their fixed fire engine. Briera walks to Alaysia's garage.

Again, Ms. Bullock takes a photo of Briera and Alaysia exchanging the fire engine for pretend money. She records her observations and continues to the next business. After 20 minutes, Ms. Bullock's chime signals to every business owner to close up shop and start cleaning up.

TEACHING FOR CLARITY AT THE CLOSE

The class will continue working in the mini-community for the week. While most of Ms. Bullock's interactions with children prompted more talking and initiated interactions between businesses, there were a few learners who moved quickly from business to business without engaging deeply in the work or who never interacted with anyone outside of their business. Ms. Bullock knows these learners need more support to grow their time on task and depth of playful learning as well as their movement into the transfer level of learning. Ms. Bullock uses the sharing time at the end of centers to make the learning intentions and success criteria more concrete.

EFFECT SIZE FOR SELF-JUDGMENT AND REFLECTION = 0.75

First, the children share with their talking partner about the plan they made and the work they did in the mini-community. This is their reflection time with the third success criterion.

EFFECT SIZE FOR IMAGERY = 0.51

Then, they come together as a whole class to look at the photos Ms. Bullock took. She displays four photos one at a time and asks the children, "What do you notice? What do you wonder?" Each photo shows at least two children from different businesses interacting. Children notice and name the jobs, clothing, tools, vehicles, and buildings. They describe actions. Some of the children in the photos describe what was said.

Ms. Bullock emphasizes the two different businesses each child came from and how and why they are interacting. "Tomorrow, we will continue working in our mini-community to see how people from different businesses can work together. You might use some of the work by your friends today to make plans for your work tomorrow," she says.

MR. HEATON AND ANIMAL HABITATS

The 3- and 4-year-olds in Mr. Heaton's class are beginning their long-term study of animal habitats with one close to home—the United Kingdom's woodland habitat. They have learned about animals living in the woodlands (badger, mouse, pine marten, deer, bat, vole, squirrel, otter, rabbit, hedgehog, hawk, fox, owl, woodpecker) and made a concept map of each woodland animal's habitat that shows what it eats, where it gets water, and what its home looks like.

EFFECT SIZE FOR CONCEPT MAPPING = 0.64

About half of the animals are initially unfamiliar to the children. Mr. Heaton knows that systems of animal habitats are a meaningful way to help the children integrate new information about animals with their prior knowledge.

EFFECT SIZE FOR STRATEGIES TO INTEGRATE WITH PRIOR KNOWLEDGE = 0.93

He also knows that making the ideas multisensory and rich with language will support children's conceptual understanding. Reading about each animal will not be enough for deep learning to occur; the children need to experience being the animals.

LEARNING INTENTIONS AND SUCCESS CRITERIA

When Mr. Heaton uses the Early Learning Goals (U.K. Department of Education, 2021) to plan his instruction, he looks for opportunities to integrate goals. In his teaching of content, such as animal habitats, he also wants to teach comprehension, language, and cooperation. The content provides a context for learning and applying these cross-curricular skills.

EFFECT SIZE FOR INTEGRATED CURRICULA = 0.40

With integration in mind, Mr. Heaton identifies the following Early Learning Goals:

- **ELG The Natural World:** Explore the natural world around them, making observations and drawing pictures of animals and plants. Understand some important processes and changes in the natural world around them.
- **ELG Comprehension:** Use and understand recently introduced vocabulary during discussions about stories, non-fiction, rhymes and poems, and during role-play.
- **ELG Speaking:** Offer explanations for how things might happen, making use of recently introduced vocabulary from stories, non-fiction, and rhymes and poems when appropriate.
- **ELG Building Relationships:** Work and play cooperatively and take turns with others.

Next, Mr. Heaton creates learning intentions and related success criteria that align with the Early Learning Goals and can be used throughout the unit. He creates a fourth success criterion (denoted with an asterisk) for the 4-year-olds who attend both the morning and afternoon sessions, also called extended day.

Content Learning Intention: We are learning about the natural systems of habitats.

Language Learning Intention: We are learning to use our words to share our connections and ideas.

Social Learning Intention: We are learning the value of each other's ideas.

Success Criteria

- We can describe the habitat of animals (food, water, air, shelter).
- We can create animal homes within a habitat using each other's ideas.
- We can explain why the habitat fits the animals' needs.
- *We can describe the relationships among animals and plants in a habitat.

The children began working toward the first success criterion as they learned about each woodland animal and its home. Today, they dive deeper into learning by creating replicas of the homes (the second criterion) and engaging in playful learning within the replica. This provides them with experiences to support explaining why each specific animal needs its specific habitat (the third criterion) and to show connections on their concept map.

During the morning session, when the class is mixed ages and the paraprofessional is present, the children formed two teams to collaboratively create an animal home and pretend to be the animals living there with the facilitation of either Mr. Heaton or the paraprofessional. Mr. Heaton's group chose to create a rabbit burrow with tunnels using cardboard boxes, blankets, and pillows. The second group chose to create a giant hawk's nest using long wooden pieces from the blocks area and pieces of fabric. In the afternoon session, when only four 4-year-olds remain with Mr. Heaton, they will choose another animal home to create and examine the relationships among the three homes in the woodland habitat.

ACTIVATING PRIOR KNOWLEDGE

EFFECT SIZE FOR REHEARSAL AND MEMORIZATION = 0.73

The cozy group of five is sitting together singing a habitat song. The children choose the animal and then they repeat the song, rehearsing the definition of a habitat and the names of woodland animals they have studied.

After singing, Mr. Heaton shares the goals of their work, "This afternoon, we're going to choose another animal home in the woodland habitat to create. We have a rabbit burrow and a hawk's nest. What's another animal home we could build?" Mr. Heaton often opens their work together with a discussion; in such a small group, the children can practice listening and responding to each other more naturally than raising hands in the whole group discussion.

EFFECT SIZE FOR SMALL GROUP LEARNING = 0.47

Hamza enthusiastically suggests a fox because he recently saw one. The others quickly agree. "What do we know about a fox's home?" Mr. Heaton facilitates.

"It's called a den," Hamza says.

"I think it's like a rabbit burrow. It's got tunnels," Croydon adds.

"Foxes eat rabbits," Arthur says, "We shouldn't build the foxes' house close to rabbits'."

"Foxes dig tunnels in the ground," Hamza explains.

"So we need to build a fox den in the ground with tunnels that will be similar to the rabbits' burrow but they can't be near each other," Mr. Heaton summarizes. "What might happen if their homes are near each other?"

"The foxes would eat all the rabbits," Evelyn predicts.

"Foxes can smell rabbit and find them," Arthur explains.

"We know foxes hunt rabbits for food. We know foxes and rabbits have similar shelters. We also have a hawk's nest in our woodland habitat. How are hawks related to foxes and rabbits?" Mr. Heaton asks the complex question related to their additional success criterion.

"Hawks swoop down and eat rabbits too," Hamza exclaims moving his hands like a hawk swooping to the ground.

"But they live high up at the top of trees in nests," says Croydon.

"Foxes and rabbits can't climb trees," adds Arthur.

"Maybe a hawk would try to eat a fox," Evelyn suggests.

"Or maybe a hawk and fox would fight each other," Croydon supposes.

"Or they could hunt for the same rabbit and see who's faster," Hamza predicts.

"Interesting ideas about what could happen. When animals share the same habitat like the woodlands, they might live near or far from each other, hunt each other, compete for the same food, or maybe even fight each other. Those are all important relationships among the animals that live in the same woodland habitat," Mr. Heaton responds. "Our first task is to build the foxes' den. Then you can decide which animal you want to be and we'll have time to explore in the woodland habitat. Our goal is to learn more about the relationships among foxes, hawks, and rabbits in their habitat," Mr. Heaton explains. "Let's make our building plan and then we'll make our plan for pretend."

EFFECT SIZE FOR COGNITIVE TASK ANALYSIS = 1.29

The small group discusses their plan, while Mr. Heaton adds a sketch of the den to the woodland habitat concept map with the rabbit burrow and hawk's nest already drawn in and labeled. Mr. Heaton is modeling planning, visualizing, connecting images with concrete objects, and map making.

EFFECT SIZE FOR PLANNING AND PREDICTING = 0.76

Then the group begins building.

SCAFFOLDING, EXTENDING, AND ASSESSING THINKING AND LANGUAGE

As the children connect long cardboard boxes to each other and place wider cardboard boxes at the ends, they talk and Mr. Heaton is always part of the conversation.

"Let's make this tunnel really long so nothing would dare to climb through it," Arthur declares.

"We should hide the open part so badgers can't find it," Hamza suggests.

"And so we can just disappear and appear to hunt rabbit. Poof!" Croydon says with excitement.

"How would a fox camouflage the den's entrance?" Mr. Heaton models language.

"It could be hidden in a tree," Evelyn says, "At the bottom by the roots."

"Not the hawk's tree!" says Arthur.

"Or it could be under a bush," suggests Hamza.

"Let's cover the enter box with green paper. Make it like a bush," Croydon says and gets out green construction paper and glue.

While camouflaging the entrance, they make their plans for enacting the woodland animals. Hamza and Mr. Heaton will be foxes. Evelyn will be a hawk. And Arthur and Croydon will be rabbits, "So fast nothing can catch us!"

EFFECT SIZE FOR COOPERATIVE LEARNING = 0.46

During much of their playful learning, Arthur and Croydon stay inside their burrow crawling along the tunnels back and forth, while Evelyn watches from her nest and Hamza and Mr. Heaton go to the rabbit burrow entrance and then hide at their den entrance.

Mr. Heaton says to Hamza, "Those rabbits are going to get hungry eventually and we'll be ready! What should we do while we wait?"

Hamza thinks for a moment, "Maybe we should go look for water or different food? We can eat some mice."

EFFECT SIZE FOR CREATIVITY = 0.58

"Do you think the hawk will also hunt for a mouse?" Mr. Heaton prompts.

"We could race her! I bet we'll be faster!" Hamza is excited. "Race you, Evelyn!"

"Okay, where's the mouse?" Evelyn asks.

"With the stuffed animals," Hamza responds and starts running toward a tub.

"You have to crawl!" Evelyn shouts as she flaps her arms and runs after Hamza.

Meanwhile, Arthur and Croydon are watching from inside their tunnel. They run out and pretend to grab grass and run back in. Then they shout triumphantly, "We got our dinner!"

Croydon brags, "We won't come out till morning now!"

When Hamza returns to the fox den, Mr. Heaton asks, "Did you capture the mouse?"

"No, when I had to crawl, Evelyn got there first," Hamza says disappointedly.

Throughout their woodland habitat game, Mr. Heaton engaged in conversation with Hamza while also modeling language and extending the play for all the children. His prompts fostered new events in their game while maintaining the children as active decision makers.

TEACHING FOR CLARITY AT THE CLOSE

At the conclusion of their woodland habitat game, Mr. Heaton brings the children back together to review what they tried and what they learned. He returns to the learning intentions and success criteria, "We're learning about natural systems called habitats. A system means everything in the system has a relationship. So everything in the woodland habitat has a relationship. What did you learn about the relationships in the woodland habitat?" This is an abstract question and Mr. Heaton does not expect all of the children to be able to articulate their ideas; but he believes that they need multiple opportunities to try to respond, and with time and practice, they will make sense of abstract questions and share their ideas.

"I learned all animals have to eat. We couldn't just stay in our house forever," Croydon reflects.

EFFECT SIZE FOR SELF-JUDGMENT AND REFLECTION = 0.75

"That's an important part of each animal's day. They need to get their own food but it also means they could be in danger," Mr. Heaton expands on Croydon's idea.

"We could have been eaten by Evelyn or you or Hamza!" Arthur continues.

"And I ate the mouse," Evelyn says with pride.

"Scientists call the animals who hunt 'predators' and the animals who get eaten 'prey.' But even prey have to eat, so they have to be sneaky," Mr. Heaton capitalizes on this noticing of a relationship to directly teach two vocabulary terms.

"Foxes and hawks are predators?" Hamza checks.

EFFECT SIZE FOR VOCABULARY INSTRUCTION = 0.63

"Yes. And who was their prey?" Mr. Heaton gives feedback and prompts practice with the new vocabulary.

"Rabbits," answers Arthur.

"And mouses!" adds Evelyn.

"Then who eats foxes and hawks?" Croydon wonders.

"Foxes and hawks have special names called apex predators. That means nothing hunts them. They have no predators. They are at the top of the food chain," Mr. Heaton introduces more vocabulary to support the continuing class discussion.

"So they live forever?" Arthur wonders.

EFFECT SIZE FOR INQUIRY-BASED TEACHING = 0.46

"That's something we should research. If no animals eat apex predators like foxes and hawks, what happens to them?" Mr. Heaton rephrases Arthur's question.

"You worked so hard to think about the relationships in the woodland habitat. That was some great thinking and talking. Tomorrow, we'll build more homes and explore more relationships. I'm wondering if there's an animal that eats rabbits and that gets eaten by foxes or hawks. What are you wondering?" Mr. Heaton has the children share their questions and records them. They are in the deep phase of learning, making conceptual connections. Their reflection about their playful learning has led to learning new vocabulary to describe relationships, vocabulary that Mr. Heaton had anticipated and was ready to teach. Tomorrow, these same four children will work with the full mixed-age classroom and share with their peers this new language and these new concepts.

Ms. Davis and Distance Playful Learning

How do you engage twelve 4-year-olds who have never met, *online*, in play that is rich with talk and interaction (also known as playful learning)? This is the challenge Ms. Davis faces each day in her distance learning prekindergarten class. Each time she asks a question about how to do something with her learners in distance learning, she reflects on the quintessential elements of that same teaching and learning in person: How do you engage twelve 4-year-olds who have never met, *in person*, in play that is rich with talk and interaction?

First, build relationships with the children and among the children. By learning about each child, their family, their interests, and their home life, Ms. Davis is able to foster relationships among the children and select materials and topics that tap into these strengths.

In a distance learning setting, this means Ms. Davis began the year with a digital library of each child reading their own *All About Me* book. Ms. Davis spends time one-on-one with six of her learners on alternating days. She also has family conferences online and communicates daily with families.

EFFECT SIZE FOR TEACHER–STUDENT RELATIONSHIPS = 0.47

Second, Ms. Davis cultivates routines that scaffold talk about work, including play. Each day, there is small group time for playful learning. At the beginning of each small group session, the children take turns making a plan for their work. The majority of the time is spent with children implementing their plans. As they work, Ms. Davis asks each child to tell about what they are doing or trying. Then, to close their session, the children take turns sharing what they did.

Third, Ms. Davis encourages constant talk. At the beginning of their time together online, Ms. Davis spoke the most. She often narrated her work. Ms. Davis was also constantly modeling ways to engage with each other verbally—ways to use each other's ideas to start and extend work, ways to role-play together, and ways to ask each other questions. With time, modeling, and familiarity, the children have begun to talk to each other without Ms. Davis's constant prompting or scaffolds. While Ms. Davis remains a conversational partner and a language facilitator during playful learning, she has shifted her focus to intentionally using language in order to practice executive processing and reasoning. She asks gradually more abstract questions, such as "What if . . . ?" and "Will that always work?"

EFFECT SIZE FOR META-COGNITIVE STRATEGIES = 0.60

Like everything else in distance learning, the children's small group time for playful learning does not look the same as in person. But it sounds the same, with children saying things like, "Anna, I made you a cupcake. Everybody sing Happy Birthday to Anna!" "My train is longer than yours, Jinson. Want to see?" "I'm making the bear puzzle. Josué, what puzzle you making?"

TIPS AND CONSIDERATIONS FOR PLAYFUL LEARNING

As you intentionally plan your language for creating rich verbal inquiry in playful learning, consider these guidelines and tips:

- Start with familiar, informal language and contexts so that children can show what they know. Use this as a springboard to connect to formal vocabulary and phrases.

- While playful learning involves a lot of adult interaction, it can still fit in child-centered classrooms where choice and hands-on tasks capitalize on children's intrinsic motivation to play.

- Remember that outdoor play should be playful learning too. Rather than thinking of outdoor play as recess, reframe this time as another choice time or centers time where you can be a conversational partner and a language facilitator.

- Songs, poems, and retellings are effective ways to engage children in rehearsal and memorization as well as spaced practice of new vocabulary and ideas.

- As you plan your language, be sure to be intentional with your questions. Plan them. Write them down and carry them with you as you interact with the children.

- Organize vocabulary instruction into hierarchical categories or taxonomic relationships, like Ms. Demchak, Ms. Bullock, and Mr. Heaton did. These meaningful groupings of words focus on relationships and conceptual understanding and they support memory.

- Adult interaction is key to making play a learning opportunity. One of your ways of interacting can be to facilitate peer interactions too. This develops multiple children's language simultaneously and supports socioemotional growth.

- Connect language to multiple and multisensory representations using concrete materials, images, actions, and symbols as well as song, dance, movement, rhyme, and rhythm.

- Encourage children to interact with you and their peers in their home languages. Their growth in home language vocabulary and comprehension supports this growth in English too.

CHAPTER 3

Visible Learning in Early Childhood Mathematics

For many of us, school mathematics can hold a mixture of emotions and experiences. Yet we engage in mathematical reasoning with confidence and ease in our daily lives outside of school. This is because the heart of mathematics is the contextualized reasoning, patterning, and problem solving that we encounter each day. True mathematical thinking begins at birth and develops as young children explore their world. At the center of their explorations are number sense and spatial reasoning. Effective mathematics teaching and learning in early childhood builds on these natural qualities of mathematical thinking while making it explicit through language. By providing rich, language-based experiences for young children, we can create opportunities for them to develop strong and positive mathematical identities and understandings.

This chapter will unpack what research tells us is critical in early childhood mathematics teaching and learning, and then we will see the Visible Learning research in action inside three early childhood classrooms. First, let's establish a common vision and language for describing effective, visible mathematics teaching and learning in early childhood.

EFFECTIVE MATHEMATICS LEARNING IN EARLY CHILDHOOD

While we may think our primary role as educators is to teach mathematical content or to engage learners in mathematical inquiry, research tells us that the most critical role of early childhood educators is the mathematization of children's ideas, representations, and language (Clements, 2004; Fuson, 2004; National Research Council, 2009; Perry & Dockett, 2008; Sophian, 1999).

Every child brings substantial, valuable informal mathematical knowledge (Civil, 1998; Muhammad, 2020). By accessing this knowledge, children develop formal mathematical understandings and mathematical identities. In order to access this knowledge, educators must help children make it explicit, transferable, generalizable, intentional, and verbal. In other words, our role as early childhood educators is not to impart knowledge but to connect knowledge. The gradual process of making nonverbal mathematical knowledge verbal is called mathematization and occurs through reflection, interaction, and communication.

MATHEMATIZATION

Educators often underestimate children's informal mathematical knowledge and perceive a gap between children's verbal and nonverbal mathematical knowledge (Baroody, 2004; Clements & Sarama, 2007; Ginsburg & Golbeck, 2004; National Research Council, 2009; Perry & Dockett, 2008). This gap should not be interpreted as a lack of conceptual understanding; instead, it is a lack of language knowledge (Baroody, 2004; Ginsburg & Golbeck, 2004: Hindman et al., 2010; Jordan & Levine, 2009; Jordan et al., 2006; Tudge & Doucet, 2004), and this is precisely where early childhood educators play a significant role.

Mathematized knowledge is language-based. Connecting precise verbal and visual representations to contextualized concepts is an important step of mathematization (Baroody, 2004). All learners develop conceptual understanding of mathematical ideas and concepts by building on and making connections among three phases of representations: concrete, pictorial, and abstract; this instructional strategy is called CRA or concrete-representational-abstract (Berry & Thunder, 2017).

Educators do this vital work through language-based interactions with learners. Teacher-to-learner and learner-to-learner talk is critical. The language should be mathematically accurate and constantly focused on making connections among words, familiar and new contexts, and concrete, pictorial, and abstract representations. We must create early childhood classrooms rich with mathematical talk.

In order to mathematize knowledge, educators must first recognize and appreciate children's informal mathematical knowledge. This requires educators to know important mathematical concepts, vocabulary, and ways of thinking as well as to be

EFFECT SIZE FOR STRATEGIES TO INTEGRATE WITH PRIOR KNOWLEDGE = 0.93

EFFECT SIZE FOR MANIPULATIVES = 0.39

EFFECT SIZE FOR IMAGERY = 0.51

EFFECT SIZE FOR CLASSROOM DISCUSSION = 0.82

In order to mathematize knowledge, educators must first recognize and appreciate children's informal mathematical knowledge.

familiar with meaningful contexts, materials, and manipulatives that cultivate opportunities to mathematize. Two mathematical concepts are foundational to all mathematical thinking and start developing at birth: number sense and spatial reasoning.

NUMBER SENSE

Number sense is understanding numbers and their relationships. There are three categories of number sense concepts, and each remains important mathematically across time: counting, value, and relationships among numbers. Table 3.1 defines each of the 11 number sense concepts (Gelman & Gallistel, 1978; Thunder, 2014; Van de Walle et al., 2019).

EFFECT SIZE FOR MATHEMATICS = 0.58

TABLE 3.1 ● Number Sense Concepts

COUNTING	VALUE	RELATIONSHIPS AMONG NUMBERS
One-to-One Correspondence Objects are counted by saying number words in a one-to-one correspondence with the objects.	**Connecting Number Symbol, Number Word, and Quantity** Numbers can be represented by a symbol, a word (oral or written), and a quantity (concrete or pictorial).	**Subitizing** Sets of objects in patterned arrangements can be quickly recognized and the number of objects can be determined without counting.
Ordinality The counting numbers follow an order.	**Relative Value or Relative Magnitude** The value of a number can be described as relative to the value of a number without knowing the actual value of the number.	**Equality and Inequality** The value of numbers can be more, less, or the same as other numbers.
Cardinality The last number word said when counting tells how many objects have been counted.		**Anchors or Benchmarks** The value of numbers can be described based on their distance to anchors or benchmarks (numbers important to our number system), such as multiples of 5 and 10.
Abstraction Counting determines how many regardless of the objects' other attributes.		**Part–Part–Whole Relationships or Decomposing Numbers** A number is made up of two or more parts. A number can be decomposed into two or more parts.
Order Irrelevance No matter where you start counting, the same number of total objects will be counted.		

Some of these number sense concepts may be familiar to you and you may already know what they look like or sound like when one of your children is showing they know the concepts in familiar contexts. Other number sense concepts may be new to you. What do you envision they would look like or sound like when one of your children shows you they know the concept? To facilitate mathematization, consider the language-based interactions you would have to help learners attach precise mathematical language to their informal knowledge and to make meaningful connections among representations, contexts, and words. When we visit Ms. Demchak, Ms. Bullock, Mr. Heaton, and Ms. Davis's classrooms, you will see examples of children knowing and showing these number concepts informally and formally.

SPATIAL REASONING

A second significant math concept is spatial reasoning. Spatial reasoning is both spatial orientation (knowing how to get around in the world) and spatial visualization (knowing how to mentally build and manipulate objects). Researchers found a strong relationship between spatial reasoning and number sense (Clements, 2004). In fact, subitizing is a combination of both number sense and spatial reasoning because it develops an understanding of numbers and number relationships while also growing spatial visualization of quantities.

EFFECT SIZE FOR IMAGERY = 0.51

Spatial reasoning may be a mathematical concept familiar to you and the work that you see your children engaging in. It can be closely related to gross and fine motor work. We often focus on teaching positional words like *over*, *under*, *behind*, and *through* as well as engaging learners in building and constructing with materials. These are ways you may already mathematize learners' informal spatial reasoning. As we take a peek inside three early childhood classrooms, you will see and hear additional strategies for mathematizing spatial reasoning.

WAYS OF THINKING AND DOING MATHEMATICS

From your mathematical thinking in daily life, you know there is more to mathematics than merely mathematical content. National standards and national curricula recognize that the core of mathematics is about the ways of thinking and doing mathematics content in context. In the United States, the Common Core State Standards for Mathematics has standards for both mathematical content and practice (National Governors Association Center for Best Practices, Council of Chief State

School Officers, 2010). The eight Standards for Mathematical Practice focus on processes and proficiencies (National Council of Teachers of Mathematics, 2020; National Research Council, 2009), such as reasoning, modeling, and constructing arguments. The United Kingdom's national curriculum includes three general mathematics aims for all pupils, such as persevering, conjecturing relationships, and using mathematical language; for some years, there are both specific mathematics content goals and specific goals for "working mathematically." Similarly, Australia's national curriculum delineates proficiency strands of understanding, fluency, problem solving, and reasoning separately from the three content strands (number and algebra, measurement and geometry, statistics and probability).

While all early childhood standards may not specify these ways of thinking and doing mathematics, it is critical for early childhood educators to focus on processes. Mathematizing is about making informal knowledge explicit, transferable, generalizable, intentional, and verbal. By mathematizing learners' ways of thinking and doing mathematics, learners will be able to mathematize their own mathematical content as they continue through school and experience the ever-expanding nature of school mathematics.

In addition, a positive emphasis on process can lay the foundation for growing learners' positive identity, agency, positionality, and authority within school mathematics contexts (National Council of Teachers of Mathematics, 2020). Australia's national Early Years Learning Framework exemplifies this vision by characterizing early childhood standards within a view of the whole child as belonging, being, and becoming (Australian Government Department of Education and Training, 2019).

> While all early childhood standards may not specify these ways of thinking and doing mathematics, it is critical for early childhood educators to focus on processes.

> **EFFECT SIZE FOR TRANSFER STRATEGIES = 0.86**

> **EFFECT SIZE FOR SELF-EFFICACY = 0.66**

This is where mathematics education research and Visible Learning research intersect: Our primary role is to mathematize or to connect learners' knowledge through language. The critical mathematical knowledge we must mathematize is number sense, spatial reasoning, and ways of thinking and doing mathematics. Now, we step into three early childhood classrooms to see and hear this intersection of playful learning and Visible Learning research in action.

MS. DEMCHAK AND NUMBERS

Ms. Demchak and Ms. Murrah collaborate within their vertical professional learning community to align preschool and kindergarten instruction, plan differentiated tasks, and prepare the preschool children for the transition to kindergarten.

Because number sense is a significant mathematics concept for early childhood, Ms. Demchak teaches multiple number units throughout the year, each one extending and deepening the previous unit to include new contexts, representations, and words.

The previous number units focused on equal sets and comparing sets, and the current number unit focuses on anchoring sets to 5.

In kindergarten, Ms. Murrah has shared that ten-frames and number charts are important mathematical tools. She often has learners who are ready to count larger collections of tens and ones, and children spend time working independently as well as with a partner to play mathematics games. These are all considerations Ms. Demchak uses as she plans her instruction.

Ms. Demchak also knows from observing and engaging with her learners and their families that the children in her class have a lot of informal mathematical knowledge about numbers. During the last few weeks, they made anchor charts about the numbers 2–5 (Figure 3.1). Together, the class has shared what they know about each value and Ms. Demchak has recorded their ideas using pictures and letters. For example, on the 5 chart, Ms. Demchak wrote the numeral 5, the word "five," and five domino dots. The children added a traced hand to show five fingers, Bindi's name with five letters, the five school days Monday through Friday, the five people in Cole's family, five candles on a cake for everyone who is 5 years old, five *Llama Llama* books, five green and speckled frogs, and more. They also drew five dots on a five-frame and a ten-frame and then found and highlighted the numeral five on a number line and a number chart.

FIGURE 3.1

An anchor chart for the number 5

LEARNING INTENTIONS AND SUCCESS CRITERIA

Today, Ms. Demchak's classroom of 4-year-olds is concluding the first week of the number unit on anchoring sets to 5. The majority of her class is working at the deep level of learning. Ms. Demchak identifies two aims from Outcome 4 of the Early Years Learning Framework for Australia as her goals for the lesson (Australian Government Department of Education and Training, 2019):

Outcome 4: Children Are Confident and Involved Learners

- Children transfer and adapt what they have learned from one context to another.
- Children resource their own learning through connecting with people, places, technologies, and natural and processed materials.

Based on these teacher-facing goals, Ms. Demchak creates mathematics-focused learning intentions and success criteria:

Content Learning Intention: We are learning ways numbers are related to 5.

Language Learning Intention: We are learning to talk about our mathematical thinking.

Social Learning Intention: We are learning to share ideas and problem solve as a team.

Success Criteria

- We can describe the number of dots and the number of empty boxes in five- and ten-frames.
- We can use what we know about building and counting to make sets using five- and ten-frames.
- We can help each other when we get stuck.

With clear goals for teaching and learning, Ms. Demchak plans how she will communicate these goals to her young learners and how she will mathematize their rich experiential knowledge through language.

ACTIVATING PRIOR KNOWLEDGE

Ms. Demchak begins with a short, multimodal mini-lesson to communicate the learning intentions and success criteria and to activate learners' prior knowledge. She says, "Today, we're continuing our work to find ways numbers are related to 5. Do you remember our song about 'Five Little Ducks'? We start with five ducklings and one mama duck."

As she talks, Ms. Demchak puts five carpet squares out in the middle of the class circle, forming a five-frame. "Let's start with a different number today. How many ducklings could there be?" she asks. The children suggest 4, 8, 10, 100, and so on.

Ms. Demchak intentionally chooses 4. "We're going to start with 4 ducklings. How do we need to change the carpet squares so we have 4?" Ms. Demchak waits as the children process her question looking at the carpet squares. Then she rephrases using guiding questions to ensure every child has access to the task, "We have 5 carpet squares. We want 4 for 4 ducklings. How is 4 related to 5? Is 4 more or less than 5?" Again Ms. Demchak waits and then she calls on a few children to share their ideas. Most of the children think 4 is less than 5 so they will need to take away carpet squares. "How can we work together to figure this out? We know how to build and count 4 and 5. How can that help us?"

Jedda suggests, "We could make 4 kids the ducklings and they can stand on the carpet squares."

Thomas adds, "Yeah, and then we'd see extra carpet squares."

Ms. Demchak points to children as the whole class counts to 4. Ms. Demchak repeats the task question, "How do we need to change the carpet squares so we have 4?" Children are pointing to and counting the four kids standing on the carpet squares.

Mirrin says, "One carpet square is empty."

Ms. Demchak explains, "We could turn that carpet square over to remind us it stays empty or we can put it away." Max flips over the carpet square. The class sings and acts out "Four Little Ducks." Then everyone returns to the circle, leaving the five-frame carpet square arrangement.

"We're finding ways numbers are related to 5. Let's think about the number 4 and our 4 ducklings on our 4 carpet squares. How did we change the 5 carpet squares to make 4?" Ms. Demchak asks.

"We turned one carpet square over," says Coen.

"Nobody sat on one carpet square," adds Ruby.

Ms. Demchak has four children return to sitting on the carpet squares and the class counts them. "We used what we know about counting and building to help us organize our 4 carpet squares into a five-frame. Can you visualize the five-frame? Let's describe what we see. How many full carpet squares are there? How many are empty?" The children share ways to describe the four "duckling" children sitting on the carpet squares as well as the one empty carpet square. Ms. Demchak continues:

> We are learning a lot about the ways numbers are
> related to 5. We used what we know about building

and counting to make a set of 4 organized in a five-frame. We described how many carpet squares were full and how many were empty on our five-frame. And when we got stuck, we worked as a team to help each other by sharing our ideas. This is the work you'll be doing today by yourself and with a partner. Remember to use what you know to build and count, remember to talk about what you see and make, and remember to help each other when you get stuck.

SCAFFOLDING, EXTENDING, AND ASSESSING MATHEMATICAL THINKING

The children get their task boxes and spread across the room to work. Each tub has an image of the success criteria.

Jacob and Noah are painting dots on five- and ten-frames with cotton swabs. Illarah and Mia are making sets of playdough balls on ten-frames. Isla and Oliver are building sets of shells on plastic ten-frames. Coen and Bindi are taking turns rolling dice and changing the number of plastic bears on a plastic five-frame to match the dots on the dice. Using a variety of materials (multiple representations), each learner is exploring the learning intentions and success criteria with the size numbers that are just right for them (Table 3.2). Some are working with numbers 1–5 and others are working with numbers 1–10; some are using five-frames and others are using ten-frames. Mirrin is working with numbers 10–20 on twenty-frames.

Ms. Demchak moves from learner to learner in order to mathematize their individual thinking and to actively connect their independent practice to the learning intentions and success criteria. Jacob and Zoe are building sets of matchbox cars on five-frames that look like parking lots. They each grab a numeral card from a bag, build the matching set, and then put the card on the five-frame as a label. They each have their own work but they talk to each other as they build and count. Jacob and Zoe are in the deep level of learning focused on making conceptual connections.

Ms. Demchak watches them work and then asks, "How are your parking lots of cars related to the number 5?"

Jacob points to his parking lots, "These are smaller than 5 and this one is 5."

Ms. Demchak mathematizes, "You're comparing the sets to 5. You noticed some sets are less than 5 and one is equal to 5. What about you, Zoe?"

EFFECT SIZE
FOR SUCCESS
CRITERIA
= 0.88

EFFECT
SIZE FOR
APPROPRIATELY
CHALLENGING
GOALS = 0.59

EFFECT
SIZE FOR
COOPERATIVE
LEARNING
= 0.46

TABLE 3.2 ● Task Box Success Criteria

FIGURE 3.2

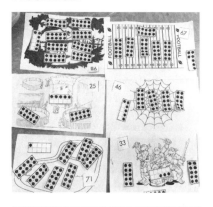

I can build a set to match a number.

I can point and count the set.

I can describe the number of dots and the number of empty boxes.

FIGURE 3.3

I can build a set to match the dice.

I can point and count the set.

I can describe the number of dots and the number of empty boxes.

FIGURE 3.4

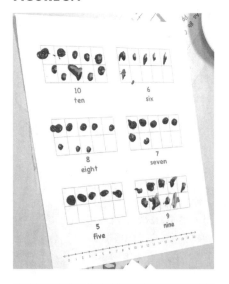

I can paint dots to show the number.

I can point and count.

I can describe the number of dots and the number of empty boxes.

FIGURE 3.5

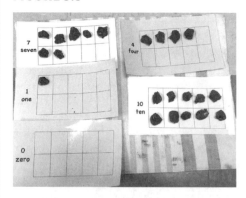

I can roll balls to build the number.

I can point and count.

I can describe the number of dots and the number of empty boxes.

"This one has 3 cars and 2 empty spaces," Zoe says as she points to a parking lot labeled 3. "And this one has 4 cars and 1 empty space," Zoe points to a different parking lot labeled 4.

Ms. Demchak asks questions to emphasize making connections between the number sense concepts of inequality and anchors to 5. "I notice Jacob's parking lot that has less than 5 cars can also be described Zoe's way. There is 1 car and 4 empty spaces. I wonder if that's always true—if you have less than 5 cars, can you always say you have some cars and some empty spaces?"

Zoe points to all of the parking lots less than 5 to check the statement and it seems true so far. Then Jacob adds, "You can always say you have some empty parking spots. All the parking lots have empty spots."

"Not always," Zoe interjects pointing to a parking lot of 5. "This one is full."

"I wonder how many cars you have if your parking lot is full," Ms. Demchak extends. Zoe quickly responds "5," while Jacob counts the five parking spaces. Ms. Demchak summarizes their work in terms of the success criteria. "You've described how many parking spaces are full and empty. You've used what you know about building and counting to make parking lot five-frames. Have you gotten stuck?"

"Zoe got a card with a 0 on it. I helped her because I know O and zero look the same," Jacob reflects.

"Yeah, Jacob helped me. It's zero so I have all empty spaces," Zoe explains.

"You have 5 empty spaces!" Jacob realizes.

"You're making a lot of connections and asking important mathematical questions. I'm excited to hear what else you notice about how the numbers are related to 5." Ms. Demchak records notes from this conference on her chart (Figure 3.6) and moves to confer with another pair.

TEACHING FOR CLARITY AT THE CLOSE

The class has spent the week exploring the ways numbers anchor to 5. Ms. Demchak has confirmed through her conferences that most of her learners are in the deep level of learning and a few are in the transfer level of learning. She wants to make explicit the importance of 5 as a benchmark using the five- and ten-frames as tools and the mathematical language of combinations.

> Many of you noticed that we can build and then describe the number of empty spaces on a five-frame. Just like

EFFECT SIZE FOR STRATEGY MONITORING = 0.58

EFFECT SIZE FOR FEEDBACK = 0.62

EFFECT SIZE FOR PROVIDING FORMATIVE EVALUATION = 0.40

FIGURE 3.6 ● Mathematics Task Boxes: Observation/Conference Checklist

Dates ______________________________

Content Learning Intention: We are learning ways numbers are related to 5.

Language Learning Intention: We are learning to talk about our mathematical thinking.

Social Learning Intention: We are learning to share ideas and problem solve as a team.

NAME	SC#L: We can describe the number of dots and the number of empty boxes in five- and ten-frames.	SC#2: We can use what we know about building and counting to make sets using five- and ten-frames.	SC#3: We can help each other when we get stuck.	SIZE Numbers (*5-frames 10-frames 20-frames*)	NOTES

online resources Available for download at **resources.corwin.com/VLforEarlyChildhood** with "Four Little Ducks" when we had one empty carpet square, you can see and count empty spaces on a five-frame. The five-frame helps make this easier to visualize. You also noticed that when the five-frame is full, there are five. I'm wondering if you can know how many dots there are just by noticing the empty spaces on a five-frame. I have some five-frames to share with you. Let's talk about how many dots and empty boxes there are.

Ms. Demchak shows some five-frames with four dots, but each frame has the empty space in a different place. With each frame, the children take turns describing how many dots and empty boxes they see. Ms. Demchak records their descriptions (Figure 3.7).

Many of them also make connections to their work: "I painted 4 blue dots" or "Bindi kept rolling 4 so we built a lot of fours." "What do you notice about the number of empty spaces when there are 4 dots?" Ms. Demchak poses. Several children notice there is one empty space on each frame.

After finding the pattern, Ms. Demchak returns to the learning intentions of the day. "Our goal today was to find ways numbers are related to 5. All of these frames have four dots and one empty space. How is 4 related to 5?" This is a cognitively demanding question so Ms. Demchak pauses. This question requires the learners to practice accessing their newly mathematized knowledge. Knowing that connecting nonverbal and verbal knowledge is a gradual process, Ms. Demchak wants to provide many opportunities over time for her learners to consider higher-level questions.

FIGURE 3.7 ● Number Talk Recording

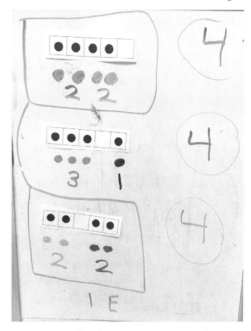

How many dots? How many empty boxes?

The children share a variety of responses: "5 is after 4." "5 is more than 4." "4 is the dots and 5 is the frame." "Here's 4 dots and 1 more is 5." "1, 2, 3, 4, 5." With practice and opportunity, the children will become more verbal with their responses and will use increasingly mathematical language.

Ms. Demchak concludes the lesson by summarizing, "You found many new ways numbers are related to 5. And you noticed a pattern: an empty space on a five-frame means there are 4 dots! Next week, we'll look for more patterns on five- and ten-frames."

MS. BULLOCK AND MEASUREMENT

Ms. Bullock has noticed her 3-year-olds always have a lot to say but they do not always have the words. Her focus is on helping them grow their vocabulary so they can effectively communicate their needs, wants, feelings, and ideas. Her learners also love to mimic adult roles and to compare their work with peers. Her measurement unit draws on these strengths to mathematize their informal knowledge of measurement tools and attributes.

LEARNING INTENTIONS AND SUCCESS CRITERIA

To begin the measurement unit, Ms. Bullock wants to assess the level of learning of the children by observing, conferring, and interacting with them as they work. Ms. Bullock identifies two early learning standards in mathematics from the Illinois Early Learning and Development Standards (Illinois State Board of Education, 2013):

Learning Standard 7.C.ECa: With teacher assistance, explore use of measuring tools that use standard units to measure objects and quantities that are meaningful to the child.

Learning Standard 7.A.ECc: Use vocabulary that describes and compares length, height, weight, capacity, and size.

Based on these standards, Ms. Bullock creates learning intentions and success criteria that she will communicate to her learners throughout the lesson:

Content Learning Intention: We are learning to measure with measuring tools.

Language Learning Intention: We are learning to describe our process and thinking.

Social Learning Intention: We are learning to try new challenges by sharing ideas.

Success Criteria

- We can describe what we measure.
- We can describe how we measure with measuring tools.
- We can try a new challenge with measuring.

Ms. Bullock's learners are highly motivated by play so today's introductory lesson will take place within their centers work or choice time—when the children choose centers to work in. Each center has a variety of play-based materials that fit the purpose of the center. For example, Costumes Area has a variety of costumes and props, Construction Zone has a variety of building materials, and Art Area has a variety of art supplies. The children are familiar with these centers and often now arrive at school with plans for what they will do and with whom in each center.

EFFECT SIZE FOR PLANNING AND PREDICTING = 0.76

Ms. Bullock will use these familiar contexts to engage her learners with new measurement tools so they can show what they know informally about measurement.

ACTIVATING PRIOR KNOWLEDGE

The class has gathered in a circle to make their plans for choice time. In the middle of the circle, Ms. Bullock has placed a variety of measurement tools: measuring tape, rulers, meter sticks, balances, scales, measuring cups and spoons, clocks, stopwatches, sand timers, calendars, and thermometers.

EFFECT SIZE FOR MANIPULATIVES = 0.39

Ms. Bullock introduces the new work and connects back to their previous studies:

> Today, we are exploring new tools. We've learned about some tools people use for their jobs like hammers and stethoscopes and cash registers. Our new tools are measurement tools. These tools help people do measuring work. Many jobs use measuring tools. People use measuring tools in their homes too. Look at the tools and see if there is one you recognize. Is there a tool you've used before or you've seen someone use?

Ms. Bullock has the children turn to sit knee-to-knee, eye-to-eye with the person next to them and they begin talking and pointing. After a few minutes, everyone turns back to the center and Ms. Bullock calls on a few children to share.

"We have those in the kitchen. We cook," Dayquan says pointing to the measuring spoons.

"We have one up there," Briera says pointing to the classroom clock.

"When I went to the doctor, I got on that," Ethan says pointing to the scale.

Ms. Bullock summarizes what was shared using precise mathematical language:

Wow, you know a lot about these measurement tools. Each tool has a name and helps us measure an attribute. Dayquan noticed the measuring cups. Measuring cups help us know how much to cook a recipe. Briera sees the clock like our classroom clock that helps us measure the time. We need the clock to know when it's time for lunch and outside time and nap time. Ethan has stood on a scale at the doctor's. A scale tells us how much something weighs. Is it heavy or light?

Next, Ms. Bullock communicates the learning intentions and success criteria:

There are lots of things to notice on a measuring tool. And there are lots of things to try with a measuring tool. So today, our work is to try a new challenge with measuring. You will choose a tool to take with you to your center and try something new using the tool. You can describe what you measure and how you measured it. You can trade in your tool to get a different tool. When we come back together after centers to share, we will share what we tried, what we measured, and how we measured it.

Each child takes a turn sharing their plan for where to work and what to do there. Each child also selects a measurement tool to take with them to their chosen center. Ms. Bullock tells each child the name of their tool. After everyone is in their area, Ms. Bullock surveys the children working and laughing in centers and chooses one to join.

SCAFFOLDING, EXTENDING, AND ASSESSING MATHEMATICAL THINKING

Carmen and Kadisha are in Art Area with a balance. They make purple playdough balls and put them on one side of the balance. Then they make red playdough balls and put them on the other side of the balance. As the purple side rises, they ooh and aah. Carmen speaks Spanish at home; in school, she usually says one- or two-word phrases in English or combinations of English and Spanish phrases with English-speaking peers while speaking Spanish with Ms. Bullock and her Spanish-speaking classmate Machele.

Kadisha says, "It's going up!"

And Carmen cheers, "Up! Up!"

When the purple side rises to the top and the red side lowers to the bottom, they laugh. "It pushed down!" Kadisha narrates.

And Carmen adds, "Fall down!"

Ms. Bullock watches their experimentation and then asks, "One side of your balance is down and one side is up. How did you do that?" She repeats the statement and question in Spanish.

EFFECT SIZE FOR QUESTIONING = 0.48

Kadisha explains, "We put more and more and more playdough in and it went down and down and down."

Carman says in Spanish, as she points to the lowered side, "There is a lot of red playdough!"

Ms. Bullock mathematizes, "This is a balance. It measures how much things weigh. I wonder which weighs more, the purple playdough or the red playdough?"

"There's more red," Kadisha responds.

"Let's feel how much they weigh," Ms. Bullock takes the cups filled with playdough from each side of the balance and holds one in each hand. Then she has each girl take turns holding both cups and asks, "Which one feels heavier?" They hold up the cup of red playdough. "The red feels heavier. Let's see what it looks like on the balance," Ms. Bullock says. The girls put the cups back on the balance and again the red side sinks down. "Which one looks heavier on the balance?" The girls point to the red cup.

EFFECT SIZE FOR SCAFFOLDING = 0.58

"It's down," Carmen notices.

Ms. Bullock repeats her initial question, "Which weighs more— the purple playdough or the red playdough?"

"Red," Carmen answers.

"It's heavy because we put more in," adds Kadisha.

Ms. Bullock summarizes and connects to the success criteria:

> There is more red playdough so the red side is heavier. The red side went down because it's heavy. The purple side is lighter. You've described measuring the weight of the playdough. You've described using the balance to measure. And you tried something new by sharing ideas. What will you do now?

"We can push down, Ms. Bullock," Kadisha shares as she pushes the purple cup down with her hand.

"Your hand weighs more than the red playdough!" Ms. Bullock notes. Then she extends their thinking in English and Spanish, "There's a measurement tool that you can use to measure how much you weigh. It's called a scale. You can stand on it."

Carmen says in Spanish, "I know!" and she goes to get the bathroom scale. She puts it on the ground and pulls Kadisha to stand on it. Then Carmen bends low to look at the arrow and says, "Three two."

"That number is 32. You weigh 32 pounds, Kadisha." Kadisha hops off so Carmen can get on and then bends over to read the numbers.

Ms. Bullock records her observations as the girls continue putting objects on the scale. They informally know the concept of weight and how to use the balance and scale as measurement tools. They are ready to learn the specific language of weight measurement: weigh, heavy, light, scale, balance. They are at the surface level of learning. Knowing this, Ms. Bullock can now select the right instructional strategies, and based on her goals, she knows she will use direct vocabulary instruction with concrete materials.

TEACHING FOR CLARITY AT THE CLOSE

After about 30 minutes of exploration in centers, Ms. Bullock brings the class together again in their circle to share. She says, "Think back to your work. When it's your turn to share, you can tell us one thing you tried, one thing you measured, and how you measured it." Each learner gets a turn to reflect on their work and use language to describe it. As they share, Ms. Bullock adds a labeled picture of their measuring tool to the visual word wall they will build over time. It is divided into sections: length, weight, volume/capacity, time, and temperature. She also places each measurement tool at the base of the wall.

EFFECT SIZE FOR CONCEPT MAPPING = 0.64

Carmen and Kadisha share about weighing each other on the scale. "You stand on it. The numbers move fast and stop. I was . . . what was I, Ms. Bullock?" Kadisha shares.

"You weigh 32 pounds," Ms. Bullock replies using precise mathematical language.

Kadisha repeats, "I weigh 32 pounds."

Ms. Bullock shows the picture of the bathroom scale and says as she puts it on the wall, "This is a scale. It measures weight."

Kayvion and Machele share about connecting trains as long as a stick. "Your train was as long as the meter stick? It was

1 meter long! Wow!" Ms. Bullock responds with measurement vocabulary.

Kayvion adds, "No, it was longer! It was longer than the meter!"

Ms. Bullock shows the picture of the meter stick and says as she puts it on the wall, "This is a meter stick. It measures length."

Alex and Jaedyn share about cooking a birthday cake. Alex used the measuring cups to pour and mix the cake. Jaedyn used the clock to know when the cake was done. "I went 'Beep! Beep! Beep! The cake is done!'"

"Oh, so you set a timer on the clock. Timers can count up and down to help us measure how much time something takes. A timer that counts down can go 5, 4, 3, 2, 1, Beep! Beep! Beep!" Ms. Bullock connects Jaedyn's use of a timer to their work with counting forward and backward. Then she shows the pictures of the measuring cups and clock and says as she puts them on the wall, "These are measuring cups. They measure capacity or how much. This is a clock. It measures time."

EFFECT SIZE FOR DELIBERATE INSTRUCTION = 0.59

After each learner has shared, Ms. Bullock brings closure by reviewing the learning intentions and success criteria and connecting their work to the next day: "You've worked so hard to measure with measuring tools today! You've tried many new things and shared what you measured and how you measured it. Many of you noticed numbers on your measuring tools. I wonder if they all have numbers. Tomorrow, we will try more new things with measuring tools and look for numbers!"

MR. HEATON AND GEOMETRY

Mr. Heaton's mixed-age class has been studying two- and three-dimensional shapes for a few weeks. While the 3- and 4-year-olds have mastered different types and numbers of shapes and their components, the majority of learners are at the transfer level of learning with regard to composing and decomposing shapes.

Just as Mr. Heaton works to create a variety of familiar contexts where his learners feel comfortable and confident showing what they know mathematically, he also works to create a variety of novel contexts where his learners can practice accessing their newly mathematized knowledge and transfer concepts and processes to new situations.

EFFECT SIZE FOR TRANSFER STRATEGIES = 0.86

Throughout their study, Mr. Heaton has kept track of the types of tasks that inspire the most excitement and creativity from each learner and now he has created problem-solving tasks based on those interests. In the morning, when all of the children are present, Mr. Heaton will present the task options and time to work. In the afternoon, when just the 4-year-olds remain at school, they will have additional time to work when Mr. Heaton can further differentiate their work by extending and deepening their mathematical thinking.

LEARNING INTENTIONS AND SUCCESS CRITERIA

The Early Learning Goals for Mr. Heaton's lesson are not strictly in the mathematics area of learning. As he plans his instruction, he considers number sense, spatial reasoning, mathematical processes, and the question "So what?" Mr. Heaton always wants his learners to experience why the mathematics matters through integration of concepts across the curriculum. His lesson focuses on transfer to new contexts and includes Early Learning Goals in mathematics, understanding the world, and arts and media (U.K. Department of Education, 2021):

ELG Numerical Patterns: Verbally count beyond 20, recognizing the pattern of the counting system.

ELG People, Culture and Communities: Explain some similarities and differences between life in this country and life in other countries, drawing on knowledge from stories, non-fiction texts and—when appropriate—maps.

ELG Creating With Materials: Safely use and explore a variety of materials, tools and techniques, experimenting with color, design, texture, form, and function; Share their creations, explaining the process they have used.

Based on these Early Learning Goals, Mr. Heaton creates learning intentions and success criteria for all of his learners and one additional success criterion (denoted with an asterisk) for just his afternoon 4-year-olds:

Content Learning Intention: We are learning to use what we know about shapes to create and build with shapes.

Language Learning Intention: We are learning to use number words to talk about shapes.

Social Learning Intention: We are learning the importance of solving problems by learning from each other.

After setting goals for his instruction, Mr. Heaton plans how he will communicate these goals to his learners and selects instructional strategies to support learners at the transfer level of learning.

ACTIVATING PRIOR KNOWLEDGE

The class sings and acts out a shape song. Mr. Heaton says, "Wow! We know a lot about shapes! We know the names of two- and three-dimensional shapes. We know the names for the parts of shapes, like side, angle, and base. We know how to break apart or decompose shapes into other shapes and to put together or compose shapes to make other shapes." He points to a big chart with a concept map of shape images, student work, and shape words. "Today, we're going to use what we know about shapes to create and build with shapes. You decide which creation challenge you'd like to work on."

Mr. Heaton continues, "The first creation challenge is called 'Can You Build It?' Here are famous structures from around the world. Your creation challenge is to build a famous structure using Legos, wooden blocks, or the polyhedral pieces." Next, he thinks aloud and models a brief example to concretely illustrate the success criteria.

I'd like to try building this structure. It's called the Parthenon and it's in a country named Greece. To build the Parthenon, I have to think about what shapes I can see. What shapes do you see? I see two triangles at the top where the roof is. And then I see oblong rectangles on the sides. Part of the oblong rectangles are made of columns, which are cylinders. There are a lot of columns. After looking at the picture to see shapes, I'm going to visualize the structure to help me build it. I'm going to use the wooden blocks because I know we have cylinders, triangular prisms, and rectangular prisms. Should I start with the roof or the sides of the structure?

EFFECT SIZE FOR COGNITIVE TASK ANALYSIS = 1.29

Mr. Heaton continues thinking aloud as he builds a quick replica of the Parthenon with wooden blocks and then he uses the success criteria to summarize his process, "I built the Parthenon with shapes and I can describe my structure. The roof is made of two triangular prisms. The sides are rectangular prisms and cylinders."

Mr. Heaton introduces the other three creation challenges:

- *Story Collage.* "We've read many books with illustrators who use collages to create the pictures. Your creation challenge is to use shapes to create a Story Collage."

- *Tiling.* "We've tiled with shapes to make floors and walls. Today, I have giant pattern blocks. Look how big they are! Your creation challenge is to use the giant pattern blocks to tile the floor of our class meeting space."

- *Number Chart Puzzles.* "These puzzles make number charts. Sometimes the numbers are missing on the pieces. Your creation challenge is to put the number chart puzzle together and then make your own."

As he presents the challenges, Mr. Heaton posts corresponding images on a chart (Table 3.3).

TABLE 3.3 ● Shape Creation Challenges

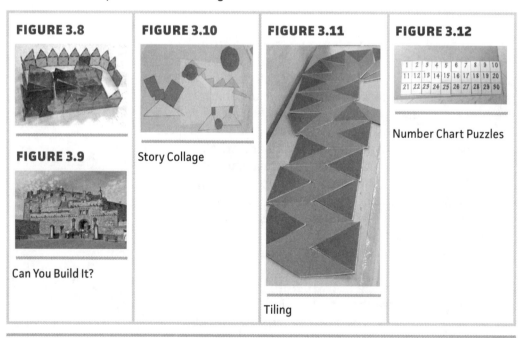

Edinburgh Castle image source: iStock.com/BMPix

The children typically make plans before they begin work. First, they turn to share their plan with a peer sitting next to them. Then they go around the circle sharing their choices. Finally, they move to sit with peers who made the same choice to make a plan for how they will share materials and either work collaboratively or independently. When each group has started working in their area, Mr. Heaton is ready to confer and mathematize.

SCAFFOLDING, EXTENDING, AND ASSESSING MATHEMATICAL THINKING

Mr. Heaton notices Amare and Bahar are sitting with blank papers in the Story Collage area. At the same table, Evelyn is cutting paper and Freddie is gluing circles.

"What are you going to create?" He asks Amare and Bahar as he sits down with them.

"We don't know," Amare says.

"I want to make the Very Hungry Caterpillar but I don't know how," says Bahar.

"Let's see if Evelyn and Freddie can help us get unstuck. Evelyn, what are you working on?" Mr. Heaton prompts.

EFFECT SIZE FOR SEEKING HELP FROM PEERS = 0.72

"I'm making a dragon. I'm cutting her body," Evelyn responds as she cuts.

"What shape is your dragon's body?" Mr. Heaton asks.

"It's rectangle but I didn't make corners so it looks like a oval," she explains.

"What other body parts are you creating?" Mr. Heaton asks.

"Dragons have two wings, a head, four legs, and a loooooong tail," Evelyn lists.

"It sounds like you're visualizing a dragon in your mind. You know what you want your dragon to look like and you're thinking about each body part," Mr. Heaton describes.

EFFECT SIZE FOR FEEDBACK = 0.62

"Yeah, the wings are going to be triangles," Evelyn describes.

"I'm excited to see your finished dragon made of so many shapes," Mr. Heaton says.

Mr. Heaton then turns to Freddie, "What are you creating?"

"A snowman. Like Olaf," replies Freddie.

"How are you using shapes to make your snowman?" Mr. Heaton asks.

"I'm using three circles. Then I'm gonna use more circles for his eyes and buttons and legs," Freddie explains.

"You are creating a dragon, you are creating a snowman using shapes, and you're describing your dragon and snowman with shape and number words," Mr. Heaton summarizes. He then returns to Bahar and Amare. "Let's see if we can use Freddie and Evelyn's ideas to help us think about how to use shapes to make our stories. Bahar, you want to make the Very Hungry Caterpillar. What shapes do you need to make him?" Mr. Heaton asks (Carle, 1994).

EFFECT SIZE FOR TRANSFER STRATEGIES = 0.86

"Circles like Freddie," Bahar responds and he finds circles in the tray to glue.

"I wonder how many circles you will need," Mr. Heaton prompts. "Amare, what do you want to create?"

"I'm making a dragon like Evelyn. But mine is red like fire," he replies.

"Think about what shapes you need to make a dragon. Visualize a dragon in your mind and on your paper. What shape will you start with?" Mr. Heaton scaffolds.

"A circle head," Amare replies and sets off to work.

Mr. Heaton pauses to record notes from these interactions. He notes who is meeting the success criteria and what geometric language each child uses. He also notes the number sense they use to visualize and create—they are connecting number word and quantity and Freddie subitizes three circles. Mr. Heaton also writes down that he wants to meet with Evelyn again in the afternoon. She is starting to explain her process of composing shapes to create a dragon and he wants to make this process explicit by talking with her about it. Mr. Heaton also has a table with shape names where Evelyn can record how many of each shape she used; this will support her description using number words and introduce her to an important mathematical tool.

EFFECT SIZE FOR APPROPRIATELY CHALLENGING GOALS = 0.59

TEACHING FOR CLARITY AT THE CLOSE

EFFECT SIZE FOR TIME ON TASK = 0.42

The children have been working with focus and now it's time to pause their work. Tomorrow, they will continue working on these problem-solving tasks so Mr. Heaton has each child store their work on a windowsill space. For the group tiling the class meeting space, Mr. Heaton takes a photo so that he and his paraprofessional can quickly reconstruct the work in progress tomorrow.

As the children gather in the circle, there is a lot of talk about their creations—they are excited. Mr. Heaton begins the share, "Today, Croydon is going to share about her progress with the Number Chart Puzzles. Here is the puzzle Croydon is working on putting together. Croydon, tell us about your number chart puzzle using shape and number words." Mr. Heaton conferred with Croydon during worktime so he is ready to facilitate her share.

EFFECT SIZE FOR SCAFFOLDING = 0.58

He puts Croydon's number chart puzzle on the easel for everyone to see. There are some missing pieces and numberless spaces.

Croydon shares, "There are a lot of square rectangles with numbers inside to count to 30. And then those are in shapes that fit together. Some oblong rectangles here and here, kind of a triangle here, and then some shapes I don't know. I'm not done yet."

Mr. Heaton engages the class in Croydon's think-aloud. "Use your eyes to spy the shapes Croydon is describing. Can you see an oblong rectangle? Can you see a kind-of triangle?" he asks. As Mr. Heaton prompts the children, he uses his finger to outline the shapes. "Look at this empty space. What shape would fit here? Try to visualize the shape that matches." Mr. Heaton pauses and several children raise their hands.

EFFECT SIZE FOR PEER- AND SELF- GRADING = 0.42

Harper stands up and points to the piece that would fit, "This one."

Mr. Heaton mathematizes her knowledge, "What is the name of that shape?"

Harper is not sure so she asks Eamon for help and he says, "Square."

"Let's see if the square rectangle will fit," Mr. Heaton directs Harper to place the piece in the empty space. "The square rectangle fits! Great visualizing!"

Mr. Heaton brings the lesson to a close, "Today, you chose a creation challenge to work on using all of the things you know about creating and building with shapes. You used shape and number words to describe your work. You visualized shapes and counted shapes. Tomorrow, we will continue our work and more people will share their creations."

Ms. Davis and Distance Learning in Mathematics

In previous years, Ms. Davis used similar tasks to Ms. Demchak for exploring numbers. This year, in distance learning, she is not able to provide hand-over-hand support or scaffold by doing parallel work with her learners. In fact, she struggles with providing feedback when learners are counting objects and with modeling one-to-one correspondence because of the choppiness of the Internet and the video conference platform.

After some trial and error, Ms. Davis has found that tasks like Mr. Heaton's "Can You Build It?" and organizing tools and questions, like Ms. Demchak's use of five- and ten-frames to discuss full and empty boxes, are great self-checking instructional strategies. Ms. Davis can allow children choice about which Can You Build It? card to create or which number to build. Then, with a document camera, she can build simultaneously and make her process and product visible to the learner. Ms. Davis can model and think aloud while creating a visual reference for her learners at home. In addition, Can You Build It? and five- and ten-frames provide an organizing tool that is self-checking because learners are matching and placing manipulatives on top of the outlines.

Feedback is easier to provide and the organizing tools create a common reference and opportunity to practice mathematizing language. For example, Ms. Davis made Can You Build It? cards with multilink cube animals and objects. Learners choose a card. Ms. Davis can model the build or both the learners and Ms. Davis can build the card simultaneously with Ms. Davis's work displayed via the document camera. Throughout their work, they talk. Ms. Davis asks questions like, "What part will you build first—the head, the body, the legs, or the tail? How many cubes will you need for the tail? How many cubes did you use for the body? How many cubes did you use for the whole fox?" The children also talk throughout their building process and compare their final product with Ms. Davis's product.

The Can You Build It? cards can feature multilink cubes, pattern block puzzles, tangrams, Cuisenaire rods, and so on.

Similarly with five- and ten-frames, Ms. Davis can roll a digital die or learners can choose a numeral card and a manipulative (plastic animals, pattern blocks, cubes, etc.). Ms. Davis can model the build or both the learners and Ms. Davis can build the numeral on the frame simultaneously with Ms. Davis's work displayed via the document

EFFECT SIZE FOR STRATEGY MONITORING = 0.58

EFFECT SIZE FOR SELF-VERBALIZATION AND SELF-QUESTIONING = 0.59

camera. Like with the Can You Build It? cards, they constantly talk as they work. Ms. Davis asks questions like, "How many boxes are full? How many are empty? How many reds do you have on your five-frame? How many cats do you have on your five-frame? How many animals did you use altogether? What is a different way you can arrange the animals in the five-frame?" The children also practice mathematical language as they work and refer to Ms. Davis's work to compare with their own.

With these two strategies, Ms. Davis has been able to give more specific feedback and support children's use of learning intentions and success criteria to evaluate their own work even in distance learning.

MATHEMATICS AND PLAYFUL LEARNING

Let's return to the ideas about playful learning in the early childhood Visible Learning classroom. Mathematics can be the content of playful learning. The materials within playful learning contexts can be used to create opportunities for children to show what they know informally and for early childhood educators to mathematize this informal knowledge through language-based interactions. By leveraging a combination of manipulatives and language, early childhood educators can mathematize mathematical understandings and maximize learning time with their learners.

As you select the materials and create the contexts for playful learning with mathematics, consider these guidelines and tips:

- Rather than naming a center or tub of materials "Mathematics," consider how the opportunity to show and connect mathematical ideas is present in all centers and materials.

- When selecting mathematical literature, check for mathematically precise language and representations. Remember, a diamond is not a geometric shape; it is a gem. The mathematically accurate shape is often a rhombus. Two-dimensional shapes and three-dimensional shapes are not the same thing; in other words, balls and wheels are not circles. They are both round, but a ball is a sphere and a wheel is a cylinder.

- When selecting counting books, check that the number symbol, word, and quantity are presented together to reinforce the number sense concept. Use counting books as a way to model the five counting principles. For example, ordinality can be counting forward by ones but it can also be skip-counting, counting backward, and counting on. You can model order irrelevance by counting the same number of objects on a page in different ways.

- Capitalize on familiar home contexts where daily mathematical thinking is used, often without even realizing it, and create those contexts in school so that children can show what they know, like Ms. Bullock did. Listen for informal language and watch for nonverbal understandings of significant mathematics concepts.

- Mathematize children's informal knowledge of significant number sense and spatial reasoning concepts by using precise mathematical language in interactions as they explore traditional early childhood toys, such as nesting dolls, shape sorters, stacking cups, trains, Legos, and puzzles.

- Build children's familiarity with primary school mathematics manipulatives by making them available for exploration while pairing this exploration with language. The "Notice, Wonder, Create" routine can be a powerful way to mathematize: What do you notice? What do you wonder? What can you create? High-engagement primary school mathematics manipulatives include pattern blocks, tangrams, pentominoes, Cuisenaire rods, multilink and Unifix cubes, base-ten blocks, polyhedral pieces, and measurement tools.

- Keep an eye out for new manipulatives that make abstract number sense and spatial reasoning concepts concrete. There are constantly new manipulatives being created. For example, there are ten-frame trains that actually make a train of 100 cubes in groups of 10, there are three-dimensional pentominoes that can be combined to make a variety of three-dimensional puzzles or silhouettes, and there is a three-dimensional binomial puzzle.

CHAPTER 4

Visible Learning in Early Childhood Literacy

Early childhood education is rich with literacy teaching and learning, which includes language development. We have many options and ideas for teaching literacy and we often have to choose what will fit within our instructional day. How do we make those decisions? How do we maximize young children's learning of literacy? We can answer these questions with a combination of thinking about who we want our learners to become as readers and writers as well as research on the most effective components of early childhood literacy instruction. Ultimately, we want to grow fluent readers and writers who use their skills to deeply comprehend the reading texts they choose and to communicate effectively through the written texts they choose, both professionally and personally. In order to support these long-term goals, we need to focus our instruction on reading comprehension and written communication.

This chapter will examine what research says is vital to develop strong reading comprehension and written communication, and specifically, what this means for visible early childhood literacy teaching and learning. When we think of literacy teaching and learning, what do we envision? Let's clarify what we mean and connect this with our knowledge for teaching literacy.

EFFECTIVE LITERACY LEARNING IN EARLY CHILDHOOD

What do you think of when you hear the word "literacy?" There are so many words associated with early childhood literacy instruction—phonological awareness, read-alouds, rhyme, letters and sounds, writing, and more. We have to make sense of many literacy words and place them within a digestible framework in order to organize our instruction around what is most important in the literacy content and to use Visible Learning research to implement effective instruction. Next, we will examine reading and writing research.

READING

The research evidence provides much support for *The Simple View of Reading* (SVR) (Gough & Tunmer, 1986), which includes two main components of learning to read:

$$\text{Word Recognition} \times \text{Language Comprehension} = \text{Reading Comprehension}$$

Word recognition includes phonological awareness, decoding, and sight recognition (Kilpatrick, 2016; Scarborough, 2001). Language comprehension includes background knowledge, vocabulary, comprehensive language skills, verbal reasoning, literacy knowledge, and attention (Kilpatrick, 2016; Scarborough, 2001). SVR can also give a zoomed-in view of early childhood reading comprehension by examining what word recognition and language comprehension mean for young learners.

Word Recognition. In early childhood with children ages 3–6, two aspects of word recognition are the primary foci: phonological awareness and letter-sound skills (part of decoding). The third aspect of word recognition called sight recognition or word-specific knowledge is not an area of focus in early childhood. Sight recognition is a reader's knowledge about specific words based on experiences that makes those words automatically known and familiar.

The first aspect of word recognition that is important in early childhood is phonological awareness, a metalinguistic skill. Phonological awareness is the ability to recognize and manipulate the sound properties of spoken words. In other words, phonological awareness enables children to make conscious and explicit the abstract concept of spoken language and to play with words and sounds.

At the syllable level of phonological awareness, children learn word play, including rhyming and alliteration, and to segment syllables by counting, clapping, and saying syllables slowly (Kilpatrick, 2016). This first level of phonological awareness is the entry point for engaging children in thinking about the sounds within words rather than the meanings of words.

Children become aware of an important rule about language: Every word is made of one or more syllables. They use this knowledge in the next level to make sense of and manipulate word sounds based on another rule: every syllable has a vowel.

At the onset-rime level of phonological awareness, children break apart syllables into two sounds: the onset and the rime (Kilpatrick, 2016). The onset of a syllable is made up of the consonant sounds before the vowel of the syllable. The rime of a syllable is made up of the vowel sound and the consonant sounds after the vowel of the syllable. Children working in this level segment single-syllable words, like bat, into two parts: the onset /b/ and the rime /at/. This work engages children with phonemes.

Phonemes are the smallest unit of sound in spoken words, whereas letters are the smallest part of written words. At the phoneme level, children recognize and manipulate individual phonemes of spoken words, including phoneme segmentation, deletion, and substitution. Children orally segment and blend phonemes of words and they take phonemes off of words and replace phonemes to create new words. Phoneme awareness is a critical part of connecting letter combinations with pronunciation. By attending to phonemes, children can later become familiar with letter strings, which support the efficient storing of words in permanent memory.

Letter-sound skills are the second aspect of word recognition important in early childhood.

EFFECT SIZE FOR PHONICS INSTRUCTION = 0.57

Letter-sound skills mean recognizing instantly the sounds that connect to letters and specific sequences of letters. There are five effective strategies for teaching the letter-sound connection (Kilpatrick, 2016). We should create multiple exposures or spaced practice across the school day and year and use multisensory methods.

EFFECT SIZE FOR SPACED PRACTICE = 0.65

We should neither teach one letter at a time (letter of the week) nor teach all letters at once; instead, we should teach a small set of letters together (Adams, 2013; Jones et al., 2012; Piasta & Wagner, 2010; Piasta et al., 2012). As we examine that small set of letters, we should make explicit the visual features of the letters, such as comparing letters with similar features and comparing uppercase versus lowercase versions of letters.

EFFECT SIZE FOR DELIBERATE INSTRUCTION = 0.59

We should teach letter sounds in a developmentally appropriate sequence by starting with easier letter sounds, like letter sounds in the letter names, and then move to letters with harder sounds. The sequence should also include an element of review for spaced practice. Finally, we should teach letter sounds using embedded mnemonic letters, which means we should teach letters with a keyword where the first letter of the keyword is drawn in the shape of the keyword. For example, we could teach /s/ for snake and show the letter s in snake drawn to look like a snake, providing a visual support.

Our work in early childhood education to develop word recognition falls in these two categories: phonological awareness and letter-sound skills.

Our work in early childhood education to develop word recognition falls in these two categories: phonological awareness and letter-sound skills. This means we should spend a large portion of our reading time intentionally playing with words to develop rhyme, alliteration, syllable segmentation, onset-rime segmentation, and phoneme awareness as well as explicitly teaching letter-sound skills.

Language Comprehension. In Chapter 2, we began our examination of the importance of language for learning, including intentionally taking on the roles of conversational partner and language facilitator during playful learning. In Chapter 3, we studied what it means to mathematize children's thinking through explicit mathematical language interaction and instruction. Now, we return to the power of language again in the context of literacy.

Language comprehension, sometimes called listening comprehension or oral language development, is the second component of reading comprehension. It is composed of background knowledge, vocabulary, comprehensive language skills, verbal reasoning, literacy knowledge, and attention. The progression of typical oral language development begins at birth and the critical years are birth through age 5 years (American Speech-Language-Hearing Association, n.d.).

Our intentional interactions and instruction can engage young children in noticing, practicing, and applying each of the components of language comprehension. This work can take place throughout our day and is not isolated to literacy instruction (see Chapter 2). We can intentionally teach language comprehension during playful learning by engaging as children's conversational partner and language facilitator. It can also take place during deliberate and inquiry-based instruction for word play. Read-alouds, including studying a book series, an author's work, or variations of a folktale, can be avenues for intentionally growing language comprehension through class discussion and identifying similarities and differences.

Once again, we see from research that language is a powerful and overarching part of early childhood teaching and learning. Strong language skills are not only significant for learning across the curriculum, but they can compensate for problems learning to read (Kilpatrick, 2016). Combined with early word recognition work, language comprehension develops the foundation of reading comprehension in young learners. The other half of literacy is writing.

WRITING

In early childhood, there can be confusion between writing and handwriting. Letter formation or handwriting intersects with letter skills and fine motor skills. Writing and growing to become a writer is about composing cohesive ideas and communicating them. Here, we focus on research on developmentally appropriate writing instruction for early childhood, which is often talking and oral storytelling.

Research points us again to the power of language in growing writers. Early writing instruction should begin by drawing upon the strengths of children as storytellers and build upon that strength by developing their oral language for storytelling (Horn & Giacobbe, 2007). When we teach young children to write, we must first teach them to tell detailed, organized, and expressive stories, whether true or pretend. Then, we can deliberately teach them to draw their oral stories with these same characteristics—details, organization, and expression. Explicitly teaching children to draw focuses on language, spatial reasoning (seeing people and objects as made up of shapes that can be drawn), and connecting the concrete with the pictorial (Berry & Thunder, 2017).

We should not wait to put writing utensils in our youngest learners' hands; instead, we should constantly connect talking, drawing, and writing. Through these meaningful connections, we focus on using oral and written language to communicate a message (Wood Ray & Glover, 2008).

When readers write, they apply word recognition and language comprehension to communicate their ideas. When writers read, they examine mentor texts that teach them about voice, decision making as a writer, and messages from fellow writers (Hansen, 2001).

Therefore, as we make decisions about what to read aloud to our young learners, we are also making decisions about what we want them to learn as both readers and writers. Reading and writing are inextricably linked and our instruction should intentionally reflect this symbiotic relationship.

Combined with early word recognition work, language comprehension develops the foundation of reading comprehension in young learners.

When we teach young children to write, we must first teach them to tell detailed, organized, and expressive stories, whether true or pretend.

EFFECT SIZE FOR DELIBERATE INSTRUCTION = 0.59

EFFECT SIZE FOR SELF-JUDGMENT AND REFLECTION = 0.75

READ-ALOUDS AS MENTOR TEXTS

Read-alouds can also serve as another type of mentor text—texts that contribute to children's identity, agency, positionality, and authority. Bishop (1990) described books as windows, sliding glass doors, and mirrors. Books as windows give children a glimpse into new worlds. Books as sliding glass doors allow children to step into these new worlds through imagination. And books as mirrors reflect back to children affirming images of themselves. When we intentionally select read-alouds as mentor texts that will positively support our learners' growth in identity, agency, positionality, and authority, we use books to their fullest extent and create spaces for children to see themselves as visible learners.

EFFECT SIZE FOR SELF-EFFICACY = 0.66

Rereading these mentor texts is also an important instructional strategy. It allows learners to gain a deeper understanding of story elements, broadens vocabulary, helps learners understand language and narrative structure, and grows their confidence and motivation as readers. Reading a text multiple times positions learners as active participants in a read-aloud, where they ask and answer questions as well as make predictions rather than passively listening (Dickinson, 2011; Dickinson et al., 2019). Reading variations of the same text allows children to engage in the cognitive routines of analyzing similarities and differences, whole-to-part complexities, relationships, and perspectives (Hammond, 2015).

EFFECT SIZE FOR ELABORATIVE INTERROGATION = 0.66

Reading variations can also increase confidence and engagement (Collins & Glover, 2015), lead to richer, more in-depth comprehension and discussion that moves beyond questions to themes and concepts (Morrow et al., 2009), and increase vocabulary acquisition (Horst et al., 2011).

EFFECT SIZE FOR CLASSROOM DISCUSSION = 0.82

This is where literacy education research and Visible Learning research intersect: To grow readers, we should focus on early word recognition work, which is phonological awareness and letter-sound skills, as well as language comprehension. To grow writers, we should focus on oral storytelling and drawing. Our instruction should also communicate clearly to children the connections between reading and writing. In fact, we should select read-alouds as mentor texts to read and reread that intentionally and positively contribute to children's identity, agency, positionality, and authority in school and in the world. Language is central to early childhood education and to our three early childhood classrooms that live the intersectionality of early literacy research and the Visible Learning research.

MS. DEMCHAK AND OUR NAMES

Just a few weeks into the school year, Ms. Demchak's 4-year-olds know the routines and schedule and have made friends with each other. They have begun their first unit of study about names. Ms. Demchak, Ms. Murrah, and their vertical PLC have each planned name units with different emphases for identity development across grades. Ms. Demchak uses the name unit as a first step to bring families into the classroom through storytelling and photos. When families visit, she wants them to see themselves in the classroom so they know they are welcome and important partners in learning.

Recognizing, reading, spelling, and writing names are all important skills in a classroom and in life to support friendships, independence, and confidence as learners. Ms. Demchak's prekindergarten unit will also use the study of names to give purpose and motivation to learning letters and letter sounds. In kindergarten, Ms. Murrah teaches a similar unit because she tends to have learners with a similar range of name and letter knowledge; the main difference is that Ms. Murrah's unit takes place primarily during her literacy learning block, whereas Ms. Demchak's unit takes place throughout the day—during class meetings, outdoor time, centers time, read-alouds, and independent work time.

On a wall in Ms. Demchak's classroom, there is a section for each child with their name and photo displayed. Families wrote the story of how they chose their child's name and shared family photos. Ms. Demchak read aloud each name story. The children introduced their family members to the class via the photos, and Ms. Demchak posted their family members' names next to their pictures. At the beginning and end of each school day, she hears the children saying to each other, "That's Isaac's dad." "Is that your sister? What's her name?" "I see your grandma, Ruby!"

The children's names are posted all over the classroom, labeling their seats and cubbies, and attached with Velcro to be moved for their lunch choice, centers choice, Question of the Day, and classroom job. Next to each child's name is an image that starts with the same initial sound, such as Zoe zipper and Bindi bear; the image is in the shape of the first letter in the child's name. Each morning, they practice saying each other's names while singing a greeting. They play with their names and the sounds in their names by breaking them into syllables, rhyming, and alliterating. They read aloud books about names, and each child has a unique name song to practice spelling their name to a tune. This week, they began examining one child's name in-depth each day.

LEARNING INTENTIONS AND SUCCESS CRITERIA

Ms. Demchak believes that studying names is a high-interest way to engage children in word recognition and language comprehension work while also celebrating each other's unique identities.

Three outcomes from the Early Years Learning Framework are central to their name unit (Australian Government Department of Education and Training, 2019):

> **Outcome 1:** Children Have a Strong Sense of Identity
>
> - Children develop knowledgeable and confident self-identities.
>
> **Outcome 2:** Children Are Connected With and Contribute to Their World
>
> - Children respond to diversity with respect.
>
> **Outcome 5:** Children Are Effective Communicators
>
> - Children interact verbally and nonverbally with others for a range of purposes.
>
> - Children engage with a range of texts and gain meaning from these texts.

Today, the class will engage in their name study routines and some new independent and differentiated tasks. Ms. Demchak has gathered formative assessment data from her interactions and observations since the beginning of school as well as some quick checks for letter identification and name spelling and writing. Her learners are spread across the three phases of learning—surface, deep, and transfer. She wants all of her learners to move forward as a community while meeting the children where they are as individuals. The learning intentions and success criteria align with the outcomes and unite the class, while also allowing for children to access them and work toward them at different rates and in different contexts.

> **Content Learning Intention:** We are learning our names.
>
> **Language Learning Intention:** We are learning to show and say our thinking.
>
> **Social Learning Intention:** We are learning that knowing our classmates' names helps us better communicate with them.

Guided by the learning intentions and success criteria, Ms. Demchak plans to activate prior knowledge and bring closure as a whole group, and to scaffold, extend, and assess individuals' literacy thinking using the right strategy at the right time as they work on their tasks.

ACTIVATING PRIOR KNOWLEDGE

The children are looking at a pocket chart with three names—Jacob, Sophia, and Illarah—as they think about Ms. Demchak's question, "What do you notice about these names?" This question is becoming familiar because Ms. Demchak always asks it. She asks it right after the child with the name of the day has sung her name song, and Ms. Demchak has written down the letters in that child's favorite color.

> EFFECT SIZE FOR CLASSROOM DISCUSSION = 0.82

As Ms. Demchak writes, she says the name of each letter and the steps for making each letter.

"I notice Jacob has a, Sophia has a, Illarah has a," says Liam.

"How many a's do they have?" Ms. Demchak extends.

"Jacob has one. Sophia has one. Illarah two," Liam responds.

"I notice Sophia and Illarah both have h," Coen describes.

"I see Sophia's h is in the middle of her name. Where is Illarah's h?" Ms. Demchak asks.

"Illarah's h is last," Mirrin says.

"Illarah has two lines," Thomas says, making lines in the air as he talks.

"She does. What is the name of the letter that is a big line down?" Ms. Demchak also writes in the air and then points to the letters in Illarah's name.

"L," responds Alinta.

"Me and Sophia have o's but Illarah doesn't," adds Jacob.

"I see a letter with a dot in Sophia's name but not Illarah," notices Jedda.

"I love the letters with dots. There are two: lowercase i and lowercase j," Ms. Demchak explicitly teaches these letter names while writing the letters in the air. "Which letter does Sophia have: i or j?"

"She has i. No one has j," says Bindi.

"I have J," Jacob states proudly.

"Interesting. Bindi says no one has a lowercase j with a dot. But Jacob knows he has a J. J is his first letter. It is an uppercase J so there is no dot. J and j are the same letter but J with a line on top is uppercase and j with a dot is lowercase. That's an important connection. Thanks, Bindi and Jacob!" Ms. Demchak makes their noticings clear using language to describe and name the letters while also air writing the letters to give a visual cue. "Let's count how many letters Illarah has in her name."

The class counts the letters, and Illarah places a numeral 7 next to her name, saying, "I have more letters."

Ms. Demchak uses the specific mathematical language, "Illarah, you have the most letters! Seven is more than 5 and more than 6."

"Now, let's do our cheer!" Ms. Demchak holds up each letter in Illarah's name and shouts, "Give me an I." And the class echoes back the name of the letter. At the end, she asks, "What does that spell?" And the class cheers, "Illarah!"

Next, Ms. Demchak moves into the new work for today. The class will work independently or in partners on task boxes, which contain name work. Some of the children know how to spell and write their names and some do not. Some know most uppercase and lowercase letters and some do not. Through her formative assessments, Ms. Demchak has noticed that all of the children need practice recognizing letters in different fonts, and the children who know most letters need to develop fluency in naming letters that look similar. She says,

EFFECT SIZE FOR PROVIDING FORMATIVE EVALUATION = 0.40

> Our work today is all about our names! You might be building your name or friends' names. As you work, be noticing the ways letters look similar and different and the ways your names are similar and different. Practice saying the names of the letters you know. When you don't know the name of a letter, ask a

teacher or friend for help, sing your name song, or sing the alphabet song to figure it out. When we come back together, we will share something we noticed in our work about letters and our names.

As each child retrieves their task box to take to their work space, Ms. Demchak reminds them of their specific work and the image on the side of the tub with a visual of their work (Table 4.1). When everyone has settled into their work, Ms. Demchak and her paraprofessional begin their intentional, individualized interactions with the children.

TABLE 4.1 ● Task Box Success Criteria

FIGURE 4.1

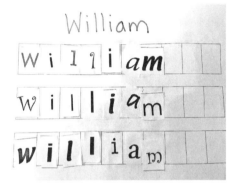

I can make a name.

I can read and count the letters.

I can compare the letters.

FIGURE 4.2

I can make a name with spices.

I can read and count the letters.

I can compare the letters.

FIGURE 4.3

I can make a name with playdough.

I can name and count the letters.

I can compare the letters.

FIGURE 4.4

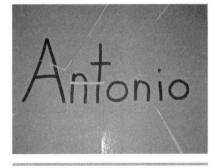

I can make a name puzzle.

I can read and count the letters.

I can compare the letters.

(Continued)

TABLE 4.1 ● (Continued)

FIGURE 4.5

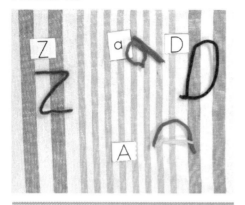

I can build a name with pipe cleaners.

I can name and count the letters.

I can compare the letters.

FIGURE 4.6

I can hole punch letters in a name.

I can name and count the letters.

I can compare the letters.

FIGURE 4.7

I can make a name with magnets.

I can name and count the letters.

I can compare the letters.

FIGURE 4.8

I can paint a name.

I can name and count the letters.

I can compare the letters.

SCAFFOLDING, EXTENDING, AND ASSESSING LITERACY THINKING

During the children's work time, Ms. Demchak alternates between interacting with the children as they do their independent and partner tasks and meeting with small groups of children for deliberate instruction. Her plan is to check in with Zoe first.

"I'm making your name, Mirrin!" Zoe calls to her friend working in another area.

"Remember my M is first!" Mirrin calls back.

Ms. Demchak joins Zoe, Max, and Oliver who are all building names with letter beads in different fonts. Zoe is building her friends' names to explore other letters; she has mastered the letters in her first and last name. Max is building his last name multiple times; he has mastered the letters in his first name. Oliver is building his first name multiple times.

"Zoe, how are you building Mirrin's name?" Ms. Demchak wonders.

"I make letter matches. This is Mirrin's name card. So I just look at her letters and then find the beads that match," Zoe responds.

"What are the letters in Mirrin's name?" Ms. Demchak asks.

Zoe names each of the letters but the last one. "I don't know. M? R?" She starts naming letters.

"Let's figure it out. Why do you think it might be m?" Ms. Demchak engages Zoe in meta-cognitive reflection and analysis of the letters.

EFFECT SIZE FOR META-COGNITIVE STRATEGIES = 0.60

"It looks like a little m like my mom's name. But it's different," Zoe connects.

"Lowercase m has two humps like this, and this letter just has one hump like this," Ms. Demchak air writes. "So it can't be m. Why do you think it might be r?"

"It looks like those r's in Mirrin's name but it's not right. Maybe it's a fancy r?" Zoe wonders, knowing that they have been looking at letters in fancy fonts.

"You're thinking a lot about all the ways r can look and comparing it to this letter. That's important noticing. This letter is not exactly like r. Lowercase r stops and this letter keeps going," Ms. Demchak air writes again. "What tool could we use to help us figure this out?"

"We could match with the ABCs. This is the same letter. It's right here, next to m," Zoe points to an alphabet strip near her work area and has already visually matched the mystery letter.

She sings the alphabet song and points to the letters. Zoe is using a strategy that Ms. Demchak has practiced with the class; it is one of many strategies they have learned to help them problem solve independently.

When Zoe gets to the mystery letter, she says "N," stops, and claps, "It's n! Mirrin, your last letter is n!"

"I know, Zoe!" And Mirrin sings her name song as she works.

As Zoe finishes making Mirrin's name with beads, Ms. Demchak summarizes Zoe's work and connects it to the learning intentions and success criteria: "Zoe, you matched letters to build Mirrin's name. You matched letters with her name card. And when you didn't know a letter, you compared letters and then matched letters with the alphabet strip to figure out its name."

Ms. Demchak records notes about her conference and then confers with Oliver. Next, she calls a small group of children to an open floor space. Isla, Alinta, Thomas, and Jedda are working on identifying the uppercase letters and letter sounds for the set of letters BMRS. Each day, they meet for 8–10 minutes to deliberately practice.

First, they practice naming the letter, keyword, and letter sound for the letters BMRS and three review letters that they all already can name AOX. Then, they sort the letters BMRS in different fonts on different materials—magnets, beads, foam pieces, wooden letters, and sandpaper letters—saying the name of the letter each time they sort. Sometimes, they sort objects and pictures that start with the letter sounds BMRS instead. Finally, they build, trace, and write the letters using a variety of different materials—wooden pieces, magnets, chalk, sand, sponges, crayons, and whiteboards. Throughout their work, they talk. They compare the letters visually and as they form them. They compare how their mouths look and feel as they make the letter sounds. They notice other letters and letter sounds that are similar, as well as names with the letters and letter sounds in them.

After meeting with a small group, Ms. Demchak returns to her conferences and the children return to their independent work. Ms. Demchak also plans to meet with Ruby today. Ruby has a large piece of paper with her name written in pencil filling the whole page. Ruby has made R and u; she puts liquid glue on her b and is now placing dried seed pods on the glue to form the letter. Ms. Demchak begins with an open question so Ruby can show what she knows in the language she feels confident and comfortable using, "What are you noticing about your name, Ruby?"

"I have letters that go up high and go low and a little letter," Ruby shares as she points to the letters.

"Which letters go up high?" Ms. Demchak asks.

"This one," Ruby points to her R and b.

"What are the names of those letters?" Ms. Demchak probes.

"That's R. I don't know that one," Ruby says pointing again to b.

"How could we figure it out?" Ms. Demchak prompts.

"Sing my song?" Ruby ponders. Together, they sing her name song, spelling the letters in her name to the tune of "Oh My Darling" while pointing to each letter. Ruby now names the mystery letter: b. Then they talk about and name each of the other letters Ruby described—the letter going low is y and the little letter is u.

EFFECT SIZE FOR SCAFFOLDING = 0.58

Next, Ms. Demchak engages Ruby in deliberate practice using a combination of her informal language, physical gestures, and the formal names of the letters. They play I Spy, taking turns to give the clues. Ms. Demchak goes first, air writing as she describes the letter, "I spy a letter with a long line that goes low on the page, like a tail hanging down." Ruby points to the y, and Ms. Demchak asks the name of the letter. After reviewing each of the letters, Ms. Demchak leaves Ruby to continue working and calls another small group to an open space on the floor. This small group is working on distinguishing between four lowercase letters—bdpq—and their letter sounds.

The small group practices with Ms. Demchak for about 10 minutes and then returns to their independent work while Ms. Demchak returns to her conferences. Ms. Demchak and her paraprofessional are constantly interacting with the children as they work. The children are listening and talking to each other and the teachers as well as engaging in self-talk. There is a constant low hum of talk in the classroom—a sign to Ms. Demchak that learning with language is happening.

TEACHING FOR CLARITY AT THE CLOSE

As the year progresses, the time to work independently will expand to allow learners to gradually increase their independent, on-task behavior through practice. This early in the year, the children work for about 20 minutes and then clean up, saving incomplete work for another day. Ms. Demchak gathers the children as a class to bring closure to their work:

We are learning our names. First, I want to check in with you about how your learning is going. One way we know we are successfully learning our names is by singing our name songs *proudly*, not shyly or quietly or silly. Think about singing your name song.

How do you feel? Give me a thumbs up if you feel like you can sing your name song proudly. Give me a thumbs down if you feel like you can't sing it by yourself yet. And give me a sideways thumb if you can sing it but maybe not proudly yet.

The children show a range of thumb signals and Ms. Demchak quickly notes who she wants to check in with.

For each of the other three success criteria, Ms. Demchak asks a child she conferred with to share. She wants to provide the other children with an example of what meeting the success criteria can look like and sound like. Zoe shares how she compared letters in Mirrin's name and matched letters by singing the alphabet song. Ruby shares what she noticed about her letters and how she matched letters by singing her name song. Isaac shares that Illarah has the most letters in her name and no one has 1, 2, 8, 9, or 10 letters in their name.

To bring closure, the class sings "Willoughby Wallaby Woo." They change the first sound of each child's name to begin with /w/ and create rhyming names, like Woah Noah and Windi Bindi. Their independent practice time comes to an end with laughter.

MS. BULLOCK AND LISTS

Ms. Bullock tries to combine what she notices her children trying with what she needs to teach in order to capitalize on their natural curiosity and connect their explorations to language.

Lately, her 3-year-olds make scribbles on small pieces of paper. This began when Alaysia announced she was making a grocery list like her mom. Then she pretended to go to the grocery store and shop. As a result, Ms. Bullock has launched a genre study of lists. She returns to their common knowledge and experiences with occupations from their study of community jobs and uses read-alouds, playful learning, and writing to extend that learning.

LEARNING INTENTIONS
AND SUCCESS CRITERIA

Ms. Bullock's deep familiarity with the learning standards enables her to plan responsive instruction that is aligned to standards while remaining child centered. She identified three Illinois Early Learning and Development Standards for the class's study of lists (Illinois State Board of Education, 2013):

> **Learning Standard 5.A.ECab:** Experiment with writing tools and materials. Use scribbles, letter-like forms, or letters/words to represent written language.
>
> **Learning Standard 5.B.ECb:** With teacher assistance, use a combination of drawing, dictating, or writing to compose informative/explanatory texts in which they name what they are writing about and supply some information about the topic.
>
> **Language Arts 1.B.ECb:** With teacher assistance, participate in collaborative conversations with diverse partners (e.g., peers and adults in both small and large groups) about age-appropriate topics and texts.

To create her learning intentions and success criteria, Ms. Bullock connected back to the familiar context of jobs and linked reading, writing, and talking. She also wanted her learning goals to be versatile so that she could use them again later to study other genres as her learners are ready.

> **Content Learning Intention:** We are learning about a type of writing called lists.
>
> **Language Learning Intention:** We are learning that lists help us to communicate our message to others.
>
> **Social Learning Intention:** We are learning about taking turns talking with classmates.
>
> **Success Criteria**
>
> - We can read and write a list to do our job.
> - We can talk about our lists.

Ms. Bullock's next step was to use the learning intentions and success criteria to plan her lesson for centers time. She thought carefully about what reading and writing mean for her 3-year-old learners. Reading can be reading an image and writing can be drawing a picture or scribbles; the important aspect of each is the communication of a message. Therefore, her instruction about lists focuses on using this genre to communicate a message, and with communication, there is language.

ACTIVATING PRIOR KNOWLEDGE

Ms. Bullock intentionally begins by positioning Alaysia as the teacher with knowledge to share from her rich experiences at home. She says, "I noticed Alaysia writing a list of groceries. Then she went shopping and bought the food on her list. Alaysia, will you show everyone your list and tell them about what you wrote?"

"This says apple juice. And goldfish. And this is cheese sticks. That's my snack. And this says dog food for my dog, Cardi," Alaysia points to a different small piece of paper with scribbles for each grocery item.

"How did you know how to write a list?" Ms. Bullock prompts.

"My mom makes a grocery list and I help. Then we go to the grocery store and buy the list. My mom says, 'If it's not on the list, we don't get it.'" Alaysia shares proudly.

"Alaysia's writing made me think about all the times people write lists and all the jobs where people need lists for their work. Alaysia and her mom make a grocery list to help them shop. I'm a teacher and I make lists of books to get from the library. When have you seen people make a list or when have you made a list?" Ms. Bullock shares to activate their prior knowledge about lists.

"The doctor makes a list. It tells medicine," Ethan shares.

"And a list of sick people," Zakeisha adds.

"Doctors make lists of prescriptions for medicine and give it to their patients. And doctors make lists of appointments to know when someone is coming to their office because they're sick," Ms. Bullock layers specific, new language onto Ethan and Zakeisha's ideas.

"In the drive-through, you say your food. Then they say it too," Jaedyn says.

"Yes, sometimes they even show a list of food to you on a screen so you can check it. And at a restaurant, the waiter takes your order and makes a list of your food too," Ms. Bullock extends.

"Toys I want for my birthday," Briera says.

"You could write a list of toys!" Ms. Bullock replies. "There are so many lists you can write and so many jobs that need lists to help them get their work done. This is my list of books that we need in our classroom. Look at my list and see if you can read it." Ms. Bullock displays a piece of chart paper that says "Book List" at the top and has a column of book covers below. She pauses while the children look at the list. Then she has them turn knee-to-knee, eye-to-eye to take turns telling a partner what they see on the list. Ms. Bullock listens in on some conversations.

EFFECT SIZE FOR CLASSROOM DISCUSSION = 0.82

"You read my Book List by reading the pictures of the book covers! I'm going to give this list to our librarian. What do you predict she will do with the list?" Ms. Bullock asks.

The children call out: "She gets out the books." "She find them." "She give the books to us."

Ms. Bullock makes explicit the purpose of lists and how to interact with the genre:

> A list helps the writer and reader keep track of ideas. Alaysia and her mom made a grocery list to keep track of what they needed to buy. I made my list of books to keep track of my ideas for what I want us to read. And our librarian will read the list to keep track of which books she can give me and which ones are already checked out. What could I do to help remember which books I have?

"My mom goes like this. That means she got it," Alaysia acts out drawing a line.

"Alaysia's mom crosses out or draws a line through the food she buys. So I could cross out The Lost House when the librarian gives me that book," Ms. Bullock models this on her list. She crosses out The Lost House (Cronin, 2016) and continues:

> Today, be thinking about how you might use a list as you work. Maybe you are a doctor and you make a list of patients coming to your office. Maybe you have a toy shop and you make a list of toys for sale. Maybe you need to buy groceries, so you make a grocery list. You may glue pictures like I did or draw pictures or use stickers or stamps to make your list. You might write letters and words like Alaysia to make your list. After our work time, we'll read and talk about the lists that you wrote.

The children make their plans for centers time and begin their work. Each center has list-making supplies, including a tray of pictures, stickers, and stamps to support their list writing.

SCAFFOLDING, EXTENDING, AND ASSESSING LITERACY THINKING

Ms. Bullock takes a quick survey of the work her learners are doing in centers. She sees Alaysia, Zakeisha, and Alex writing a grocery list; they are looking at the pictures to decide which ones to glue onto their paper. Kayvion and Sabina are putting animal stickers on a page, taking turns asking each other, "Do you want an elephant?" If they say "yes," the sticker goes on the page to make a list of animals they want as pets. Kadisha is making phone calls on the pretend phone and writing something. Ms. Bullock is curious so she joins her.

EFFECT SIZE FOR SELF-VERBALIZATION AND SELF-QUESTIONING = 0.59

Kadisha flips through the class phone book and stops at Dayquan's phone number. She matches numerals in order to dial the phone number and then stops, saying aloud, "Is that 9 or 6? It looks like that one," pointing to the numeral 6 on the phone.

Ms. Bullock asks, "How could we figure it out?"

Kadisha points to each button and counts, "1, 2, 3, 4, 5, 6." She says, "It must be 6. And that must be 9," pointing to the numeral 9 on the phone.

Ms. Bullock says, "You figured out which is 6 and which is 9 by matching and counting. Now, you can call Dayquan's house."

Kadisha finishes dialing the number, "Hello, can I talk to Dayquan's mom? I'm Dayquan's teacher. You're invited to our Family Play Day." When she hangs up, Kadisha makes a scribble on her paper.

"What are you writing?" Ms. Bullock asks.

"I'm making lists. That say 'Dayquan.' I call his house," Kadisha explains.

"Why do you need a list?" Ms. Bullock probes.

"So I know who next," Kadisha responds. She turns to the pages in the class phone book and stops at Machele. "Machele."

"How will you know when you've called everyone in our class?" Ms. Bullock wonders.

"They be on the list," Kadisha points to her list.

EFFECT SIZE FOR TEACHER EXPECTATIONS = 0.42

"You're writing a list of names to keep track of who to call about Family Play Day. I should do that when I call families too. Thank you for the great idea," Ms. Bullock again intentionally places Kadisha in a position of knowledge by saying she gave Ms. Bullock an idea.

"I wonder how many names will be on your list when you've called everyone."

"Maybe 20 or 100," Kadisha starts dialing Machele's number.

Ms. Bullock records notes from this interaction. She also makes a note to put out lists of the children's names in each center and use Kadisha's interaction as the model for one way to use the list.

Again, Ms. Bullock looks around at centers. Alaysia, Zakeisha, and Alex are now pretending to be doctors. Alaysia has a clipboard with a paper and says importantly, "Who sick? Zakeisha, you sick?" This group could show another way to use a class list.

Ethan and Dayquan are looking outside and pointing at a flock of geese that has landed in the school yard. Ms. Bullock writes a note to make an image list of things to spy outside with the children; she can tape the list to the window.

EFFECT SIZE FOR TASK VALUE = 0.46

Then, Ms. Bullock notices Carmen and Briera gluing pictures at a table and giggling. She wonders what they are working on, so she joins them. Carmen and Briera are gluing down pictures of a frog and dog next to each other while laughing. "What are you working on?" Ms. Bullock asks.

"A list," Carmen says in Spanish.

"A list of what?" Ms. Bullock probes in Spanish and then repeats the question in English.

"Frog. Dog," Carmen replies, pointing to each picture.

"They rhyme! Down by the bay, where the watermelons grow . . ." The girls sing together, "Did you ever see a frog walking a dog?!" And they erupt in laughter.

"Frog and dog rhyme so they're on your list! What else will be on your list?" Ms. Bullock prompts.

The girls pull out more pictures from the tray, saying the name of each picture. When they see house, they look back at the pictures to get the mouse image. They hold the pictures up and sing "Down by the Bay" again, "Did you ever see a mouse painting his house?! Mouse house rhyme!" They laugh and glue the pictures down next to each other.

"Frog dog. Mouse house. You're making a list of words that rhyme. I can read your list by reading your pictures," Ms. Bullock makes a note about this type of list—a list to show what they know. She will need to have the girls share this new reason for making a list.

TEACHING FOR CLARITY AT THE CLOSE

At cleanup time, Ms. Bullock asks different groups of children if she can share their lists. She collects their papers and they all meet in the circle. "So many of you wrote a list today! You wrote many different types of lists for many different reasons. Now we're going to see if we can read and talk about your lists." Ms. Bullock puts the children in pairs and gives them each one of the lists made during centers. They talk and read the pictures—animals, food, rhyming words. Then each pair takes a turn telling the whole class about the list they read, and the authors of each list explain why they wrote the list.

EFFECT SIZE FOR SUMMARIZATION = 0.74

Ms. Bullock summarizes their work by connecting back to the learning intentions and success criteria: "Today, we learned about a new type of writing: lists. You might have tried writing, reading, and talking about lists. Be watching at home to see when someone in your family writes a list. Tomorrow, we'll do some more work with lists."

From her interactions, Ms. Bullock has several ideas for new ways to move their learning about lists forward.

MR. HEATON AND ANANSI THE TRICKSTER SPIDER

Each year, Mr. Heaton watches his 3- and 4-year-old learners become avid retellers and rereaders of texts that become familiar over time. He capitalizes on their retellings to explicitly teach playful learning. He intentionally teaches about the roles, materials, tools, actions, and dialogue involved in planning and implementing play as well as the processes of problem solving and collaboration. The children assign character roles and create settings, share repeated lines with great inflection, use their bodies to act out their emotions, and use new language to describe the story events, settings, and problems. They also take on the perspectives of the characters and make decisions about how to solve the story problems in their own variations.

EFFECT SIZE FOR COLLABORATIVE LEARNING = 0.39

Mr. Heaton interacts with them before, during, and after their playful learning to extend each of these important intentions for learning. By sharing texts, his class becomes a community of readers, storytellers, writers, problem solvers, learners, and friends.

Currently, the class is reading tales about Anansi the trickster spider. They began by reading and comparing variations of *Anansi and His Children* (Dobkin, 2010). Then, they dove into a stack of books about Anansi's mischievous adventures. The classroom library is now full of Anansi books and there are spider-like creations in every area around the room. The children know Anansi well from reading and rereading his tales. Mr. Heaton has observed and interacted with his learners as they act out Anansi stories outside and inside, while wearing costumes, building scenes with blocks and playdough, and using puppets. They are telling their own Anansi variations. Now, Mr. Heaton wants to capitalize on this deep familiarity and storytelling to engage them in practicing meta-cognitive skills as readers and writers.

LEARNING INTENTIONS AND SUCCESS CRITERIA

Mr. Heaton knows teaching writing is different from teaching handwriting, which is actually letter formation. In fact, writing grows out of storytelling and drawing; therefore, Mr. Heaton teaches both storytelling and drawing with writing and often uses playful learning as a context for practicing. As a result, when Mr. Heaton plans his reading/writing instruction, he draws upon the Early Learning Goals in both reading and expressive arts and design (U.K. Department of Education, 2021):

ELG Comprehension: Demonstrate understanding of what has been read to them by retelling stories and narratives using their own words and recently introduced vocabulary.

ELG Creating With Materials: Make use of props and materials when role-playing characters in narratives and stories.

ELG Being Imaginative and Expressive: Invent, adapt and recount narratives and stories with peers and their teacher.

Mr. Heaton's emphasis is always on language as he considers how to create meaningful learning intentions and success criteria based on the Early Learning Goals. He wants his learners to talk, engage in discussion, interact, and also create.

Content Learning Intention: We are learning that stories can have similar characters and story structures.

Language Learning Intention: We are learning the language of Anansi storytelling.

Social Learning Intention: We are learning about ways to share our reading and writing with peers.

Success Criteria

- I can compare stories by saying, "I notice" and "I wonder."
- I can use what I know about characters and story structures to make predictions.
- I can create my own variations with similar characters and story structures.

After creating the goals for teaching and learning, Mr. Heaton plans how to communicate these to his learners through his language, examples, and tasks.

ACTIVATING PRIOR KNOWLEDGE

EFFECT SIZE
FOR META-
COGNITIVE
STRATEGIES
= 0.60

Mr. Heaton is reading *Anansi and the Magic Stick* (Kimmel, 2002). He has planned specific places to pause and engage his audience by asking them what they notice, wonder, and predict. For example, when Anansi spies on Hyena and learns about his magic stick, Mr. Heaton says, "Let's think about what we know about Anansi and use that to help us make a prediction. What do we know about Anansi?"

The children call out a list of descriptions: "tricky," "lazy," "likes to eat," "likes to sleep," "has six children and a wife," "wants things other animals have," and "smart." Mr. Heaton continues, "Now, what do you predict will happen next? What would make sense?" The class is unanimous that Anansi will take the magic stick; some predict Anansi will trick Hyena into giving it to him and others predict Anansi will sneak to take it.

The book ends with Anansi planning new tricks. This is the perfect springboard to creating their own variations of Anansi stories. Mr. Heaton says,

> We've been reading and comparing a lot of Anansi tales. We are Anansi experts. And we know stories can have similar characters and similar events. So today, I'm going to write my own Anansi story. It might have similar animals and similar things happen as other Anansi books we've read. But some parts will be different because this is my own Anansi story. Just like when you play your own Anansi story, we can also write our own Anansi stories.

Mr. Heaton thinks aloud to plan his Anansi story using some of the children's earlier descriptions as inspiration. In his story, Anansi uses honey instead of building a web (because he's "lazy" and "likes to eat") and tries to trick Butterfly into landing on it. Mr. Heaton says, "Sometimes Anansi is successful with his tricks and sometimes he's not. I'll have to decide if Anansi will be successful in my story."

EFFECT
SIZE FOR
DELIBERATE
INSTRUCTION
= 0.59

Mr. Heaton has told his story aloud and now he retells his story while pointing to a blank piece of chart paper, planning where he will draw each part. Next, he draws, describing his decisions about colors and shapes throughout, "A spider has three parts to his body that look like circles. One circle will be his head with his eyes and mouth. And he has eight legs, which are straight lines connected to his body." Finally, he goes back and labels Anansi with the letter A, honey with the letter H, and Butterfly with the letter B.

Mr. Heaton says, "Today during Writing Workshop, you can write about anything you want. You might decide to write your own Anansi story like I did. You are Anansi experts. Use what you know about Anansi to create your story." The children turn knee-to-knee, eye-to-eye with their talking partner and share what they will write about. This way each child can orally rehearse their storytelling idea. Then the children begin their writing.

SCAFFOLDING, EXTENDING, AND ASSESSING LITERACY THINKING

All of the children are drawing and most are talking as they work. Mr. Heaton joins a table of writers and says, "Yasmin, tell me about your writing."

"Anansi want melons. He lazy and no climb trees," Yasmin draws swirls as she talks.

"What will Anansi do to get the melons?" Mr. Heaton asks.

"He yell at crow. Crow knock 'em down. Flap, flap, flap! It a accident but Anansi no care," Yasmin continues drawing and talking.

Mr. Heaton recognizes the inspiration for Yasmin's story and wants to make this transfer explicit for her. "Your story reminds me of *Anansi and the Mangoes*. Some parts are the same and some parts are different. What is different?" he asks.

"Yasmin has melons like *The Talking Melon*," Hunter interjects.

"But she just have crows. Not all the animals," Mabel connects.

"Anansi yell at crow in my story. He scary," Yasmin explains.

"You changed how Anansi tricks the crows. Why did you make Anansi scary instead of nice?" Mr. Heaton asks a meta-cognitive question.

EFFECT SIZE FOR META-COGNITIVE STRATEGIES = 0.60

"I want Anansi scary. Not always pretending he nice," Yasmin replies.

"You noticed Anansi always pretends to be nice and you wanted him to try being scary. Well, both are good ways to trick someone!" Mr. Heaton records Yasmin's story and explanation in his notes and then turns to Hunter, "Hunter, what are you writing about today?"

Hunter has drawn a recognizable spider next to a web. He is now drawing a head, body, arms, and legs in yellow. "Anansi is capturing the lion with his web so he can be king," Hunter explains.

EFFECT SIZE FOR ELABORATIVE INTERROGATION = 0.66

"How did you decide to write this story?" Mr. Heaton again asks a meta-cognitive question.

"Anansi always wants what the other animals have. I think he wants to be king. And he can wrap up the lion like he wraps up the snake on the log. The lion is sleeping. And Anansi is fast with his web," Hunter tells his story and his decision-making process as he continues drawing the lion and then he scribbles gray over him. "Now he's trapped."

"That's so tricky!" Mabel comments.

"Anansi is slow. Not fast," argues Eamon.

"No, Anansi is lazy. Sometimes that means he's slow. But he can also be fast. He's fast to catch the snake so he's fast in my story too," Hunter explains his reasoning. Conversations like this one arise throughout their writing time.

"That's interesting, Hunter. Lazy and slow aren't the same thing. You know from *Anansi Does the Impossible* (Aardema, 2000) that Anansi can be fast when he wants to be, so he's lazy but not slow," Mr. Heaton makes this inference explicit as feedback for Hunter and for the other children at the table. Before conferring with the next child, Mr. Heaton prompts, "I wonder what letters you could use to label your writing."

Hunter says as he writes, "A for Anansi and L for lion." Mr. Heaton records Hunter's story and reasoning (Figure 4.9).

TEACHING FOR CLARITY AT THE CLOSE

At the end of writing time, the children bring their writing to the circle. They turn and share their writing with their talking partner and now turn back to the circle. Mr. Heaton introduces one child to share with the whole group based on his conferences with children during writing, "Amare is working on his own story about Anansi. Amare, will you show and tell us your story of Anansi?"

"Anansi very hungry. He eats a banana, apple, pear, sausage, cupcake, melon, cheese, everything! Anansi still hungry," Amare holds his picture for the class to see as he tells his story. There is a black circle with lines coming out—Anansi—and there are different colored swirls for the food.

FIGURE 4.9 ● Observation/Conference Chart

Dates: _____

Content Learning Intention: We are learning stories can have similar characters and story structures.

Language Learning Intention: We are learning the language of Anansi story telling.

Social Learning Intention: We are learning about ways to share our reading and writing with peers.

Success Criteria:

● I can compare stories by saying "I notice" and "I wonder."

● I can use what I know about characters and story structures to make predictions.

● I can create my own variations with similar characters and story structures.

NAME	NARRATION	ANANSI INSPIRATION

online resources → Available for download at **resources.corwin.com/VLforEarlyChildhood**

EFFECT
SIZE FOR
COGNITIVE
TASK
ANALYSIS
= 1.29

"Think about Amare's story and look at his writing. What do you notice? What do you wonder?" Mr. Heaton engages the class in a discussion to model the success criteria.

The children notice: "Anansi likes to eat!" "Anansi eats a lot." "Anansi sounds like the Very Hungry Caterpillar!" "He likes melons."

The children wonder and Amare answers:

"Why is Anansi eating so much?" "He's very hungry."

"Whose food is that?" "The hippo."

"Is the hungry caterpillar there too?" "No, he's a butterfly now."

"Where is the hippo?" "Sleeping."

"Now, let's use what we know about Anansi to make some predictions about what could happen next. What would make sense?" Mr. Heaton asks.

Mr. Heaton moves the conversation to making predictions and the children have many. Each time, Mr. Heaton asks the predictor to explain why their idea makes sense: "Anansi could look for more food. Because he's still hungry." "The hippo could wake up mad. Because Anansi ate his food and always tricks them." "Anansi could go to sleep too. Because he's lazy and likes to sleep."

"Amare, your friends have some great ideas for what could happen next with your story. Maybe you'll write more about Anansi tomorrow or maybe another friend will write what happens next." Mr. Heaton connects their sharing discussion with their writing work for tomorrow.

With deliberate practice, they are making sense of what it means to notice, wonder, and predict. The now-familiar context of Anansi stories provided the space for growing and transferring this language and these ideas.

Ms. Davis and Distance Learning in Literacy

To create her distance learning classroom, Ms. Davis relied on Visible Learning and literacy research. She knew language must fill her classroom through interaction.

Ms. Davis reflected on her in-person classroom to identify the times when language-based interactions with literacy ideas were most prevalent. Writing Workshop was always a time of constant talk, exchanging of ideas, and practicing of new language. Reading aloud mentor texts at the beginning of Writing Workshop would be a way to maintain the reading and writing link. Ms. Davis also realized that much of their whole group word recognition work happened within routines, structures, and songs while the differentiated pieces of word recognition teaching and learning took place in small groups.

In her distance learning prekindergarten classroom, Ms. Davis has Writing Workshop each day, meeting with half of her class and then the other half. By keeping the number of learners smaller, she is able to increase the talking time of each individual child and increase the number of peer-to-peer interactions. She begins each Writing Workshop with a read-aloud of a mentor text that connects to the writing mini-lesson. As children write, there is constant discussion, sharing ideas, asking each other questions, and showing each other their work. Ms. Davis continues to emphasize storytelling and drawing in order to grow her writers.

> EFFECT SIZE FOR CLASSROOM DISCUSSION = 0.82

Like Mr. Heaton, Ms. Davis reads aloud series, books by the same author, and variations of folktales. When her class reads Anansi tales, her lessons sound very similar to Mr. Heaton's. The children notice, wonder, and predict about Anansi. They use their Anansi expertise to tell and draw their own Anansi stories. Typically, in order to scaffold retelling and reenacting stories, Ms. Davis would place materials in her centers for the children to build, make, and dress up like Anansi and other characters. This year, Ms. Davis sends home paper puppets to make Anansi and other characters. This provides meaningful fine motor skill practice in coloring and cutting and engages the children in retelling and reenacting stories. The puppets create a home–school connection as the children tell stories to and with their family members. And the children begin to tell their own versions of Anansi tales, which they then draw and share with peers.

> EFFECT SIZE FOR FAMILY INVOLVEMENT = 0.42

Singing together, greeting each other, and participating in other routines like Ms. Demchak's "Name of the Day" are all ways Ms. Davis engages her whole class as a community of learners in word recognition work. Ms. Davis intentionally selects songs, greetings, and activities that work on phonological awareness skills, such as rhyme, alliteration, syllable segmentation, and phoneme awareness, as well as letter-sound skills. Phonological awareness work adds a unique layer of challenge to Ms. Davis's planning because she wants to

(Continued)

(Continued)

provide visual cues while encouraging the children to orally play with words and their sounds. As a result, she uses puppets to visually cue, model, and scaffold these skills. Ms. Davis knows the importance of multimodal, multisensory, and multiple context practice for letter and letter-sound identification so she sends home materials for building, forming, and sorting letters. She also differentiates this work during her daily one-on-one sessions with individual children so that each child is working on their just-right skill at their just-right pace with their just-right instructional strategy.

LITERACY AND PLAYFUL LEARNING

Let's consider literacy as the content of playful learning in the early childhood Visible Learning classroom. Remember, playful learning can be pretend play, inquiry and exploration, and deliberate instruction. In other words, writing, read-alouds, word recognition, and language comprehension can be both playful and intentional if you focus on language-based interactions. As you plan literacy instruction, select materials and create contexts that facilitate rich opportunities for interaction. Then, as you capitalize on these opportunities as a language facilitator and conversational partner, be intentional with your language. The materials and contexts you create directly affect the language that you and your learners will practice. Consider these guidelines and tips:

- As texts become familiar, they can be fantastic springboards for contextualized problem solving about taking turns, sharing, talking out problems, having empathy, counting and comparing, seriation, measurement, describing and classifying attributes, and sequencing. Familiar texts storify problem solving and enable learners to access the content and show what they know (Hammond, 2015).

- Environmental print is an important way to engage children in noticing letters and words and attaching these to meaning. Label storage, materials, manipulatives, and classroom library shelves with images and words. The words can be in English as well as other home languages.

- Rhythm is a powerful tool for supporting memory across the curriculum. In literacy instruction, use songs, poetry, and spoken word in rhythm to play with words and practice new vocabulary.

- Multisensory, multimodal literacy materials engage the brain in multiple ways simultaneously to develop word recognition and language comprehension. For example, in both playful learning and deliberate practice, engage children in exploring different textures for letters and letter formation. Make letter puzzles available to grow children's visualization of letters. Practice sky writing while saying the letter formation steps to support orthographic mapping.

- Remember, children grow simultaneously across areas of phonological awareness, so our instruction should not focus on just one area at a time nor should we wait until a child reaches mastery in one area before exploring another.

- Read-alouds are a discretionary space. Discretionary spaces are the moments that are not dictated by policies or curriculum, but they are places where we make countless decisions, such as how to facilitate a discussion or how to manage a small classroom event (Ball, 2020). Each of these decisions within discretionary spaces is an opportunity for us to disrupt injustice. And it's a space where we can intentionally choose to grow each of our learners' identity, agency, positionality, and authority (Berry & Thunder, 2012).

....

CHAPTER 5

Visible Learning and Understanding the World in Early Childhood

From slime to gears, blocks to animals, family histories to classroom communities, and social justice to maps, the teaching and learning about children's physical and social environment allows young learners to acquire and consolidate knowledge about how the world works. As young children grow in their awareness and efficacy to explore, understand, and contribute to the world around them, early childhood educators intentionally create learning experiences about the natural and physical world, cultures and communities, and their histories. Understanding the world is the ideal area to balance learners' curiosity with educators' expertise and knowledge for activating intentional learning. The very nature of the content is engaging and offers a diverse pallet of topics, ideas, and concepts for a wide range of learners' interests.

This chapter focuses on the following questions: What works best in early childhood learning as children learn about their world? How do we activate learning in our young learners in ways that help them better understand the world, even if they do not ultimately become a scientist, historian, or geographer? Understanding the world around us and having tools for exploring and making sense of it is part of being an informed citizen of the world. This work starts in the early childhood classroom.

EFFECTIVE LEARNING TO UNDERSTAND THE WORLD IN EARLY CHILDHOOD

Science, humanities, and social sciences engage children in making sense of their physical and social environment, gradually learning about their expanding community, and cultivating a positive view of themselves as citizens. These content areas exist in meaningful integration within children's lives and are more than simply content.

BIG IDEAS, PROCESSES, AND WAYS OF KNOWING

Science is a body of knowledge about the physical and biological components of our environment, a set of processes for engaging with the environment, and a way of knowing about the environment (Bell, 2008). The body of knowledge includes the facts and figures of science—laws, principles, properties, and interactions. The body of science knowledge is built through a set of scientific practices or processes (see Table 5.1) that foster active, cognitive engagement with that body of knowledge. In other words, when children are doing science, they are building or even refining their knowledge of science.

TABLE 5.1 ● Processes of Science

Observing
Classifying and sequencing
Communicating
Measuring
Predicting
Hypothesizing
Inferring
Experimenting
Interpreting
Analyzing
Evaluating
Modeling

Adapted from Virginia Department of Education. (2012). *Practices for science investigation: Kindergarten-physics progression.* Author.

Scientists operate under the belief that we understand our world through hypothesis generation and testing. With that belief, scientists also come to understand that the current knowledge about how the world works is tentative and does not represent absolute truth. Progress in science is continuous. The way we know in science is not from seeking evidence that confirms our hypotheses, but attempting to verify them through replication.

EFFECT SIZE FOR SCIENCE LABORATORY PROGRAMS = 0.57

In other words, we use the practices and processes of science to test and see if our hypothesis holds up to repeated experiments across multiple contexts and time. Thus, Visible Learning in the early childhood classroom seeks to build this distinct way of knowing in young learners.

EFFECT SIZE FOR SELF-JUDGMENT AND REFLECTION = 0.75

Humanities and social sciences are composed of social systems, social concepts, and processes (National Council for the Social Studies, 2019). Social systems include relationships and interactions as well as the related societal norms and values, both explicit and implicit. Children gradually examine social systems beginning with their identity development, their family,

EFFECT SIZE FOR SELF-CONCEPT = 0.47

their classroom and neighborhood communities, and eventually, their culture, country, and society (Bronfenbrenner, 2005).

Social concepts are big ideas that can both inspire and answer big questions about the world, such as continuity and change, perspectives and action, interconnections, cause and effect, power, authority, governance, resources, and diversity. Like science, humanities and social sciences also emphasize processes or action-oriented strategies for making sense of these social systems and concepts, including research, interviews, discussion, collaboration, data, evidence, and chronological awareness.

To effectively and truly learn science, humanities, and social sciences in early childhood, children must actively engage in processes to make sense of new knowledge and to access a new way of knowing. Therefore, effective early childhood teaching about the world must be more than relaying facts or replicating a process; it must engage children as scientists, historians, and geographers within their meaningful contexts so they can intentionally experience the depth and breadth of the content, processes, and ways of knowing.

COMPLEX QUESTIONS AND HIGHER-ORDER THINKING SKILLS

EFFECT SIZE FOR META-COGNITIVE STRATEGIES = 0.60

Much attention has been given to the development of critical thinking skills or, in the United States, what is more commonly called the profile of a learner (Battelle for Kids, 2021). There are many variations of these skills based on how schools around the globe assimilate these skills and dispositions into their own vision for their learners (see Battelle for Kids, 2021). At the root of each profile variation are these four skills, often referred to as the four Cs: critical thinking, communication, creativity, and collaboration. Learning with our youngest students lays the foundation for subsequent growth and development in these four Cs (e.g., Samarapungavan, 1992; Schulz & Bonawitz, 2007; Sodian et al., 1991).

EFFECT SIZE FOR SELF-REGULATION STRATEGIES = 0.54

EFFECT SIZE FOR CREATIVITY = 0.58

EFFECT SIZE FOR COLLABORATIVE LEARNING = 0.39

Science teaching and learning in the Visible Learning classroom contributes to the building of problem-solving skills (Rahayu & Tytler, 1999). When learners engage in the practices and processes of science within the context of authentic interactions with scientific phenomena, they begin to develop and apply problem-solving skills (e.g., Tytler & Peterson, 2003). In addition to critical thinking, young learners develop processes of higher-order thinking and reasoning (Gelman & Brenneman, 2004; Stein & McRobbie, 1997).

Similarly, the social systems and concepts of humanities and social sciences inspire complex questions and investigations that develop learners' critical thinking skills (Mindes, 2015). By emphasizing the processes of humanities and social sciences, early childhood educators can engage young children in purposeful debate, discussion, decision making, critical thinking, and problem solving (National Council for the Social Studies, 2019). Young children can also actively experience being a community member, collaboration, and diversity through their relationships and interactions with classmates (National Council for the Social Studies, 2019).

The progression of thinking in learners requires not only that they learn higher-order thinking skills (e.g., predicting, inferring, analyzing, etc.), but they also have multiple opportunities to practice these thinking skills within the context of authentic science, humanities, and social sciences content.

> EFFECT SIZE FOR SPACED PRACTICE = 0.65

Therefore, as early childhood educators, we must capitalize on children's curiosity as they encounter the world. When they wonder and experiment, we should intentionally select instructional strategies to emphasize higher-order thinking skills. And we should embrace rather than avoid complex questions about significant science ideas, social systems, and social concepts.

> EFFECT SIZE FOR TEACHER EXPECTATIONS = 0.42

For example, in Chapter 2, Ms. Demchak and Ms. Murrah's classes are engaged with the big idea of classification and sorting: *How are things (animals, vehicles, etc.) alike and different?* Meanwhile, Ms. Bullock and Mr. Heaton's classes are grappling with complex questions about interconnections and systems. Ms. Bullock's class is exploring, *How do businesses in a community rely on each other?* Mr. Heaton's class is examining, *How do animals in a habitat rely on each other?*

COMMUNICATION

Communication, both as one of the four Cs and as an essential part of learning, requires that learners effectively exchange ideas. For young children, oral language development lies at the foundation of the effective exchange of ideas. One piece of oral language development is vocabulary.

> EFFECT SIZE FOR VOCABULARY INSTRUCTION = 0.63

Science, humanities, and social science are rich in academic vocabulary. Making vocabulary visible enhances the vocabulary of learners by putting words into context and creating opportunities for learners to engage in academic discourse around science and social phenomena.

> EFFECT SIZE FOR CLASSROOM DISCUSSION = 0.82

This academic discourse relies on three tiers or types of academic vocabulary (Beck et al., 2013):

- **Tier 1 Vocabulary**—these are words or terms that are utilized in everyday life and are common in spoken language, and they typically do not have multiple meanings. Examples of Tier 1 words include *green, walk, tree,* and *window.* In many cases, this vocabulary is built through conversation. For our young English language learners and children with language needs, Tier 1 vocabulary may need to be deliberately taught and practiced.

- **Tier 2 Vocabulary**—this cluster comprises frequently used academic vocabulary terms that cross multiple subject areas and may have multiple meanings. For example, the processes of science, humanities, and social sciences (e.g., predict, infer, analyze, evaluate, etc.) are Tier 2 words because many of these processes are significant across the curriculum. Tier 2 words, such as *table, bark,* and *shade,* have different meanings depending on the context. Learners need to know and understand these terms, as they will be part of their learning experience across all content areas and outside of the classroom; therefore, this vocabulary should be the focus of much of our deliberate instruction for all children in early childhood.

- **Tier 3 Vocabulary**—this set of words includes terms that are domain-specific. This means that these terms have one meaning and are key to understanding specific concepts in a content area, such as science. Examples of Tier 3 words in science include magnets, motion, and liquid.

Through the planning, designing, and implementing of high-quality, high-impact teaching and learning in early childhood, we foster the effective exchange of ideas.

EFFECT SIZE FOR MANIPULATIVES = 0.39

EFFECT SIZE FOR IMAGERY = 0.51

In Chapter 2, we examined research around teaching and learning language, including academic vocabulary. In Chapters 3 and 4, we extended this research and included research on another way to effectively exchange ideas: representations. The CRA (concrete-representational-abstract) method and writing progression are two important guides for growing children's use of representations to express scientific, historical, and geographical ideas. We will see that science, humanities, and social sciences provide yet another context for language development and growth in the use of multiple representations.

The combination of developing both academic discourse and academic representation in young learners further enhances their academic vocabulary (Graham et al., 2020).

GROWING GLOBAL CITIZENS

Every early childhood classroom holds a vast number of discretionary spaces. Discretionary spaces are the moments that are not dictated by policies or curriculum, but are places where early childhood educators make countless decisions (Ball, 2020). One significant decision is whether to intentionally teach science, humanities, and social sciences and another is how to teach these big ideas and processes.

High-quality, high-impact teaching and learning in the early childhood science classroom is correlated with the development of interest in science-related areas. When we intentionally teach science, we capitalize on children's wonderings and expose them to the opportunities and ideas of science. In fact, when we develop children's interest in science early, their interest has long-range educational outcomes (Tai et al., 2006) and can open the doors to science-related occupations.

When we embrace diversity and social justice, when we intentionally counter bias and inequity in our early childhood classrooms, we set the tone for children's engagement as global citizens (National Council for the Social Studies, 2019). Early childhood educators can create "dialogical safe spaces" for children where dialogue around issues of bias and inequity can reflect children's real experiences, tentative thinking, and critical questions (Husband, 2010). In order to do this work well, early childhood educators need to develop their cultural competency (National Council for the Social Studies, 2019).

When early childhood educators plan and teach, it is important for us to keep an eye to the future: We are growing children who should have choice and voice in their futures as informed citizens of the world.

EFFECT SIZE FOR COLLECTIVE TEACHER EFFICACY = 1.36

When we intentionally teach science, we capitalize on children's wonderings and expose them to the opportunities and ideas of science.

EFFECT SIZE FOR TEACHER CREDIBILITY = 1.09

CHILDREN ALREADY KNOW

Children come to school each day with significant knowledge about themselves, their families, their communities, nature, race, oppression, and much more (Husband, 2010; Mindes, 2015; National Council for the Social Studies, 2019; National Science Teachers Association, 2014). Children experience their community and the world in ways that reflect the ways their families experience their community and the world. Therefore, early childhood teaching and learning to understand the world should begin with familiar experiences that bridge home and school and move to creating shared experiences for the class.

In humanities and social science, this means beginning with examinations of self, then family, community, and culture in

EFFECT SIZE FOR STRATEGIES TO INTEGRATE WITH PRIOR KNOWLEDGE = 0.93

EFFECT SIZE FOR INQUIRY-BASED TEACHING = 0.46

EFFECT SIZE FOR FAMILY INVOLVEMENT = 0.42

EFFECT SIZE FOR INTEGRATED CURRICULA = 0.40

EFFECT SIZE FOR FAMILY INVOLVEMENT = 0.42

ways that respect and appreciate diversity (National Council for the Social Studies, 2019). This also means examining complex questions—"How do people and places change over time?" and "How do we share power and resources?"—through the familiar experiences of daily life and community connections. In a farming community, farm life could be the context for examining these questions; in an immigrant community, the context might change, but the children and their families would remain rich resources for investigating these questions.

This work can also be integrated across the curriculum.

We see this in Ms. Demchak's classroom. In Chapter 4, her class shares their name stories to learn letters. In Chapter 6, her class learns about respecting and appreciating different perspectives. Finally, in Chapter 7, her class learns fine art and motor skills while developing self- and family identity and celebrating the class's diversity by creating family portraits.

In science, this means incorporating home-familiar materials and experiences that illuminate scientific knowledge, processes, and ways of knowing. In this way, we can model replicating experiments from home to school in order to gather empirical evidence and to make explicit the science processes. As early childhood educators, we can also foster this home–school connection by having families share their experiences. Families' hobbies, chores, or regular activities indoors and in nature are often rich with scientific knowledge, such as cooking, construction, gardening, nature walks, hunting, and cleaning (Chawla, 2007).

> From birth, children seek to understand the world around them, and our role as early childhood educators in this process is significant.

This is where science, humanities, and social sciences education research and Visible Learning research intersect: From birth, children seek to understand the world around them, and our role as early childhood educators in this process is significant. By choosing to intentionally teach science, humanities, and social sciences, we lay the foundation for their continued interest in and their embrace of diversity and social justice. By valuing children's home experiences, we allow all children access to big ideas, higher-order thinking skills, and the communication of their ideas. As we see and hear this intersection of science, humanities, and social sciences education research and Visible Learning research in action, note the ways our three early childhood educators intentionally make decisions to connect research and practice.

MS. DEMCHAK
AND STEM CHALLENGES

Over the first semester, Ms. Demchak has observed her 4-year-old learners growing in their sense of agency and identity as members of the classroom community. The children often solve problems that arise during their interactions and make plans together for creations and pretend play. But Ms. Demchak wants them to grow more intentionally as a community of learners. She wants them to practice listening to each other's differing ideas and to collaborate on a science, technology, engineering, and mathematics (STEM) task.

In their vertical PLC, Ms. Demchak, Ms. Murrah, and the other teachers have been planning STEM challenges with the disciplines "turned up" or "turned down" depending on the learning intentions (Neill & Patrick, 2016). This turning up and down of the STEM disciplines allows the teachers to create tasks with meaningful integration.

> EFFECT SIZE FOR INTEGRATED CURRICULA = 0.40

Ms. Demchak and Ms. Murrah have decided to use a variety of familiar texts as springboards into their STEM challenges in order to contextualize or storify (Hammond, 2015) the tasks.

> EFFECT SIZE FOR STRATEGIES TO INTEGRATE WITH PRIOR KNOWLEDGE = 0.93

Ms. Demchak's class has read many versions of *The Three Little Pigs*, including *The Three Little Javelinas* (Lowell, 1992). Retelling and reenacting the story has quickly become a class favorite.

Ms. Demchak's class has also been exploring natural resources. They have sorted living and nonliving natural resources and concluded that some living things cannot move on their own (like plants) and some natural resources were alive but are not anymore (like sticks). They have categorized and classified natural resources based on their physical properties and realized surprising facts—for example, sand and soil can pour like liquids but they are solid.

Now, the majority of learners are in the transfer phase of learning. They are ready to analyze natural resources' properties to determine which will make a strong house.

> EFFECT SIZE FOR ELABORATIVE INTERROGATION = 0.66

LEARNING INTENTIONS
AND SUCCESS CRITERIA

Ms. Demchak always has more than one goal in mind for her children's learning. She considers the content of their work as well as the processes for engaging in the work. She also values the dispositions or attitudes that the children can learn through these interactions. For this STEM challenge, Ms. Demchak identifies three targeted outcomes (Australian Government Department of Education and Training, 2019):

Outcome 4: Children Are Confident and Involved Learners
- Children develop dispositions for learning such as curiosity, cooperation, confidence, creativity, commitment, enthusiasm, persistence, imagination, and reflexivity.
- Children develop a range of skills and processes such as problem-solving, enquiry, experimentation, hypothesising, researching, and investigating.

Outcome 2: Children Are Connected With and Contribute to Their World
- Children develop a sense of belonging to groups and communities and an understanding of the reciprocal rights and responsibilities necessary for active community participation.

Ms. Demchak translates these outcomes into learning intentions and success criteria, which she calls the engineering design brief. She refers to each group as a "team of engineers." She turns up the science and engineering disciplines and turns down the technology and mathematics disciplines for her STEM challenge, "The Three Little Pigs' New House" (Thunder & Demchak, 2020).

Content Learning Intention: We are learning to analyze natural resources in order to identify the strongest material.

Language Learning Intention: We are learning to name plant, soil, rock, sand, and mineral resources.

Social Learning Intention: We are learning to actively listen to and include each person's contributions to meet a goal.

Success Criteria

- Your house must have walls, a floor, a roof, and a door. Two pigs must fit inside.

FIGURE 5.1

- Your house must be made of natural resources from plants, soil, rocks, sand, or minerals (like quartz).
- Your house must have a name based on its natural resources that you can explain and defend.
- Your house must withstand the howling wind of the Big Bad Wolf for 5 seconds (Figure 5.1).

Image source: Pixabay.com/OpenClipart-Vectors

To complete the engineering design brief, Ms. Demchak adds the story or context (Thunder & Demchak, 2020):

The Three Little Pigs' New House

> The first and second Little Pigs are tired of living with their brother in the brick house. They are ready to build their own houses. And this time, they are working carefully to build strong houses that can't be blown down by the Big Bad Wolf. They have hired you to design and build one of their strong houses.

Now, Ms. Demchak is ready to plan how to communicate the learning intentions and success criteria through the lens of an engineering design brief.

By analyzing student work, Ms. Demchak's vertical PLC has noticed that the planning phase of the STEM challenges needs to be elongated and scaffolded.

Without this, learners tend to rely on trial and error and do not carefully consider and incorporate the contributions of each team member. In other words, without planning, the intentional transfer of learning does not take place. Ms. Demchak uses this feedback from the learners to refine her implementation of STEM challenges, and so, today is strictly about planning.

EFFECT SIZE FOR PLANNING AND PREDICTING = 0.76

ACTIVATING PRIOR KNOWLEDGE

Ms. Demchak has just finished reading aloud the engineering design brief, including the success criteria, which are displayed as an enlarged visual checklist (Figure 5.2). The children are sitting with their assigned team of three engineers. "That was a lot of information! Who can tell us: What is our challenge?"

EFFECT SIZE FOR PROBLEM-SOLVING TEACHING = 0.67

"We have to build a strong house," Noah summarizes.

"Strong like the brick house so the Big Bad Wolf can't blow it down!" Alinta adds.

"Yes, and each member of your team has to help plan and build the strong house," Ms. Demchak adds. "Let's look back at the success criteria. This is how we'll evaluate each house to see if it succeeds at meeting the challenge." This time, as Ms. Demchak rereads the success criteria of the engineering design brief, she engages the class in discussion to make sense of them using the familiar cognitive routine, Notice and Wonder. She asks, "What do you notice about the success criteria? What do you wonder?"

EFFECT SIZE FOR SELF-JUDGMENT AND REFLECTION = 0.75

As the children notice, they use their own words to rephrase the success criteria.

FIGURE 5.2 ● Engineering Design Brief: The Three Little Pigs' New House

The first and second Little Pig are tired of living with their brother in the brick house. They are ready to build their own houses. And this time, they are working carefully to build strong houses that can't be blown down by the Big Bad Wolf.

They have hired you to design and build one of their strong houses.

Success Criteria:

● Your house must have walls, a floor, a roof, and a door. Two pigs must fit inside.

● Your house must be made of natural resources from plants, soil, rocks, sand, or minerals (like quartz).

● Your house must have a **NAME** based on its natural resources that you can explain and defend.

● Your house must withstand the howling wind of the Big Bad Wolf for 5 seconds.

Image sources: iStock.com/marvod, iStock.com/runna10, iStock.com/wingmar, iStock.com/malerapaso, iStock .com/Spiderplay, iStock.com/dirkbaltrusch, iStock.com/DevMarya, pixabay.com/OpenClipart-Vectors

Source: Adapted from Thunder and Demchak (2020).

As the children wonder, they ask clarifying questions. "Do we only use one resource or can we combine?" "Can we use water to make the sand wet?" "Can we use glue?" "Does the house need rooms or windows?" "Does the roof have to be pointy?"

Some of their wonderings offer opportunities for Ms. Demchak to remind them about their prior learning for transfer to this new challenge.

For example, when Mirrin asks if sticks are natural resources, Ms. Demchak engages the class in a discussion to activate their prior learning about plants. She points out the class-created "Plants" anchor chart with drawings, photos, and magazine images of plants, including sticks. She also shows them the table covered in plant materials for the challenge. Teams of engineers turn and talk about what natural resources are plants. Ms. Demchak says,

> Today, we are only making a plan. We will construct houses tomorrow. As a team of engineers, you will record your plan by drawing a picture of your house. You will label its parts and the materials you will use. You can name your house. You might need to test something to help you make a decision about your plan. Testing something means you're asking, "What would happen if . . . ?" If you want to see if something will work for your plan, you can test it today. Everyone in your team of engineers must contribute ideas to your final plan. At the end of work time, we'll share the materials you will use to build your house.

SCAFFOLDING, EXTENDING, AND ASSESSING STEM THINKING

As teams move to their work areas, Ms. Demchak joins a team where one person seems to be dominating the planning. She wants to scaffold the social learning intention for this group. "I hear Zoe sharing a lot of her great ideas! One of our goals for today is to make sure we listen to and understand everyone's ideas. What's a strategy we use when we talk together as a whole class to make sure everyone's voice is heard?" Ms. Demchak wants to make this whole group strategy explicit so they can transfer it to their small group work.

"We take turns around the circle," responds Isla.

"Let's see how we can take turns around this little circle of just three people. Zoe, you've started sharing your ideas. Who will share next?" Ms. Demchak points around the small circle.

"Liam is next," Zoe says and turns to face him.

Liam shares his ideas, followed by Isla. Zoe wants to build a stick and mud house, Liam wants to build a rock and mud house, and Isla wants to make a sandcastle-like house.

EFFECT SIZE FOR COGNITIVE TASK ANALYSIS = 1.29

"You've listened to each person's ideas by taking turns around the circle. Now, how will you make a plan for your strong house that includes everyone's ideas?" Ms. Demchak breaks down the social learning intention to help the group identify their next step.

"We all want to use something sticky to make the house strong," Zoe points out.

"My sand could be a sticky floor for the walls," Isla offers.

"Rocks and mud make strong walls," says Liam, who has been building many rock and mud walls outside.

Isla walks to the visual checklist of the success criteria and points as she says, "Sand floor. Rock and mud walls. Zoe, can your sticks make a roof?"

"Sure! They can make anything!" Zoe responds.

EFFECT SIZE FOR STRATEGY MONITORING = 0.58

"Wow! Each of you is contributing your idea to make one part of your strong house. Let's look at the visual checklist again like Isla did," Ms. Demchak points to each part of the house image as she says, "Isla's sand floor, Liam's rock and mud walls, Zoe's stick and mud roof . . . What else do you need?"

"We need a door!" Liam reads the image.

"Sand does not make strong doors," Isla admits.

"I could find one flat rock for a door," Liam suggests.

"Or I could make a mud and stick door," Zoe adds.

"Let's go look at the materials for a flat rock. If we can't find one, Zoe, you can make the door and roof!" Liam proposes.

EFFECT SIZE FOR FEEDBACK = 0.62

"It sounds like you're listening to each other and making sure everyone's ideas are included. You're even making a backup plan! You have almost all of your house parts. You're using a combination of natural resources. You still need to draw your plan, label it, and name your house. I'll be back to see how your work is going." Ms. Demchak summarizes their progress toward the learning intention and leaves the group as they look for a door. She makes notes about their progress and then moves to meet with two other teams of engineers.

Jedda's group is testing whether clumps of moss will balance on sticks. Ruby's group is testing what happens when they mix soil, sand, *and* water. After meeting with those groups and noting their questions and discoveries, Ms. Demchak returns to Zoe, Isla, and Liam, who are debating who will draw the plan.

"What are you trying to decide?" Ms. Demchak inquires.

"Isla wants to draw the house, but that's not fair," Liam says.

"Why isn't that fair?" Ms. Demchak probes.

"Because we want to draw too," Liam explains.

"I see. Everyone contributed ideas to create your strong house plan. And now, you want everyone to contribute to the recorded plan also," as Ms. Demchak says this, Liam and Zoe nod in agreement. "Let's think about what you still need to do and figure out a way for everyone to contribute. You need three things for your plan: you need to draw the house. And what else?"

"Label it," says Zoe.

"Name it," says Isla.

"Three things for your plan and three people on your team of engineers. That's interesting. Your house needs four parts." Ms. Demchak points to the parts on the visual checklist as the children name them: floor, walls, door, roof. "Four parts of the house and three people on your team. Also interesting." Ms. Demchak waits quietly. She wants to point out options but allow the children to make the decision for how to contribute.

"If Isla draws, I can label. I'm good at letters. And Liam can name the house," Zoe suggests.

"Or Isla can draw the floor and label it, and I can draw the walls and door and label it, and Zoe, you can draw the roof and label it," Liam provides an alternative.

"But who would name the house?" Isla wonders.

"We all could!" Zoe exclaims.

Again, the team has identified a strategy for including everyone's contributions while also transferring their understanding of natural resources to this new context. Ms. Demchak adds to her notes. All of the teams are drawing their plans.

> EFFECT SIZE FOR SMALL GROUP LEARNING = 0.47

TEACHING FOR CLARITY AT THE CLOSE

During their share, each team of engineers shows their house plan and explains the materials they will use. Because

Ms. Demchak has conferred with the teams as they planned, she is able to facilitate the class discussion. She asks questions that engage the class in noticing similarities and differences in plans as well as in tests the groups conducted during planning time.

"Jedda's team of engineers wondered if moss could balance on sticks. Sophia, what did you discover?"

"If it's just one stick up like this, then it'll fall over when moss is on top. Or it'll break," Sophia explains while holding a stick vertically.

"I thought it would work because I've seen moss on tree branches," Jedda explains his connection.

"But if the sticks are like this, then you can put moss on top and it'll stay! And it's stronger than just sticks," Noah adds holding a bunch of sticks horizontally.

"You observed moss in nature and that inspired your question. Then you collected important empirical evidence about how to use sticks and moss together. What did you decide based on your experiments?" Ms. Demchak asks.

"We're making a whole roof of sticks and then moss on top," Jedda responds, pointing to their picture representation of their house.

Now, Ms. Demchak turns to the whole class, "How is this experiment similar to Ruby's team of engineers' experiment?" The teams turn and talk to each other. Many children point out that the groups were testing what happens when you combine natural resources. As a class, they conclude that often combining natural resources makes a stronger structure. Tomorrow, they will refer back to their picture plans, actually build their strong houses, and then test every structure against the blowing wind of the Big Bad Wolf!

MS. BULLOCK AND BEING A SCIENTIST

Ms. Bullock knows that when children are familiar with materials, their depth of inquiry and investigation increases. She begins her school year with home-familiar materials throughout her classroom. Gradually, she introduces new materials in the now-familiar context of school.

Today, Ms. Bullock is ready to deepen her 3-year-olds' examination of new materials. Most of the children are at the surface phase of learning as they begin a study of physical properties. Ms. Bullock wants her learners to recognize themselves and their families as already engaging in scientific practices. She also wants to connect their rich experiential knowledge with new scientific language, concepts, processes, and a distinct way of knowing.

Ms. Bullock has assembled exploration trays. Each tray contains materials for scientific exploration:

- Prisms, mirrors, glass pebbles, and flashlights
- Kinetic sand and sand tools
- Slinkys
- Seashells and magnifying glasses
- Magnet wands, magnet balls, paperclips, toothpicks, buttons, and washers
- Block ramps, cardboard tubes, and marbles

She will interact with the children as they engage with the exploration tray materials. Through this formative assessment, Ms. Bullock will learn what types of questions the children are already asking, what connections they are making, what language they are using, and what investigations would be appropriate next steps.

LEARNING INTENTIONS AND SUCCESS CRITERIA

When Ms. Bullock selected the Illinois Early Learning and Development Standards for her first exploration tray lesson, she was surprised to see the focus on communication embedded with the science learning goals (Illinois State Board of Education, 2013). Yet this makes sense to Ms. Bullock because, regardless of the content, she knows that language is the linchpin of early childhood teaching and learning.

- **Science 11.A.ECa:** Express wonder and curiosity about their world by asking questions, solving problems, and designing things.
- **Science 11.A.ECf:** Make meaning from experience and information by describing, talking, and thinking about what happened during an investigation.
- **Science 11.A.ECg:** Generate explanations and communicate ideas and/or conclusions about their investigations.

Ms. Bullock's big idea for learning is "Scientists ask questions and investigate answers." She anticipates learners will ask six types of questions that she calls BIG questions because there are many possible answers:

- How does this work?
- How is this made?
- How is this the same or different?
- Why?
- What would happen if . . . ?
- Will it always work?

These questions reflect significant scientific processes. Each exploration tray holds materials to unpack a different scientific concept. Her learning intentions and success criteria unite these different materials by focusing on process and communication. A big part of communication is exchanging ideas, which requires talking as well as actively listening and responding to another person's ideas.

Content Learning Intention: We are learning that scientists ask questions and investigate answers.

Language Learning Intention: We are learning to communicate our questions and answers using words and actions.

Social Learning Intention: We are learning to think about what friends are saying.

Success Criteria

- I can ask BIG questions.
- I can try different ways to answer my questions.
- I can show and tell my questions and answers.
- I can think about friends' words when they share.

Ms. Bullock knows her learners bring a wealth of knowledge related to these learning intentions. They are inquisitive and attentive children. She also knows she will need to differentiate to meet each learner where they are and move them forward. As Ms. Bullock observes and interacts with her learners, she will use her formative assessment data to inform her next instructional steps and to determine which instructional strategies are most effective for which learners (Figure 5.3).

FIGURE 5.3 ● Observation/Conference Chart

Date _____

NAME	EXPLORATION TRAY	CONNECTIONS	LANGUAGE	QUESTIONS	NOTES

Content Learning Intention:

We are learning scientists ask questions and investigate answers.

Language Learning Intention:

We are learning to communicate our questions and answers using words and actions.

Social Learning Intention: We are learning to think about what friends are saying.

Success Criteria:

- I can ask BIG questions.
- I can try different ways to answer my questions.
- I can show and tell my questions and answers.
- I can think about friends' words when they share.

Anticipated BIG Questions:

- How does this work?
- How is this made?
- How is this the same or different?
- Why?
- What would happen if …?
- Will it always work?

ACTIVATING PRIOR KNOWLEDGE

Ms. Bullock finishes reading *Ada Twist, Scientist* (Beaty, 2016), saying, "Ada has the heart of a young scientist and so do you. Today, we're going to show each other our scientist's hearts by doing the work of scientists, speaking and thinking the words of scientists, and listening to each other as scientists." Ms. Bullock pulls out one exploration tray. "Scientists ask questions and investigate answers. Today, everyone will get an exploration tray to explore. You can ask questions about the materials in the trays and you can investigate answers. Let's try one together."

Ms. Bullock shows the contents to the class: prisms, mirrors, glass pebbles, and flashlights. She picks up each item and thinks aloud. As she holds the prism, Ms. Bullock wonders, "I've never seen this before. It looks like it's made of glass. I can kind of see through it. I wonder what it is. Does anyone know what this is?" There is silence. "Ms. Thompson, do you know what this is?" Ms. Bullock asks the paraprofessional who is sitting in the circle with the children.

EFFECT SIZE FOR HELP SEEKING = 0.72

"Yes, that's a prism," Ms. Thompson responds.

"It's a prism," Ms. Bullock holds it up to the light and looks through it. Next, she picks up the flashlight, "I have one of these at home. I use it to see in the dark, like when the electricity goes out. I forget what it's called. Do you remember?" Ms. Bullock turns the flashlight on and off as she asks the class.

Several call out, "Flashlight!"

"Right! It's a flashlight!" Ms. Bullock continues pulling out the mirror and the glass pebbles, making connections to the mirrors in the classroom and the glass pebbles at the light table. "I wonder why these are together. What can I try with them?" Ms. Bullock pauses to allow the children to think with her. "I'm wondering . . . What would happen if I shine the flashlight at each one? What questions are you wondering?" Ms. Bullock has several children share their questions: "What can you build with them? Will they break like glass? What can you see in the mirror?"

Ms. Bullock continues,

EFFECT SIZE FOR META-COGNITIVE STRATEGIES = 0.60

Scientists ask questions and investigate answers. We asked some small questions like, *What is this called?* And we asked some BIG questions like, *What would happen if I shine the flashlight on each item?* Now I'm going to investigate answers by trying different strategies. I'm going to show and tell you about my answers. And you can be thinking in your head about my words.

Ms. Bullock proceeds to shine the flashlight at the prism, the mirror, and the glass pebbles. She summarizes her answers as she shines the flashlight on each item again: "I can see the light go through the prism and the glass pebbles. I can see the light shine on the mirror and it shines back into my eyes. That's called a reflection. The light reflects on the mirror. Are you thinking about my words?" Many children shake their heads yes. "We are being scientists!"

"Today as you investigate your exploration tray, ask questions and try different ways to answer your questions. Then, we'll show and tell what we discover," Ms. Bullock says. Each child picks an exploration tray and goes to a work area to begin their investigation. When they are done with their tray, they can trade it in for another tray. Ms. Bullock and the paraprofessionals confer with the children as they explore.

SCAFFOLDING, EXTENDING, AND ASSESSING SCIENTIFIC THINKING

Through her interactions as children work, Ms. Bullock notices that the magnet trays are the most popular. As she confers with Kayvion, she notes that he uses the magnet wand to push the magnet balls across the table.

Kayvion shouts proudly, "Look! It's moving! I'm not touching!"

"Wow, you're using the magnet wand to push the magnet balls across the table. But the wand and balls aren't touching! Scientists ask questions. What are you wondering, Kayvion?" Ms. Bullock prompts Kayvion to consider the learning intentions and success criteria.

"Why is it doing that?!" Kayvion wonders excitedly.

"Why? is a BIG question!" Ms. Bullock records Kayvion's observation and question. She also notes that he is invested in experimenting with the magnet materials but without using their names. Kayvion says this is his first time using the magnets.

Ms. Bullock also confers with Sabina as she works with magnets. Sabina uses the word "magnet" and shares that she has letter magnets on her fridge at home. Her mom uses the magnets to make her pictures "stick" to the fridge. "What are you wondering about magnets, Sabina?" Ms. Bullock asks.

"How work? What inside?" Sabina shakes the magnet balls and wands. They can hear something shifting.

"How do magnets work? is a BIG question! *What are magnets made of?* is another BIG question! Scientists ask questions *and* investigate answers. What could you try to answer your questions?"

Ms. Bullock records Sabina's connections to home and her BIG questions. Sabina begins to touch the magnet wand to each item in the tray until all of the magnet balls, washers, and paperclips are attached.

"They stick!" Sabina points to the magnet wand and then points to the toothpicks and buttons in the bottom of the tray and says, "They don't. Why no stick?"

"You touched each item with your magnet and some stuck to it and some did not. Now you have another BIG question: *Why do some things stick to a magnet and some do not?*" Ms. Bullock notes Sabina's investigation and question.

Ms. Bullock also notices that some children try the same strategy—stacking—regardless of the materials and others either only ask questions about objects' names or do not ask any questions and rather tell about the materials.

FIGURE 5.4

Record of children's discoveries

TEACHING FOR CLARITY AT THE CLOSE

To bring closure to the lesson, Ms. Bullock facilitates the children's sharing about their exploration trays. This provides the children with another opportunity to practice as well as model for each other the learning intentions and success criteria.

Ms. Bullock records the children's discoveries and introduces new language for talking about the materials (Figure 5.4). At the same time, Ms. Thompson records the children's questions so that Ms. Bullock can analyze the types of questions they are asking and use this to guide her instruction.

As the children worked today, Ms. Bullock gathered feedback from the learners about her instructional decisions. Magnets are a high-interest topic to dive deeply into next, and there are children at the surface and deep phases of magnet learning. The exploration trays were effective for her initial assessment of children's language, questions, and connections, but they were ineffective for some of her learners to meet the learning intentions and success criteria today. Ms. Bullock knows she needs to use a variety of instructional strategies and, especially for her learners at the surface phase of questioning and problem solving, she needs to use deliberate instruction and practice, modeling, guiding questions, and direct vocabulary instruction as they continue learning to ask BIG questions and problem solve.

EFFECT SIZE FOR EXPLICIT TEACHING STRATEGIES = 0.57

Tomorrow, the learning intentions and success criteria will emphasize scientific communication and problem solving with magnets:

Content Learning Intention: Today, we are learning that magnets make things move.

Language Learning Intention: We are learning ways to describe movement with words and actions.

Social Learning Intention: We are learning to work together to try many strategies to solve a problem.

Success Criteria

We'll know we have it when . . .

- We can answer the question "How do magnets make things move?" with words and actions.
- We can show different ways magnets make things move.

Ms. Bullock plans to read aloud *Magnets Push, Magnets Pull* (Adler, 2017). She will give the children a variety of supplies, including magnetic tape, cardboard, cardboard tubes, scissors, paper, fabric, tape, paperclips, washers, magnet balls, and magnet wands. As teams of scientists, they will create objects that can be pushed or pulled along a pathway using magnets. Based on her feedback from learners today, Ms. Bullock is able to select the right instructional strategies at the right time for her children and to refine and differentiate her instruction to move their learning forward tomorrow.

EFFECT SIZE FOR PROVIDING FORMATIVE EVALUATION = 0.40

MR. HEATON AND MAPS

Treasure maps, story maps, maps for field trips, underground transportation maps, map puzzles—the children in Mr. Heaton's class are really excited by maps. They have even found "maps" in the end pages of books. Most of the children have surface knowledge about maps. They know maps show where things are, maps have small pictures of places and sometimes symbols like "X marks the spot," maps often have roads or paths, and maps are useful if you are lost (Figure 5.5).

Mr. Heaton wants to deepen their understanding of how maps represent a place; he wants to engage the children in creating

FIGURE 5.5

Children drawing "maps" with chalk, showing what they already know

a three-dimensional space and then translating this place into a two-dimensional representation—a map. He believes that through the creation process, his learners will better understand how a map is made and, therefore, grow their spatial reasoning to read, use, and create other maps.

The class has created a three-dimensional box town by cutting doors and windows into large cardboard boxes, painting the boxes, and creating signs to name each "building." Outside, they ride tricycles and walk between the buildings as peers pretend to live or work inside them (Figures 5.6 and 5.7).

FIGURES 5.6 AND 5.7

Constructing and playful learning in the three-dimensional box town

To deliberately practice constructing miniature towns with familiar materials, Mr. Heaton has blocks, Legos, and train kits available inside as well as floor mat maps for miniature vehicles (Figures 5.8–5.11).

EFFECT SIZE FOR DELIBERATE PRACTICE = 0.79

FIGURES 5.8, 5.9, 5.10, AND 5.11

Constructing and playful learning with miniature towns using familiar materials

Next, the class worked together to build a miniature version of the box town using small cardboard box buildings placed along a grid of roads (Figure 5.12). Again, they cut doors and windows, painted the small boxes, and created signs to name the "buildings."

FIGURE 5.12 ● The Three-Dimensional Miniature Box Town

EFFECT
SIZE FOR
MANIPULATIVES
= 0.39

EFFECT
SIZE FOR
IMAGERY
= 0.51

Today, the class is translating this three-dimensional representation of their box town into a two-dimensional map.

They will choose images to represent each building and then place those images on a replica of the town's road grid.

LEARNING INTENTIONS AND SUCCESS CRITERIA

Mr. Heaton knows that maps capture significant concepts and processes, including representation, spatial reasoning, and the relationship between geography and the social system of a neighborhood (U.K. Department of Education, 2021). Reading and using maps can lead to discussions about interconnections, changes over time, distribution of resources, and comparisons between places. Mr. Heaton identifies three goals for their map learning:

- **ELG People, Culture and Communities:** Describe their immediate environment using knowledge from observation, discussion, stories, non-fiction texts and maps.

- **ELG Creating With Materials:** Safely use and explore a variety of materials, tools and techniques, experimenting with color, design, texture, form, and function; Share their creations, explaining the process they have used.

- **ELG Listening, Attention and Understanding:** Listen attentively and respond to what they hear with relevant questions, comments and actions during whole class discussions and small group interactions.

With these big ideas and processes in mind, Mr. Heaton creates learning intentions and success criteria that will guide his instructional decision-making process. He anticipates that both he and his learners will make mistakes as they use position words to describe where to place images on the map, so he uses the learning intentions and success criteria as another opportunity to make learning about mistakes both positive and intentional.

Content Learning Intention: We are learning that maps have images that represent specific places.

Language Learning Intention: We are learning position words to describe things on a map.

Social Learning Intention: We are learning that mistakes are a chance to be kind and to learn.

Success Criteria

- I can use images to represent buildings.
- I can use words to describe where images go on a map to match the buildings in our town.
- I can use kind words when someone makes a mistake.
- I can learn something new from a mistake.

These learning intentions and success criteria serve as guideposts as Mr. Heaton plans each part of his lesson. The tasks, materials, his questions, and his feedback are all aligned to the learning intentions and success criteria.

ACTIVATING PRIOR KNOWLEDGE

Mr. Heaton begins, "Today, we are cartographers. Cartographers make maps. We are making a map of our tiny town. We will use the map to hide treasure for each other to find using our code-apillars tomorrow." By previewing future work, Mr. Heaton gives purpose to today's work.

> I started our map by making the roads. The roads are exactly the same as the roads of our tiny town. Now, we need our buildings. But this is a map. We can't put buildings on here! I want to be able to fold this map up and put it in my backpack. What could we do instead of actually placing the tiny buildings on the map?

The children suggest drawing pictures and using stickers or stamps. They also add that matching the color of the building with its sticker or using the name of the building on the picture would help.

"Those are great suggestions. Maps have images that represent specific places, like our tiny buildings. And, we can use images or pictures that match what the building really looks like—maybe they're the same color or maybe its name is on the image." Mr. Heaton pulls out a variety of images he has gathered to glue onto the map. Some are just colors. Others are symbols or pictures. He places the images on the floor in the middle of the circle.

"You will work on using images to represent the buildings you constructed. I'll show you how. I'm going to work on using an image to represent the building I constructed," Mr. Heaton cues the children to pay attention because he is going to model what they will do later.

"Do you remember what I built? It's my favorite place to eat."

The children shout, "Pizza!"

"Yes, I made the pizza restaurant because I love pizza. I love to walk my dog from my house, down the street, to the pizza restaurant and eat dinner," As he talks, Mr. Heaton walks his fingers along the road of the tiny town to the pizza restaurant. Then he carefully picks it up and places it on the ground in front of him. "Look at the images. Which one could represent the pizza restaurant? Which one reminds you of this building?"

EFFECT SIZE FOR DELIBERATE PRACTICE = 0.79

In pairs, the children turn and talk about which image they think Mr. Heaton should use to represent the pizza restaurant. Mr. Heaton purposefully included multiple options that would work so the children can practice making a decision and justifying it.

After rehearsing their thinking with their partner, the children take turns sharing their ideas with the whole group.

"It should be the pizza slice. That's what you eat there," Harper says.

"Use green. It's green," suggests Bahar, who is matching the color of the sticker with the color of the building.

"See the circle with the little circles inside. It looks like pepperoni pizza," Aurora explains.

"Pizza starts with /p/ for P. Put the P for pizza," connects Hamza.

Mr. Heaton says, "Each of you has good justification for your choice of image to represent the pizza restaurant. I'm going to combine some ideas. I'm going to use the green sticker because it matches the color of the building. And I'm going to draw a pizza slice and a P on the sticker. I'm also going to make a matching green image with a pizza slice and the letter P for our key." Mr. Heaton adds the picture and letter to two green stickers. He models placing one in the key and writing "Pizza Restaurant" next to it.

> Now, where should I put my pizza restaurant sticker so that it matches the tiny town? I'm going to need a partner to help me. Mabel, will you help me please? I'm going to look at the tiny town and use my words to describe where you should place my pizza sticker. We will probably make mistakes as we do this work but mistakes are important. We can help each other when we make a mistake. We can use kind words and we can learn something new.

Mabel holds the sticker as Mr. Heaton stands over the tiny town and describes where to place the sticker. Together, they model talking through positional words, like *down*, *top*, and *next to*. Mr. Heaton is careful to model making a mistake and using kind words when Mabel makes a mistake. Eventually, the class agrees that they have found the right location for the pizza sticker and Mabel places it.

SCAFFOLDING, EXTENDING, AND ASSESSING GEOGRAPHICAL THINKING

The map making is one choice during work time. Mr. Heaton facilitates this work while the paraprofessional circulates and interacts with children working in other centers (Figure 5.13).

FIGURE 5.13

Translating the three-dimensional miniature box town into a two-dimensional representation (map) with a key

Amelia and Hunter are excited to select their images for the map. One of Hunter's buildings is the library because he loves to read books. Amelia constructed a zoo, her favorite place to go with her family. Amelia and Hunter first point out their buildings to each other in the tiny town—looking and talking about it has retained a high level of interest.

Then they begin to look through the images while talking:

"I need a lot of animals, not just one," Amelia thinks aloud, "Or a rainbow. My zoo is rainbow colors."

"Yeah I need a lot of books too," Hunter agrees. "Or B for books or L for library or R for read."

"That's a lot of letters. I need /z/. What letter goes /z/?" Amelia asks Hunter.

"Z. Look, you wrote zoo on your sign. You need Z-O-O," Hunter points to her tiny building.

Mr. Heaton notes that Amelia and Hunter are engaged in powerful conversation filled with opportunities for growing self-efficacy and language through peer modeling and feedback. Mr. Heaton is listening carefully so that he can extend their language and thinking. He is also hopeful that this interaction will be an effective place for the children to practice learning from and being kind about mistakes.

Hunter and Amelia are now ready to place their images on the map. Hunter walks back and forth between the three-dimensional tiny town and the map while Amelia walks. Mr. Heaton asks, "Hunter, what are you thinking about?"

"I'm trying to remember where my library is so I can put it on the map. But it looks different," Hunter looks perplexed.

"How does it look different?" Mr. Heaton probes.

"These are tall and this is flat," Hunter visually compares the completed tiny town with the incomplete map.

"The map is flat with images representing the buildings," Mr. Heaton affirms Hunter's observation and uses the learning intention language. "Do you remember how I placed my image on the map? Mabel helped me. Maybe Amelia can help you."

Amelia walks to the tiny town and starts describing the location of the library, "Do you see Yasmin's grocery store? Your library is next."

"I don't know where Yasmin's grocery store is," Hunter responds, getting frustrated.

"Let's look at the key," Mr. Heaton scaffolds. "This says grocery store and here is Yasmin's image representing her grocery store."

EFFECT SIZE FOR EXPLICIT TEACHING STRATEGIES = 0.57

"It's grapes! Yasmin loves grapes!" Hunter finds the image of grapes and puts his image (the letter L next to a stack of books) to the right. "We did it!"

"You used an image to represent your building and Amelia used the words *next to* to describe where your library is located. Remember when I made a mistake describing where my building was and Mabel helped me fix it? How can we check to make sure your library is in the right place?" Mr. Heaton refers back to his mini-lesson to prompt their self-evaluation.

EFFECT SIZE FOR STRATEGY MONITORING = 0.58

Hunter walks to the tiny town and says, "It goes school, library, grocery store." He walks back to the map, "I see school, grocery store, library. Wait. That's not the same."

"Library is *next* to grocery store," Amelia emphasizes as she repeats.

"And it's *next* to school," Hunter adds.

"That's tricky! In the tiny town, your library is next to two buildings but on the map it is only next to one building. What are different words we could use to describe where the library is?" Mr. Heaton targets positional language.

"They *beside* each other," Amelia suggests.

"The library is *beside* the grocery store and school. That's true!" Mr. Heaton rephrases.

"It's in the *middle*," Hunter adds.

"Yes, the library is in the *middle* of the grocery store and school buildings. There's even another word we could use: *between*. The library is *between* the grocery store and school," Mr. Heaton directly teaches this new positional word.

EFFECT SIZE FOR VOCABULARY INSTRUCTION = 0.63

Hunter moves his image. Mr. Heaton connects their interaction to the success criteria again. "We made a mistake when we first placed Hunter's image on the map. But we used kind words to find the mistake and fix it. And we learned new words to describe where buildings are; we learned *next to*, *beside*, *in the middle of*, and *between*!" Mr. Heaton makes notes about this interaction as Hunter and Amelia work together to place Amelia's image on the map.

TEACHING FOR CLARITY AT THE CLOSE

"Look at our amazing map of our tiny town! I heard many people make mistakes, use kind words to talk about their mistakes, and then learn something from their mistakes. Turn and tell your partner about a mistake you made and what you learned." Mr. Heaton gives everyone a chance to talk and then focuses the whole class discussion on one pair, "Bahar and Evelyn, will you share about your mistake?" Mr. Heaton has already met with Bahar and Evelyn to ask them to share with the group and to practice what they will say. He wants the children to feel confident and safe as they share with the whole class.

"I told Bahar start at the top and go down two streets. Bahar thought this was the top," Evelyn explains pointing to one end of the map. "And I thought this was the top," pointing to a different end.

"How did you talk about your mistake with kind words?" Mr. Heaton facilitates.

"I say, 'My pet shop no fit.' And Evelyn come look and see. And we know is mistake. She say, 'Oops!' And I say, 'Oops!' And it's no big deal," Bahar recalls.

Mr. Heaton retells the story while Bahar shows with his fingers. Bahar started at his "top" and walked down two streets to discover the whole block is full of buildings. Then Evelyn uses her fingers to start at her "top" and walks down two streets to where Bahar's pet shop image is now located.

"'Oops!' And 'It's no big deal.' Those are kind words to talk about a mistake. Then you figured out why you were thinking differently about the word *top*." Mr. Heaton focuses the conversation on the success criteria and asks, "What did you learn from your mistake?"

"Top isn't good for maps," Evelyn states.

"What words did you use instead?" Mr. Heaton probes.

"Evelyn say, 'Start fire station,' and then I know," Bahar explains.

"Lots of places could be the top of a map but we just have one fire station. That was a great way to describe where Bahar's image should go!" Next, Mr. Heaton brings closure to the lesson by previewing why this emphasis on language is so important. "Tomorrow, we are going to hide treasure in our tiny town. And we will have to tell the code-pillar where to go to find the treasure. We have to use precise words to describe location. We can use what we learned from our mistakes today to help us be precise tomorrow."

Ms. Davis and Distance Learning to Understand the World

When Ms. Davis plans, she tries to maximize the unique opportunities that distance learning presents. Her families now regularly exchange video documentation of their children learning with her. Most families include siblings, who often want to teach their younger prekindergarten siblings or learn with their older prekindergarten siblings. Some families include grandparents or aunts and uncles who are helping with childcare during school hours. Distance learning means Ms. Davis can create learning opportunities at home and in the neighborhood that include multigenerational family members. She can also capitalize on family interactions to facilitate intentional learning with families.

> EFFECT SIZE FOR FAMILY INVOLVEMENT = 0.42

As the children study the past and develop chronological awareness, Ms. Davis asks community members, including some who attended the same school, to video record themselves telling about how the community has changed over time. She asks indigenous community members to share the story of their families reaching back to the first people living in Virginia. These videos form an oral history library for the class. Ms. Davis then encourages the children to interview their family and friends to learn about their life experiences within the community and to document their own life timelines. She sends home materials so families can create a physical timeline of their child's life. In these ways, her children intentionally learn their histories from and with their families.

> EFFECT SIZE FOR SELF-CONCEPT = 0.47

An important part of their community is the intersection of neighborhoods and businesses with nature. In previous years, Ms. Davis's class went on seasonal walks along the same nature trail to note the ways it changed with the seasons. Often family members would join these hikes. In distance learning, Ms. Davis videotapes herself on the seasonal hike and asks the children to notice and wonder with her as they watch. She asks families to share their own videos, drawings, and stories of their family walks across the seasons. Some

(Continued)

(Continued)

families hike trails with historic home sites. Some families walk the city routes with historic markers or simply walk to the grocery store. Others document noticings in their backyard or at their favorite park. Ms. Davis also collects nature items from her walks and sends them home for the children to physically explore. As a class, they play *I Spy*, *Pictionary*, and *Charades* using the nature items.

Even from a distance, Ms. Davis values the experiences children share with their families and facilitates children intentionally learning about the world around them.

EFFECT SIZE FOR DELIBERATE PRACTICE = 0.79

UNDERSTANDING THE WORLD AND PLAYFUL LEARNING

As you intentionally select the materials and create the contexts for learning with science, humanities, and social sciences content, skills, and understandings, consider these guidelines and tips:

- Rather than a science center, provide science content and the opportunity to apply science practices and processes throughout the classroom (e.g., informational or nonfiction text). Science is more than just one area of the classroom.

- When selecting science informational or nonfiction texts, make sure the content does not ignite or perpetuate scientific misconceptions. As an example, the four seasons (summer, fall, winter, and spring) are not caused by the distance of the Earth from the sun! Common misconceptions can be found in Table 5.2.

TABLE 5.2 ● Common Misconceptions in Science

- Animals are living because they move, but plants are nonliving.
- Anything that pours is a liquid.
- When liquids evaporate, they just disappear.
- Electric current is used up in bulbs, and there is less current going back to a battery than coming out of it.
- Light rays move out from the eye in order to illuminate objects.
- Loudness and pitch are the same thing.

- Suction causes liquids to be pulled upward in a soda straw.
- Earth is flat.
- The phases of the moon are caused by shadows from Earth falling on the moon.
- Seasons are caused by the changing distance of Earth from the sun (see Driver et al., 1994).

- Like mathematics learning, capitalize on familiar home contexts where practices and processes are used, often without even realizing it, and create those contexts in school so that children can show what they know. Listen for informal language and watch for nonverbal understandings of significant science, humanities, and social sciences concepts, skills, and understandings.

- When learners utilize informal language or demonstrate nonverbal understandings, be ready to explicitly teach science, humanities, or social sciences vocabulary. When we engage in this content and these skills and understandings, we must ensure that we use precise academic vocabulary.

- Build children's familiarity with science tools, models, and materials by making them available for exploration while pairing this exploration with language. Use guided questioning, think-aloud protocols, and teacher modeling to make science knowledge, practices, processes, and this distinct way of knowing visible to all learners.

- Keep an eye out for models that make science concepts, ideas, and phenomena concrete. These models come from many sources (e.g., home, playground, grocery store, etc.). Do not limit your source of models to science catalogs or textbooks.

- Integration is critical. In science, humanities, and social sciences, you may have already noticed many connections to social learning, self-concept development, classroom community development, and much more. You can read and reread the chapters in this book through different lenses. For example, you might notice in Chapter 4 that children are learning their name story, which is an oral story history that supports identity development and values the diversity of their classmates. In Chapter 7, while the children are developing fine motor skills, they are also examining the similarities and differences between the physical properties of slime and playdough and analyzing and celebrating the diversity of their families through family portrait creation. Chapter 2 is full of playful learning in science, humanities, and social sciences, including constructing animal habitats, acting out occupations in the community, and sorting forms of transportation, animals, and so much more.

- Background knowledge is vital to reading and language comprehension. Intentionally teach science, humanities, and social sciences to build this background knowledge. Be sure to intentionally move learners through the phases of learning, from surface to deep to transfer learning, so that this learning is memorable and accessible in the future.

CHAPTER 6

Visible Learning in Early Childhood Social and Emotional Development

In early childhood education, we ardently plan teaching and learning that considers the whole child. While learning the content of mathematics, reading, writing, and science is important, planning intentionally for the whole learner means also teaching and learning social and emotional skills. As multiple domains develop in early childhood, including social and emotional skills, language, literacy, mathematics, executive functioning, reasoning, problem solving, and fine and gross motor skills, our instruction must integrate instruction across these areas.

This chapter will unpack the research on effective social and emotional development in early childhood education by addressing both why it is important and how to effectively teach it. Then, we will step into two classrooms to see and hear the research in action.

EFFECTIVE SOCIAL AND EMOTIONAL DEVELOPMENT IN EARLY CHILDHOOD

Self-care, attachment and relationships, initiative, and self-regulation create the core of both intra- and interpersonal processes significant to children's social and emotional development. In particular, social and emotional skills are composed of regulating and managing emotions, setting and working toward goals, empathizing, forming relationships, and decision making, which are reliant on and mediated by language skills. Social and emotional skills are a significant facet of early childhood education with strong links to learning outcomes (Garner et al., 2014). In addition, social-emotional competence affects learners' ability to recall and attend as well as their quality of engagement.

EXPLICIT INSTRUCTION

EFFECT SIZE
FOR
TEACHING
COMMUNICATION
SKILLS AND
STRATEGIES
= 0.35

Social and emotional skills can be explicitly taught through language, modeling, and coaching (Murano et al., 2020). Their development cannot be left to chance, mere experience, or independent inquiry. While children will learn through experiences and inquiry, our intentional instruction creates spaces for intentional practice and rehearsal so that children have social and emotional skills in their toolboxes when they experience a need.

EFFECT
SIZE FOR
VOCABULARY
INSTRUCTION
= 0.63

We should explicitly teach targeted social and emotional skills to the whole class as well as tailor our instructional content and strategies to meet individual needs. Our deliberate instruction should include emotion content by modeling emotions, using and labeling emotion words, and coaching emotion language.

EFFECT SIZE
FOR GOAL
COMMITMENT
= 0.40

Another effective strategy is to partner with children to set a goal, identify behaviors to achieve the goal, and facilitate the progress toward the goal.

EFFECT
SIZE FOR
PROBLEM-
SOLVING
TEACHING
= 0.67

We should also capitalize on problem-solving learning by coaching in the moment and facilitating social problem-solving dialogue to foster positive relationships and interactions among peers.

This means that, as early childhood educators, we must grow our own social and emotional awareness in order to notice, think aloud, and intervene with our learners (Jennings & Greenberg, 2009; Zinsser et al., 2016).

CONTINUITY WITH HOME

Children's social and emotional development is influenced by family, peers, and community. In fact, the ways children express their social-emotional competence can be specific to the children and their families' sociocultural characteristics, experiences, and values (Garner et al., 2014). Therefore, to be effective, our social and emotional skill instruction must be aligned and compatible with children's home life, sensitive to children's sociocultural characteristics, experiences, and values, and focused on social-emotional competence beyond simply the classroom setting.

EFFECT SIZE FOR SELF-CONCEPT = 0.47

The most effective social-emotional teaching and learning is a multilayered approach where families are partners who collaborate to parallel the coaching, modeling, and language facilitation at home (Murano et al., 2020). In order for this to happen, the social-emotional teaching and learning must be responsive to families (Gross & Grady, 2002) and early educators must be culturally competent (Garner et al., 2014).

EFFECT SIZE FOR FAMILY INVOLVEMENT = 0.42

SOCIAL AND COMMUNICATION SKILLS

When considering a developmentally appropriate sequence of social and emotional skills, our deliberate instruction should first target social and communication skills within the category of relationship skills (Pianta et al., 2016). These interpersonal skills are developing in the preschool ages. Explicit instruction through modeling, coaching, and language facilitation about forming relationships and responding to peers will meet the in-the-moment needs of young children.

Explicit instruction through modeling, coaching, and language facilitation about forming relationships and responding to peers will meet the in-the-moment needs of young children.

At 4 years old, children begin to develop self-regulation, which includes meta-cognitive skills. They can begin to internalize social and communication skills in order to develop intrapersonal skills, such as regulating and managing emotions, setting and working toward goals, empathizing, and decision making. Therefore, our teaching and learning can shift to focus on self-regulation and self-direction in prekindergarten and kindergarten (Pianta et al., 2016).

EFFECT SIZE FOR SELF-REGULATION STRATEGIES = 0.54

And all of these skills lead to developing respect for self and others.

QUALITY OF INTERACTIONS

Deliberate instruction to grow social and emotional skills does not take place only within specific social-emotional competence lessons. Children develop social-emotional competence through the quality of interactions within a classroom, especially the teacher–learner interactions. These interactions can be during transitions, routines, or instruction, taking place inside and outside, and are often embedded within teaching and learning about academic content.

EFFECT SIZE FOR TEACHER–STUDENT RELATIONSHIPS = 0.47

The quality of these ongoing interactions is a powerful contributor to children's social and emotional development.

Positive experiences in a responsive preschool lead to better cognitive and academic achievement and fewer negative behavior issues in elementary and middle school (Pianta et al., 2016). When educators are sensitive to individual needs, provide support for positive behavior, and stimulate language and cognitive development, they are also growing children's social-emotional competence (Pianta et al., 2016). The quality of instruction also matters; children learn more academically, socially, and emotionally when their teachers communicate with clarity, focus on conceptual understanding, provide feedback that extends children's thinking, and engage in intentional, positive conversations with children (Pianta et al., 2016).

Therefore, our most effective interactions with children are differentiated, take place across content areas and throughout the day (including academics), are language-based, emphasize open-ended questions, and model positive interactions.

For children to learn and internalize social-emotional competence, our instruction must reflect cultural competence through meaningful partnerships with families.

This is where social and emotional education research and Visible Learning research intersect: Social and emotional development is so critical to early childhood that we must deliberately teach it and integrate it across the curriculum. For children to learn and internalize social-emotional competence, our instruction must reflect cultural competence through meaningful partnerships with families. Our youngest learners should focus on social and communication skills and then move into self-regulation skills involving meta-cognition. Our roles as conversational partners and language facilitators remain paramount as we constantly model high-quality, positive interactions with our learners, whether we realize it or not; social-emotional competence is a part of every interaction we have with learners. The Visible Learning research complements social-emotional education research and provides a practical means for implementing quality interactions and instruction in the early childhood classroom.

MS. DEMCHAK AND PERSPECTIVES

All day long, the 4-year-olds in Ms. Demchak's prekindergarten class are interacting with their peers and teachers. Ms. Demchak knows each interaction is an opportunity—an opportunity to model, coach, provide feedback, and build a positive relationship. As a result, she is constantly attending to the interactions, noticing patterns that inform her explicit instruction, and sharing these patterns with her vertical professional learning community to problem solve together.

Ms. Demchak has noticed a pattern in the children's emotional responses to each other. When a child asks another to do a specific activity and the other child says no, there is a feeling of hurt, and she often hears, "They don't want to be my friend!" When there is a disagreement about materials, there is a feeling of unfairness and Ms. Demchak often hears, "Give it back! I was using that first!" Ms. Demchak mediates these disagreements and the children are becoming proficient in expressing their own feelings; however, while they listen to their peers' feelings, they do not empathize yet.

Empathy is an abstract concept. Ms. Demchak does not expect her 4-year-olds to master empathy, but she wants to begin their development of empathy through perspective-taking.

EFFECT SIZE FOR SELF-REGULATION STRATEGIES = 0.54

Ms. Demchak uses read-alouds to scaffold the children's understanding of multiple perspectives in a friendship and to provide examples of their roles as decision makers and communicators within these relationships. This year, her learners love reading and rereading the *Elephant and Piggie* series by Mo Willems, and many of the children check out the books to take home and have siblings read to them. Ms. Demchak knew the series would be popular among siblings from Ms. Murrah and the vertical professional learning community. As a team, they look for ways to use familiar texts to storify problem solving and enable learners to access content to show what they know; they storify problems using familiar texts in every content area, including social and emotional development. Ms. Demchak plans to use the children's familiarity with the characters and plots in the series in order to focus their rereading on making sense of each character's unique perspective.

EFFECT SIZE FOR STRATEGIES TO INTEGRATE WITH PRIOR KNOWLEDGE = 0.93

LEARNING INTENTIONS AND SUCCESS CRITERIA

The Early Years Learning Framework is centered around three life processes: belonging, being, and becoming (Australian Government Department of Education and Training, 2019). Ms. Demchak uses the framework's outcomes to create cohesive instruction with a clear message: Children's sense of belonging, being, and becoming are of the utmost importance. The framework also keeps Ms. Demchak's expectations high for her learners because they express a long-term view of the whole child who is constantly becoming.

This enables Ms. Demchak to create studies about accessible yet abstract concepts like empathy, where developing an emerging understanding is the goal.

EFFECT SIZE FOR TEACHER EXPECTATIONS = 0.42

Outcome 1: Children Have a Strong Sense of Identity

- Children feel safe, secure, and supported.
- Children develop their emerging autonomy, interdependence, resilience, and sense of agency.
- Children learn to interact in relation to others with care, empathy, and respect.

Outcome 3: Children Have a Strong Sense of Well-Being

- Children become strong in their social and emotional well-being.

To create the learning intentions and success criteria, Ms. Demchak makes the abstract concept of empathy accessible by using familiar language. The class has worked on describing how they think and feel as individuals and why they feel and think that way. Now, they will begin to transfer that emotion language to appreciate other's perspectives.

Content Learning Intention: We are learning that other people may think and feel differently than us.

Language Learning Intention: We are learning ways to respectfully communicate how we think and feel.

Social Learning Intention: We are learning the value of acknowledging friends' thoughts and feelings.

Success Criteria

- I can describe how two people might feel and think differently in the same situation.
- I can explain why they might feel or think that way.

Typically, Ms. Demchak draws upon actual classroom interactions and incidents as examples. Today, she wants to remove any attachment of who is right or wrong by relying on two familiar characters: Gerald the elephant and Piggie. She will use the rereading of a book to create an exemplar situation for the class to analyze and discuss. Then she will scaffold the children's transfer of perspective-taking skills as they engage in centers.

ACTIVATING PRIOR KNOWLEDGE

Ms. Demchak reminds the class of a book they have read multiple times, including yesterday. As she talks, she turns pages describing the action.

Remember in *Are You Ready to Play Outside?* when Gerald and Piggie are so excited to play outside but it starts to rain? They are so disappointed. They have such awesome plans. They don't think anyone could have fun in the rain. And then it rains and rains. But something happens. Someone has a different perspective about the rain. Do you remember?

For this reread, she is zooming into one moment in *Are You Ready to Play Outside?* (Willems, 2008), not rereading the whole book. Ms. Demchak stops on a page and the children take turns describing it, even remembering the lines: "The worms are jumping!" "Splish, splash, splish, splash!" "Worms love the rain!"

Ms. Demchak reads aloud the next few pages and then asks an abstract question, "Why do Gerald and Piggie decide to try playing in the rain?"

"They see the worms having fun," Isla replies.

"The worms have a different perspective about the rain. Gerald and Piggie notice the worms feel happy because they think playing in the rain is fun. The worms' perspective helps Gerald and Piggie decide to try playing in the rain too." Ms. Demchak intentionally uses the language of the learning intentions and success criteria within the context of the book as a model.

EFFECT SIZE FOR TEACHER CLARITY = 0.84

"And then Piggie loves playing in the rain!" Max remembers.

"And so does Gerald!" Coen adds.

"Gerald and Piggie change how they think and feel about rain after considering a different perspective," Ms. Demchak again uses the language of perspective-taking to connect the familiar context of the story with this new, abstract concept.

> Thinking about other people's perspectives is important for understanding how they think and feel differently than you. It's especially important to understand your friends' perspectives so that you can be better friends who respect each other. Today, as you work in centers, talk to each other about how you feel and what you're thinking. You might notice that you have different perspectives sometimes. Talking about it will help you solve problems as a team.

Ms. Demchak knows these statements are grand and that her learners only have an emerging sense of empathy, but she also knows that building language and experiences around empathy through perspective-taking is a first and significant step.

SCAFFOLDING, EXTENDING, AND ASSESSING SOCIAL-EMOTIONAL THINKING

The interactions during centers are play based and just as important for modeling, coaching, providing feedback, building positive relationships, and deliberately practicing perspective taking. Ms. Demchak has noticed that some centers and materials naturally inspire reenactments of real-life interactions, which provides her with opportunities to model and practice social and communication skills in the moment. Today, she is looking and listening for opportunities to engage children in the learning intentions and success criteria through her intentional language.

Alinta and Jacob are working with the dollhouse. They have placed furniture to create two apartments—one for Alinta's family and one for Jacob's. Alinta holds a figurine and shouts, "You're too loud! Stop that racket!" Jacob makes his figurine shout back, "I like loud music!" Alinta and Jacob continue shouting. They are smiling so Ms. Demchak knows they are pretending, possibly recreating an interaction they have witnessed.

Ms. Demchak grabs a figurine and uses it to knock on Alinta's family door, "Excuse me. I can hear shouting. It sounds like something is wrong. Can you tell me what's happening? What's your perspective?"

Alinta explains that Jacob's music is too loud and will wake her sleeping baby.

Ms. Demchak intentionally says, "Oh, the music is too loud because it will wake up your baby! Does Jacob know your baby is sleeping? It might change his perspective."

Alinta shrugs.

Ms. Demchak then takes her figurine to Jacob's door and repeats her statement and question.

Jacob replies, "It's my sister's birthday. We're playing music and dancing. Then we're going to play hide-and-seek."

Ms. Demchak purposefully says, "Oh, I didn't know that! Happy Birthday to your sister! Does Alinta know you're playing music because this is a birthday party? It might change her perspective."

Jacob thinks and then says, "No. I'll tell her." He walks his figurine to Alinta's door and knocks, "Hey, Alinta. It's my sister's birthday. We're dancing to the music. Do you want to come to the birthday party?"

"I love birthday parties. But my baby is sleeping. That's why the music is too loud," Alinta responds.

"I'll turn it down till she wakes up and then come dance," Jacob offers.

"Okay! Oh, she's awake. We're coming over now," Alinta says.

"You did a great job explaining your thinking and feelings to each other. And you did a great job listening to understand your friend's perspective. When you understood why you were both upset, you found a solution together," Ms. Demchak gives feedback to Alinta and Jacob by connecting back to the success criteria.

> EFFECT SIZE FOR FEEDBACK = 0.62

And with that, Jacob and Alinta are back to their pretend birthday dance party.

Ms. Demchak makes quick notes after this interaction so that she can facilitate their sharing later and track who she has practiced perspective-taking with and in what context. Ms. Demchak works with four other groups today. Noah, Bindi, and Mia use puppets to reenact a school scene. Ruby and Thomas disagree about design ideas as they build trains. Oliver and Zoe reread the pictures of *A Big Guy Took My Ball!* (Willems, 2013), another favorite in the *Elephant and Piggie* series. Finally, Isla, Coen, and Max pretend they are at the laundry mat. Each time, Ms. Demchak is intentional with her language, using the language of empathy and perspectives as she engages in and facilitates conversations.

> EFFECT SIZE FOR DELIBERATE PRACTICE = 0.79

TEACHING FOR CLARITY AT THE CLOSE

Ms. Demchak engages the children in a brief formative assessment to practice self-evaluation and meta-cognition.

> EFFECT SIZE FOR SELF-JUDGMENT AND REFLECTION = 0.75

> Give a thumbs up if you thought about how someone else was thinking or feeling and why. Give a thumbs down if you did not notice how someone else was thinking or feeling. Give a sideways thumb if you noticed someone was thinking or feeling differently than you but you didn't spend time thinking about how or why.

She makes a quick note of how each child responded so that she can follow up with them. Ms. Demchak notes that most of the children she interacted with during centers have their thumbs up, which accurately reflects their perspective-taking practice.

Ms. Demchak pairs the children with their thumbs up with the other children and asks them to tell about when someone was thinking or feeling differently and why. She wants the children to use their own words to engage each other in talking about perspectives.

As she listens to partners sharing, Ms. Demchak hears phrases like, "I didn't know," "That's why," and "We decided." She notes this language so she can integrate it into her next mini-lesson.

The class returns to the circle. Ms. Demchak says,

> We are learning that other people may think and feel differently than us. Their ideas and feelings are important. Understanding their perspectives can help us be better friends and solve problems. Let's keep looking for chances to notice when a friend thinks or feels differently. Oliver and Zoe noticed different perspectives again with Gerald and Piggie! So tomorrow we'll reread the book they found—*A Big Guy Took My Ball!*

Ms. Demchak's learners began by learning the language and self-awareness to identify their own emotions, and now they are transferring this to understand each other's emotions. She knows empathy takes time to develop and her learners have started.

MR. HEATON AND GOAL SETTING

Throughout the school year, Mr. Heaton engages his learners in gradually more abstract and academic-focused goal setting.

At the beginning of the year, after getting to know each other and forming relationships with peers, the class celebrated the big idea, "We all are teachers and we all are learners." Each child taught another child something new. For example, Bahar taught Hunter to throw a frisbee, Mabel taught Freddie to use tweezers, and Hamza taught Harper to write an H. Then Mr. Heaton made a video showing each pair doing the new task and talking about it. He shared this video with families, which inspired families to talk about things they taught each other. By the second half of the year, the children will be setting academic goals, making plans to meet their goals, and tracking their progress.

This week, Mr. Heaton introduces the concept of goal setting. He builds on the idea that every child is an expert while also ready to learn something new. He begins with nonacademic interests so that children identify goals and make plans to attain their goals in familiar, low-risk contexts focused on playful learning (Thunder & Demchak, 2017). He also talks with each family about their goals for their child and how they will communicate and share progress toward child-, family-, and teacher-identified goals moving forward.

LEARNING INTENTIONS AND SUCCESS CRITERIA

Mr. Heaton knows that goal setting requires abstract thought about self-regulation, meta-cognition, and decision making. His 4-year-olds are ready to engage deeply in this work and his 3-year-olds are ready to be exposed to these ideas at the surface level of learning. He also knows that by communicating clearly the collective class goals for learning, by modeling and coaching, and by focusing on the quality of interactions across the day, he will teach important social and emotional skills while also growing visible learners.

EFFECT SIZE FOR STRONG CLASSROOM COHESION = 0.53

During their work to celebrate "We all are teachers and we all are learners," Mr. Heaton focused on building positive peer relationships, strong home–school connections, and a collaborative classroom community. He relied on the following Early Learning Goals (U.K. Department of Education, 2021):

ELG Building Relationships: Show sensitivity to their own and to others' needs.

ELG Self-Regulation: Show an understanding of their own feelings and those of others, and begin to regulate their behaviour accordingly.

ELG Speaking: Express their ideas and feelings about their experiences using full sentences including use of past, present, and future tenses and making use of conjunctions, with modelling and support from their teacher.

Now, Mr. Heaton will build on this foundation so the children can look inward to their personal goals while continuing to rely on their peer relationships, family, and classroom community for support and encouragement:

EFFECT SIZE FOR SELF-EFFICACY = 0.66

> **ELG Self-Regulation:** Set and work towards simple goals, being able to wait for what they want and control their immediate impulses when appropriate.
>
> **ELG Managing Self:** Be confident to try new activities and show independence, resilience and perseverance in the face of challenge.

Mr. Heaton is careful to align his learning intentions and success criteria with the Early Learning Goals and to communicate these to his learners. He knows this is one way to create quality interactions with his learners.

> **Content Learning Intention:** We are learning that setting and working toward goals is one way to learn.
>
> **Language Learning Intention:** We are learning about ways to talk about and reflect on our goals.
>
> **Social Learning Intention:** We are learning to encourage our friends as they work on goals.
>
> **Success Criteria**
>
> - I can think about what I can do and what I can't do yet and set a goal to learn something new.
> - I can make a plan to work toward my goal at home and school.

Next, Mr. Heaton plans his language for introducing goal setting and how he will use his strong family connections to extend their learning to home.

ACTIVATING PRIOR KNOWLEDGE

Mr. Heaton begins by activating learners' knowledge.

> Before we go outside today, instead of sharing your plan for what you will do, I'm going to ask you two different questions. First, what is something you can do outside easily? It is not hard for you; you can just decide to do it. Maybe pumping your legs on a swing is easy for you. Maybe doing the monkey bars is easy for you. Maybe riding a scooter is easy for you. Let's go around the circle and everyone will take a turn saying something you can do outside easily.

There are many different responses, the ones Mr. Heaton anticipated and more: monkey bars, swinging, riding a scooter, balancing on the beam, sliding down the pole, climbing to the top of the climbing wall, making sand castles, bouncing a basketball.

After everyone has shared, Mr. Heaton poses his next question: "What is something that is hard for you to do outside? Maybe you want to try it but you don't know how. It might be something that is easy for someone else in our class and that's okay because we know everyone is an expert about something. It is hard for me to do monkey bars."

Again, each child shares around the circle. This question takes more thought for some but everyone has an answer.

Some answers are what other children can do easily. Some are new: climb up the slide, shoot a basket, play hopscotch, pedal the tricycle.

"Isn't that interesting?! We know we can teach each other how to do things that are easy for us. And there are some things that each of us wants to try but they're hard right now," Mr. Heaton says. "Today, when we're outside, I'm going to ask you to set a goal. A goal is something you want to try but it is hard at first. You might not even know how to do it, but you want to try. A goal takes practice over time to accomplish. And after you set your goal, we'll make a plan for how to practice to reach your goal on purpose."

With that explanation, the class lines up to go outside. The children regularly make a plan for what they will do outside and then share a reflection about what they actually did afterward. This routine facilitates the concept of making a plan and helps the children make collaborative plans so that everyone is included before playful learning begins.

SCAFFOLDING, EXTENDING, AND ASSESSING SOCIAL-EMOTIONAL THINKING

Earlier in Mr. Heaton's career, he treated outdoor time as recess where he was merely an observer to make sure everyone stayed safe. Now, he sees outdoor time as another context for playful learning where his interactions with children are essential (Figure 6.1). This shift has expanded his instructional time as well as the spaces where learning and language can ake place.

FIGURE 6.1 ● Outdoor Goal-Setting Observation/Conference Checklist

Dates _____

Content Learning Intention: We are learning that setting and working toward goals is one way to learn.

Language Learning Intention: We are learning about ways to talk about and reflect on our goals.

Social Learning Intention: We are learning to encourage our friends as they work on goals.

NAME	SC #1: I can think about what I can do.	SC #1: I can think about what I can't do yet.	SC #1: I can set a goal to learn something new.	SC #2: I can make a plan to work toward my goal at school. (*Peer teachers?*)	SC #2: I can make a plan to work toward my goal at home. (*Family teachers?*)

online resources 🖰 Available for download at **resources.corwin.com/VLforEarlyChildhood**

Mr. Heaton walks to a playground structure with a fire pole. Children wait in line to take turns sliding down the pole and then running up the stairs or climbing up the slide to rejoin the line. Arthur is watching the group but not joining. Mr. Heaton wants to capitalize on this moment and asks, "Arthur, what is something that you want to try outside but it's hard?"

"I can't do the pole," Arthur responds.

"The pole is hard," Mr. Heaton commiserates. "But it's something you can learn to do with practice. Would you like to learn how to slide down the pole?"

"Yes!" Arthur says excitedly.

"What a great goal! Your goal is to slide down the pole. Hmmm, what do you think you need to do to learn?"

"I'm watching," Arthur points to the kids sliding down one at a time over and over.

"Watching someone else is a great way to notice how they do something. What have you noticed?"

"Hold on. Slide down. Go up. Get in line," Arthur is noticing a pattern.

Mr. Heaton wants to help him analyze the task of sliding down the pole. He decides to build on their previous work of teaching each other something new and says, "Let's go over and ask Aurora to tell us how she slides down the pole."

When it's Aurora's turn, she narrates as she quickly holds onto the pole and slides down, "Hands on. Legs on. Slide down!"

Mr. Heaton repeats Aurora's words as they watch three more children slide down the pole. "Arthur, do you want to give it a try? I can help."

Arthur is eager to try and joins the line. But when it is his turn, Arthur stands unsure at the top of the pole. He reaches out to grab the pole and freezes.

"Your goal is to slide down the pole. First, let's take a picture of you at the top," Mr. Heaton takes a quick picture to document Arthur's goal setting and then prompts, "Let's remember Aurora's advice. Hands on. You've got your hands on. What's next?"

"Legs on. Slide down." Arthur remembers the chant. "I can't put my legs on. It's too high."

EFFECT SIZE FOR APPROPRIATELY CHALLENGING GOALS = **0.59**

EFFECT SIZE FOR HELP SEEKING = **0.72**

EFFECT
SIZE FOR
COGNITIVE
TASK
ANALYSIS
= 1.29

"Let's try one leg at a time. I'll help. I won't let you fall," Mr. Heaton holds his arms out. Arthur slowly puts one leg out and Mr. Heaton directs, "One leg on—wrap your leg around the pole like a snake. Put your foot around to the other side." Arthur tries. Mr. Heaton then says, "Now two legs on—pull your body up to hold onto the pole. I'll hold your shoulders for extra help." Mr. Heaton breaks down Aurora's advice in the spot that is challenging to Arthur.

He puts his hands under Arthur's shoulders. With that extra support and reassurance, Arthur awkwardly lifts his other leg off the platform, and Mr. Heaton slowly lowers Arthur while saying, "Hands on. Legs on. Slide down!" When Arthur is standing at the bottom, Mr. Heaton says, "You did it!"

They high five. "Wow! Your goal is to slide down the pole! You watched kids do it. Then you asked Aurora for help. Then you tried her advice. And now you've slid down the pole!" Mr. Heaton summarizes Arthur's process.

Arthur smiles and says, "Yes! But I want to do it by myself!"

"That means you'll need to practice. Get back in line and remember: Hands on. *One leg on. Two legs on.* Slide down!" Mr. Heaton emphasizes the part that Arthur needed the most help with. Mr. Heaton stays nearby interacting with other children while watching Arthur, calling out the mantra when it is Arthur's turn, and moving closer to the pole in case he needs help. Mr. Heaton takes a short video of Arthur saying his mantra. After a few tries, the pole sliding turns into a game of chase and Arthur is off running with the other children.

By engaging in goal setting with Mr. Heaton, Arthur watched children play because he did not know how to do the activity and moved to actively joining their play and trying something new. This evolved into a chasing game that Arthur joined without hesitation. Mr. Heaton notes this to share with Arthur's family, who expressed their goals for him to develop initiative and build friendships.

Mr. Heaton confers with four more children during their time outside, asking each one about something hard they want to try, and for those interested, taking a first try together. Each time, Mr. Heaton snaps a picture next to the object for visual documentation of their goal setting, and he sometimes takes a brief video of their first try in action. Later today, Mr. Heaton will send these pictures and videos home to families with a brief note about each child's goal. He will also connect the child's self-selected goal with the family's goals for their child, explaining how he sees them overlapping and beginning a conversation about how both Mr. Heaton and the family will help the child practice and document this practice.

TEACHING FOR CLARITY AT THE CLOSE

Each day, after their playful learning outside, the class sits in a circle and shares what they did.

Today, Mr. Heaton asks the children to share something new they tried or played. First, Arthur and the other four children who set goals today share.

"I tried going down the fire pole," Arthur shares.

"Arthur, you set a goal about the fire pole. What is your goal?" Mr. Heaton uses goal-setting language to emphasize the special thinking they did.

"To go down the fire pole by myself," he states.

"You started practicing already! What did you do today to practice your goal of going down the fire pole by yourself?" Mr. Heaton extends.

"I watched. Then Aurora told me how to do it. And Mr. Heaton helped. And I went down *three* times!" Arthur remembers.

"Do feel like you've met your goal or do you want to practice some more?" Mr. Heaton asks a question that engages Arthur in self-evaluation and progress monitoring.

"I'm gonna practice more. I want to be fast with no help!" Arthur moves his hand like it is sliding down the pole quickly.

"Working toward a goal is hard work and takes practice. If you see Arthur working on his goal of sliding down the fire pole, remember to encourage him!" Mr. Heaton gives Arthur feedback while building on their collaborative community.

The rest of the children share what they tried or played outside. At the end of sharing, Mr. Heaton says, "I wonder if any of the new things you tried today will become your goal that you want to practice. If you haven't set your goal yet, be thinking about it and we'll share more goals tomorrow." Mr. Heaton closes by encouraging the children to continue thinking about the ideas from today in order to scaffold their meta-cognition and decision making.

> EFFECT SIZE FOR SELF-REGULATION STRATEGIES = 0.54

> EFFECT SIZE FOR STRATEGY MONITORING = 0.58

Ms. Davis and Distance Social-Emotional Learning

Getting to know Ms. Davis's learners feels very different this year because her children are engaged in distance learning. Ms. Davis has whole group, small group, and one-on-one meetings with her children every day, yet her time with the children feels shorter and the interactions are less frequent and less varied. Her instructional goals remain the same, so Ms. Davis must transfer and revise what she knows about in-person learning to distance learning. She is also trying to take advantage of unique aspects of distance learning and use these to inform her instructional strategies.

EFFECT SIZE FOR SELF-CONCEPT = 0.47

Ms. Davis is in the midst of her "Being Me" unit, which explores and communicates children's experiences, expressions, and management of emotions as well as their personal identities, including interests, physical traits, and family life.

She began by asking each family to create an *All About Me* book with their child and then record themselves reading it. Along with her own video, Ms. Davis made a virtual library of the videos so that families and children could watch and get to know their classmates.

EFFECT SIZE FOR FAMILY INVOLVEMENT = 0.42

This virtual library of read-aloud videos and songs has become a family favorite. It helps bridge school and home by bringing the shared books and songs into families' homes. Ms. Davis is able to include read-aloud videos and songs in each child's home language as well as create her own videos with closed captioning in English, Spanish, or Arabic. Families have begun sharing traditional songs, stories, and books from their childhood so that the virtual library is truly a community library.

Today, the children are learning emotion words. To plan her lesson, Ms. Davis first identified Virginia's Early Learning and Development Standards (Virginia Department of Education, 2021):

> **Emotional Competence:** Begins to recognize their own emotions before reacting. Communicates how other children or adults may be feeling and why.
>
> **Communication:** Begins to demonstrate understanding of implied messages based on speaker's tone and/or gestures.

Then, Ms. Davis created learning intentions and success criteria in child-friendly language based on the standards:

Content Learning Intention: We are learning to notice how we show our emotions with our face, body, thoughts, and voices.

Language Learning Intention: We are learning to name and describe emotions.

Social Learning Intention: We are learning to look and listen to notice friends' emotions.

Success Criteria

- I can see and hear clues to notice how friends feel.
- I can name and describe how friends feel.

In previous years, Ms. Davis has created a visual anchor chart to show the connection between each emotion word and a facial expression, body stance, and thoughts. This year, she has made three changes: she is adding vocal expression, she is using puppets as models and conversational partners, and she has sent home materials for families to create their own version of the emotions anchor chart with labels in their heritage languages (Figure 6.2).

EFFECT SIZE FOR CONCEPT MAPPING = 0.64

FIGURE 6.2 ● Emotions Anchor Chart

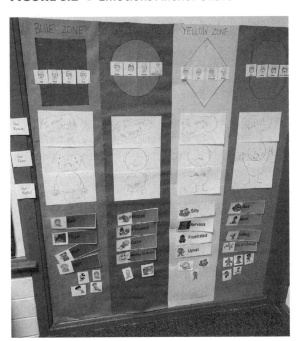

(Continued)

(Continued)

This year, the class has four puppet "classmates" and their favorite is Tashi the Tiger, who calls herself Super Tashi and wears a red cape. After the class sings and dances to an emotions version of the "Hokey Pokey," Ms. Davis holds Tashi in front of the camera and speaks into the microphone with her "Tashi" voice.

> Hey friends! We're going to play a mystery game today! I love mysteries! Remember yesterday you made a chart about feelings with Ms. Davis? Every feeling shows how your face looks, how your body looks, and what your brain might be thinking when you feel that way. Today, I'm going to change my voice to show you how I'm feeling. You can look at the anchor chart to remember the emotions we talked about. Ready?

Twelve 4-year-olds peer back at Tashi through their cameras with smiles and nodding heads. Tashi's voice is slow and soft with some sniffs and sighs, "Can you hear with your ears how I feel? Listen to my voice. Which emotion am I showing you with my voice?" Then Tashi models using the anchor chart by pointing to the emotion and asking, "Do I sound happy?" Children shake their heads and say "no." "Do I sound surprised?" Again, children shake their heads and say "no." "Do I sound sad?" The children nod their heads and shout "yes." Some clap and others jump up and down. "Braylen, why do you think I'm sad?"

"You're talking like this," Braylen mimics Tashi's slow, soft voice.

"And you sound like you're crying," Nya adds.

"Yes, my voice is slow and soft. I sound sad because I feel sad. You solved my mystery!" Tashi's voice changes to be loud and gruff, deep with some yelling and roaring, "I'm not sad anymore! Can you hear with your ears how I feel now? Listen to me! What emotion can you hear in my voice?" This time, the children are shouting "angry!" "Mercy, why do you think I'm angry?" Tashi asks.

"YOU'RE SO MAD! YOU'RE YELLING SO LOUD!" Mercy shouts back and makes her face angry in the camera.

"ROAR!" Shaheed yells, followed by a series of roars by the other children.

"ROAR! I am mad. I am angry. I yell and roar and make my voice so loud when I feel angry. You solved my mystery!" The game continues with Tashi's voice changing to show three more emotions. Then she says goodbye and Ms. Davis pops back into the camera view.

Ms. Davis describes the transition from whole group time to a screen break to small group Writing Workshop:

> You're noticing how we all show our emotions with our face, body, thoughts, and even our voices! Today in Writing Workshop, I'm going to write about a time when I was very scared. I'm going to draw me with my face looking scared and my body looking scared. I'm going to make my mouth into a circle because my voice will be screaming and sounding scared. And I'm going to tell you what my brain was thinking and why. During our screen break, think about what you will write about. Maybe you will write about a time when you were feeling scared or frustrated or excited or mad.

Talking, drawing, and writing is another place where Ms. Davis can maximize learners' interactions with her, with peers, and with the content of emotions. This was true during in-person learning and remains true in distance learning.

After Writing Workshop, families will have time to create their own version of the emotions anchor chart with labels in their home languages. They often send Ms. Davis photos of their work or videos of their child and family members explaining what they did. Ms. Davis saves this documentation in each child's digital portfolio.

SOCIAL AND EMOTIONAL DEVELOPMENT THROUGHOUT THE DAY

Because social and emotional development in early childhood occurs throughout the day, within interactions, and embedded within teaching and learning about academic content, it is critical that we plan with intentionality. Consider these tips and guidelines:

- Our deliberate instruction should include emotion content by modeling emotions, using and labeling emotion words, and coaching emotion language throughout the entire learning experience.

- Partner with children to set a goal, identify behaviors to achieve the goal, and facilitate the progress toward the goal. One important aspect of goal setting and attainment is to also model and discuss how to handle setbacks (Thunder & Demchak, 2017).

- Make social-emotional engagement a staple in the classroom. This begins with class meetings that allow learners and their teachers to meet face-to-face or through a distance learning platform. Use this protected time to integrate the two previous tips and guidelines into the classroom. Class meetings can be used to demonstrate or practice specific social skills (greeting, apologies, requests, etc.).

- As learners progress toward greater assessment capability, allow them to assume a greater role and level of responsibility in facilitating class meetings. For example, some learners may select meeting topics. Furthermore, learners can eventually co-create success criteria, norms, and processes that are adopted for class meetings. By the time learners transition into kindergarten, they may be able to run class meetings on their own—with you participating as a member of the community.

- With regard to success criteria, norms, and processes, establish these for all discussions and social-emotional challenges and conflicts. Record them with your class using visual anchor charts that you can refer to throughout the year. This front-end commitment will not only support learners in building their self-reflecting, self-monitoring, and self-regulation, but it will lay the foundation for them to engage in future challenges and conflicts beyond the walls of our learning environments (e.g., on the playground, on the bus, and at home).

- For many of our learners, the majority of their waking hours are spent with us. Help learners find consistency and predictability in our early childhood classrooms. Foster, nurture, and sustain this consistency and predictability by at least starting and ending every learning day with a personal connection. Continually look for ways to show that you care about your students as both learners and people.

- Begin with an asset-based perspective about all children, all families, and all cultures. Partner with families to ensure that social-emotional instruction at school aligns with children's learning at home and in the community. Acknowledge and respect differences across homes and communities. Look for common social and emotional communication strategies and be explicit about when and why they may be different at school and at home.

- Now, take a look inward. As early childhood educators, we must be socially and emotionally healthy if we are to be present and engaged, fully, with our learners. Find ways to attend to self-care by implementing stress relief techniques and engaging in positive collegial relationships. This is required for effective modeling.

- Finally, ensure that we are communicating that "I've got you" to our learners and not "gotcha." Each time we have the opportunity to interact with our learners, we should ensure that we are effectively providing feedback that helps support their learning and move them forward in their learning journey. When our learners know that we've "got them" and not "gotcha," they are more likely to engage and take on challenges. This building of teacher credibility, based in relational trust, accelerates learning.

CHAPTER 7

Visible Learning in Early Childhood Creative Arts and Motor Skill Development

When children are young, there are multiple critical domains developing simultaneously and often seemingly interdependent of each other. It is hard to tease out each big idea and skill, fully separating it by domain, perhaps because children's true experience of the world, its concepts and skills, is the integration of life. Effective instruction reflects this integration and engages children in learning that makes ideas and skills explicit while also meaningfully interconnected.

Like each of the previous chapters, we will unpack what research tells us is critical for early childhood expressive arts teaching and learning as well as for motor development. We will highlight the significant big ideas and skills of each content area; but as you will see, it is impossible to fully assign each to just one domain. Instead, we will examine these intersections and how intentionally planning for integration is effective.

EFFECT
SIZE FOR
INTEGRATED
CURRICULA
= 0.40

Finally, we will see and hear this research in combination with the Visible Learning research come alive in early childhood classrooms.

EFFECTIVE ARTS AND MOTOR LEARNING IN EARLY CHILDHOOD

Multisensory explorations and expressions of creativity, identity, relationships, and the natural world are central to children's engagement in the arts and artistic processes. The artistic processes are avenues for engaging in both gross and fine motor development; they provide opportunities to see mathematics, literacy, and science concepts and skills come to life and for engaging in collaborative and individual expressions of self. Research shows why the arts and motor development are important for early childhood education, ways to engage in the arts and motor development, and the potential for integrated teaching and learning experiences.

MUSIC

Early music education can include receptive music, active music making, and musical performance. Receptive music is listening to music, either active listening or music played in the background of other activities, such as centers or naptime.

Music making means children are actively singing and playing instruments, composing and improvising music, and working in a group or as an individual. Music making in early childhood has positive impacts on language, literacy, social-emotional development, and spatial reasoning (Barrett et al., 2018). Music making at home as a family can positively affect parenting practices and children's identity development (Barrett et al., 2018). Children's opportunity to engage in music making is highly dependent on the presence of instruments or the ability to recognize and use found instruments, such as pots and spoons (Barrett et al., 2018).

Musical performances can include formal or informal concerts as well as playing instruments and singing songs embedded in content instruction. Often, music in early childhood is used to teach language acquisition (name songs and songs that identify objects and parts of children's world), number sense (counting songs), sequencing and seriation (story songs), and patterning (repeating, cumulative, and interlocking patterns) (Barrett et al., 2018; Shilling, 2002). The rhythm of music and synchronized movement can serve as scaffolds for memory and recall as well as reflect culturally responsive teaching (Hammond, 2015).

EFFECT SIZE FOR WORKING MEMORY = 0.68

EFFECT SIZE FOR REHEARSAL AND MEMORIZATION = 0.73

Beat-based processing links music to reading development because the listener uses rich contextual regularities of rhythmic music to make predictions—a similar skill is needed for reading (Ozernov-Palchik & Patel, 2018).

Another way of engaging in music education involves a combination of all three—receptive music, active music making, and musical performance. By integrating physical education with music programs, children improve not only their motor skills but also their auditory and language skills; in fact, integration was more effective than teaching each content isolated from the other (Brown et al., 1981; Zachopoulou et al., 2004).

What does this mean for early childhood music education? We need to integrate receptive music, active music making, and musical performance with gross and fine motor teaching and learning as well as other content areas, such as mathematics, literacy, science, and social-emotional teaching and learning. Children need opportunities to engage with instruments (found or prepared), combine music with movement, and use the connections between music and content to explore and understand each area more deeply. We also need to connect with families to engage them with music making at home and to bring familiar cultural songs into our classrooms.

VISUAL ARTS

Parallel to music education, early visual arts education can include art viewing and art making with an emphasis on process and product. Four teaching strategies effectively engage young children in art viewing: questioning, storytelling, game play, and deliberate technical instruction (Eckhoff, 2008). These strategies reflect what we know about using games, stories, and talk to engage in culturally relevant teaching (Hammond, 2015).

Art making can include drawing, painting, photography, construction, sculpture, printmaking, and collage, where both the expressive objects (the artworks or the products) and the expressive acts (the art making or the processes) are significant and interwoven (Richards, 2018). Like all learning, the focus of art making is on sense-making either pairing artwork and art making with narratives or with inquiry. Children may ask, "What happens if?" to embark on an art inquiry or they may use art media to examine a topic of interest or personal importance and to express the meaning they discover. The connection between home and school continues to be important in early art experiences (Richards, 2018).

Six components are necessary for effective early art teaching and learning (Richards, 2018). First, children must find personal relevance in either art making or viewing.

> Children need opportunities to engage with instruments (found or prepared), combine music with movement, and use the connections between music and content to explore and understand each area more deeply.

EFFECT SIZE FOR FAMILY INVOLVEMENT = 0.42

EFFECT SIZE FOR TASK VALUE = 0.46

Then educators should add a layer of new stimuli that extend and deepen this connection.

Children need a sense of audience and purpose for their art making as well as access to art materials, including their previous work to continue or revise.

Art making takes time for children to deeply engage, explore big ideas, revisit, experiment, and make mistakes. Creating an art routine or schedule can support this protected art-making time.

Finally, children need to engage in conversation during art making and afterward. Language-based interaction continues to be at the heart of all learning, and it can be intentionally planned through teacher questions and class discussion.

With these six components in place, children can experience the ways art connects people and events and grow from recognizing artistic strategies to perceiving artistic objects and acts to intentionally engaging in art actions (Richards, 2018).

The development of visual arts skills, specifically pictorial imagery (Kindler & Darras, 1998), follows similar and intersecting trajectories with the development of written composition (oral storytelling, drawing, writing) and mathematical representation (concrete, representational or pictorial, abstract). As we saw in Chapter 4, young children's written composition development is founded in their development of oral language for storytelling, followed by drawing these stories, and finally, writing these stories with words (Horn & Giacobbe, 2007). With each new mathematical concept and skill, learners' sense-making begins with concrete representations that are then translated into pictorial representations and finally abstract or symbolic representations (Berry & Thunder, 2017). Each representation can then be connected to each other to extend and deepen meaning-making.

In visual arts, children begin developing pictorial imagery through sensory and motor explorations combined with cognitive awareness and examination of identity, similarity, and difference. Children's movements and gestures lead to explorations of rhythms, repetition, and variations.

Next, children examine and intentionally create traces, imprints, and marks, which lead to the creation of closed figures, starting with circles. Eventually, children create objects and worlds with their images.

Simultaneously, their narration of sensory-motor explorations, comparisons, movements, repetitions, traces, closed figures, and later objects and worlds also develops. At each stage of

EFFECT SIZE FOR CONCENTRATION/ PERSISTENCE/ ENGAGEMENT = 0.54

EFFECT SIZE FOR GOAL COMMITMENT = 0.40

EFFECT SIZE FOR TIME ON TASK = 0.42

EFFECT SIZE FOR CLASSROOM DISCUSSION = 0.82

In visual arts, children begin developing pictorial imagery through sensory and motor explorations combined with cognitive awareness and examination of identity, similarity, and difference.

EFFECT SIZE FOR MANIPULATIVES = 0.39

EFFECT SIZE FOR IMAGERY = 0.51

these parallel developments, the role of the adult is significant; adults can urge this development forward in their interactions with children by constantly seeking to recognize the children's creations and asking questions to make meaning of their representations.

These developmental trajectories can inform our instruction across the curriculum where language, narration, and representation are significant. They also point to the importance of motor development to connect movement to fine motor expressions of those movements and gestures.

What does this mean for early childhood visual arts education? We need to integrate art viewing and art making with gross and fine motor teaching and learning as well as other content areas in order to simultaneously develop motor, language, narration, and representation skills. Children need access to regular time and materials in order to create artistic expressions that hold personal relevance while allowing for inquiry and new discovery. Language-based interaction is paramount during art making as well as reflecting on the art process and product. We also need to connect with families to engage them with art making at home and to bring familiar cultural and natural materials into our classrooms.

GROSS MOTOR DEVELOPMENT

Gross motor skills cover a wide variety of physical activities, including locomotor skills, object manipulation, stability skills, bilateral body coordination, gait and postural control, strength and flexibility, and catching and interceptive action. Gross motor skills also include cross-curricular skills, such as rhythmic coordination and spatial working memory.

Gross motor development is interconnected with cognitive development, visual processing, and fine motor development. Gross motor and cognitive development share the underlying processes of sequencing, monitoring, and planning. Sensoriperceptual function and sensorimotor anticipations, which are essential for gross motor development, are also necessary for executive function to develop. Gross motor skills overlap with several executive function skills, working memory, and meta-cognitive skills, such as inhibition (reaction time), cognitive flexibility, planning, and attention.

Gross motor skills are the basis for fine motor skills. In fact, there is a positive correlation between cognitive skills and fine motor skills, bilateral body coordination, and timed performance in movements (van der Fels et al., 2015).

What does this mean for early childhood gross motor development? Gross motor development is a critical part of children's learning and should be intentionally taught. Recall that integrating physical education with music programs led to more effective growth in motor, auditory, and language skills (Brown et al., 1981; Zachopoulou et al., 2004), which means it is important to meaningfully connect gross motor teaching and learning with music (rhythmic coordination) and potentially other content areas, such as spatial reasoning in mathematics (spatial working memory). And throughout this interaction, we know that intentional, language-based interactions with adults play a significant role in learning overall.

FINE MOTOR DEVELOPMENT

Fine motor skills include graphomotor skills, cutting with scissors, manipulating small objects, and performing self-care tasks, like using clothing fasteners and eating utensils. Each of these fine motor skills involves a series of associated skills related to body structures and functions and contextual demands, such as visual perceptual skills, motor planning and execution, kinesthetic feedback, and visual-motor coordination. At the foundation of fine motor skills are gross motor skills. Fine motor skills, language, and cognitive skills are predictors of academic success (Cameron et al., 2012; Duncan et al., 2007; Pagani et al., 2010).

Effective fine motor teaching and learning in the early childhood classroom is multisensory and sensorimotor based with a focus on sensory integration (Jasmin et al., 2018). Fine motor instruction should engage the whole class through integrated approaches, including integration with art, music, physical education, and literacy, as well as be differentiated to deliver targeted, deliberate instruction to small groups and individuals (Bazyk et al., 2009; Jasmin et al., 2018).

EFFECT SIZE FOR SMALL GROUP LEARNING = 0.47

The connection between home and school for fine motor practice should work both ways with school-based materials available at home and daily life home-based materials available at school (Bazyk et al., 2009; Bhatia et al., 2015). When fine motor instruction is integrated with other content areas, all areas improve. And, once again, the most effective fine motor instruction is filled with language and adult interactions (Jasmin et al., 2018).

EFFECT SIZE FOR CLASSROOM DISCUSSION = 0.82

What does this mean for early childhood fine motor development? Like gross motor development, fine motor development is a critical part of children's learning and should be intentionally taught. Fine motor teaching and learning should be integrated across the curriculum, be connected to home life, and be rich in talk.

> When it comes to the expressive arts and motor development, this is where this research intersects with Visible Learning research: Integration is essential. We must partner with families to build meaningful home–school connections. Our language-based interactions with children matter, so we must plan our questions, interactions, and language. Let's see and hear how this intersectionality of research comes alive in two early childhood classrooms.

MS. DEMCHAK AND FAMILY PORTRAITS

Ms. Demchak and her vertical professional learning community have been working to deepen partnerships with families. Ms. Demchak's families expressed interest in helping their children become strong readers and writers. They also want their children to be proud of who they are, confident, and good friends. She knows her families feel comfortable and enjoy drawing together.

EFFECT SIZE FOR FAMILY INVOLVEMENT = 0.42

With this in mind, Ms. Demchak adjusted her usual self-portrait unit to be a family portrait unit. She wants to tap into each family's expertise and communicate the value of each unique family.

The family portrait unit began with family read-alouds, viewing and talking about family and self-portraits, examining their faces with mirrors, identifying similarities and differences among classmates and family members, tracing over family photographs in plastic page protectors with crayon pencils and oil pastels, and learning to build and then draw a person using shapes. The class sings a song about body parts to help them remember the names of the body parts, then how to build a person with concrete shapes, and now how to draw a person using circles and lines.

EFFECT SIZE FOR REHEARSAL AND MEMORIZATION = 0.73

As the class moves deeper into the unit, the children are working on creating multimedia self- and family portraits. They explored and experimented with a variety of art materials and tools: photographs, collage, paint with kitchen tools, eyedropper painting with watercolors, and sensory finger painting on cardstock using paint mixed with rice, sand, pasta, and beads. The children choose who to create and which materials to use while Ms. Demchak and her paraprofessional confer with the children to learn about their decisions, creation processes, and final portraits.

LEARNING INTENTIONS AND SUCCESS CRITERIA

Ms. Demchak identified the outcomes for the unit by noting where families' goals intersected with the Early Years Learning Framework (Australian Government Department of Education and Training, 2019). She chose three outcomes:

Outcome 1: Children Have a Strong Sense of Identity
- Children develop knowledgeable and confident self-identities.

Outcome 3: Children Have a Strong Sense of Well-Being
- Children become strong in their social and emotional well-being.

Outcome 5: Children Are Effective Communicators
- Children express ideas and make meaning using a range of media.

Using these outcomes, she created today's learning intentions and success criteria. They are accessible to all the children whether they are working at the surface, deep, or transfer phases of learning and will take several days for the children to master.

Content Learning Intention: We are learning to represent who we are and our families.

Language Learning Intention: We are learning that portraits are a way to communicate a message about what it feels like to be that person.

Social Learning Intention: We are learning to listen and respond with what we notice and wonder.

Success Criteria

- I can create recognizable people using shapes.
- I can tell about each person in my family: who they are, where they are, and what they're doing.
- I can explain my decisions about how to make each person in my family.

Today, Ms. Demchak will return to creating recognizable people using shapes by focusing on hair. She will continue to emphasize that each portrait shows who someone is, where they are, and what they are doing and that the decisions of what to portray are significant, based on each person's unique identity and role in the family. These aspects of portraits (who, where, what) will become their guideposts for writing stories.

The multimedia materials combined with their person-making song create a sensorimotor experience that includes concrete materials and pictorial representations.

As they work, the children talk to each other and the teachers; these language-based interactions focus on their growing narration and meta-cognitive skills.

ACTIVATING PRIOR KNOWLEDGE

"What do you notice about how Zuri is drawn in this book?" Ms. Demchak asks a familiarly framed question.

She has just finished reading *Hair Love* (Cherry, 2019), one of a series of read-alouds to practice noticing how people are artistically represented.

"Zuri has different hairdos when she's a princess and a superhero," Alinta notes.

"I notice her eyes are always big brown circles," Isaac adds.

"She has eyebrows that go like this and like this," Liam says, making finger and eyebrow movements up and down.

"Zuri doesn't always smile. She frowns when her dad accidentally pulls her hair," Zoe points out.

"Interesting. Zuri does her hair differently depending on what she's doing. And her eyebrows and mouth look different depending on how she's feeling," Ms. Demchak models explaining the reasons for the differences in the images.

"She loves her gray cat," Coen notices.

"How do you know?" Ms. Demchak asks.

"It's always with her," he replies.

"I notice Zuri always wears pink," Sophia shares.

"Why do you think she always wears pink?" Ms. Demchak asks.

"Maybe it's her favorite color," she infers.

"Wow! You can really learn what it feels like to be Zuri by looking at these drawings of her. Sometimes she's happy pretending or she's hurt when her hair is pulled. She loves her cat and pink clothes," Ms. Demchak summarizes. "What did you notice about how Zuri's dad is drawn in this book?"

"He can do a lot of hairstyles," Ruby says.

"He's strong," Jacob adds.

"How do you know?" Ms. Demchak probes.

"He has muscles," Jacob points out.

"I notice he has long hair," states Max.

"He loves Zuri," Noah decides.

"How do you know?" asks Ms. Demchak.

"He helps her and hugs her," says Noah.

Ms. Demchak continues,

> You're doing a great job noticing the decisions artists make when they create an image of a person. When you make portraits of you and your family, you make a lot of decisions too. You decide what materials to use, who to represent, where they are, and what they're doing. You have to really think about the person you're representing to help you make decisions about their clothes and hair, where they like to spend their time, and what they like to do. When we look at your portrait, we should be able to see a person and notice things about the person just like we noticed about Zuri and her dad. Be thinking about who you might create today and what materials you want to use.

Ms. Demchak directs the children to sit knee-to-knee and eye-to-eye to make their plans.

Ms. Demchak has expanded the Art Center to allow more children to work on family portraits at their own pace and as they are interested. She is still allowing children to choose other activities for either the whole work time or part of it. As work time begins, Ms. Demchak checks her plan for which children to confer with today; she is also tracking who has completed their self-portrait with a transcribed narration as well as family portraits with transcribed narrations (Figure 7.1).

SCAFFOLDING, EXTENDING, AND ASSESSING THINKING

Jedda is looking at the art supplies. Ms. Demchak joins her and asks, "What are you thinking about?"

"I want to make my mom today. I don't know how," Jedda responds.

FIGURE 7.1 ● Self-Portrait Observation/Conference Checklist

Questions:

- What do you notice?
- How do you know?
- Why do you think …?
- What does it feel like to be …?
- Where do they like to spend their time?
- What do they like to do?
- What do you need to decide next?
- Why …?
- What is the same about making ____ and making ____?
- How can you make shapes with ____ ?
- How will you show …?
- What is something that you want people to know about ____ ?

Language/Vocabulary:

- Shapes, Colors, Textures
- Body Parts
- Who, Where, What
- Portrait, Decide
- Art materials and tools: photographs, collage, paint with kitchen tools, sensory finger painting with rice, sand, pasta, and beads on cardstock, and eye dropper painting with water colors

Success Criteria:

- I can create recognizable people using shapes.
- I can tell about each person in my family: who they are, where they are, and what they're doing.
- I can explain my decisions about how to make each person in my family.

NAME	SELF-PORTRAIT NARRATION	FAMILY MEMBER PORTRAIT NARRATION	FAMILY MEMBER PORTRAIT NARRATION	FAMILY MEMBER PORTRAIT NARRATION

 Available for download at **resources.corwin.com/VLforEarlyChildhood**

"What material could you use to make your mom?" Ms. Demchak asks questions to scaffold her planning.

EFFECT SIZE FOR SCAFFOLDING = 0.58

Jedda looks at all the art materials. "Finger paints," Jedda points to the colorful sensory finger paints with rice, sand, beans, and pasta mixed into some of the colors to create textures.

"Why do you want to use finger paints to make your mom?" Ms. Demchak asks a decision-making question.

"Her clothes are lots of colors," Jedda pauses still thinking and looking at the paints, "And she cooks rice and beans and noodles."

"The finger paints will help you make your mom's colorful clothing and show her talents as a cook," Ms. Demchak replies. "What do you need to decide next?"

"The paper. I think white," Jedda contemplates aloud.

"Why would your mom be on white paper?" Ms. Demchak asks, reminding her again to make active decisions related to the learning intentions and success criteria.

EFFECT SIZE FOR TEACHER CLARITY = 0.84

Jedda exclaims, "My mom loves snow!"

"Will she be outside in the snow?" Ms. Demchak clarifies.

"Yes," Jedda replies.

"And what is your mom doing? What's something that you want people to know about your mom?" Ms. Demchak asks.

Jedda thinks and then says, "She's singing."

"You're making your mom, standing in the snow and singing. Wow! I feel like I'm getting to know who your mom is from your art! What's next?" Ms. Demchak's conversation serves to share the creation process with Jedda and vocalize her decisions.

EFFECT SIZE FOR COGNITIVE TASK ANALYSIS = 1.29

"I have to make her. I don't know how," Jedda repeats this same statement.

"I know you made your self-portrait. Let's see if looking at that can help us," Ms. Demchak and Jedda walk to the wall with a section for Jedda's portrait work. To better understand Jedda's dilemma, Ms. Demchak asks, "How did you make yourself?"

Jedda pauses, looking at her self-portrait, "I glued a tan circle for my head and a light brown oval for my body." With that, she continues describing each piece of her collage and how she used it to create an image of herself.

"Hmmm, I wonder what would be the same about making you and making your mom," Ms. Demchak says in a quiet wondering voice.

EFFECT SIZE FOR TRANSFER STRATEGIES = 0.86

"I need a head and a body and arms and legs and hair and a face," Jedda starts to list body parts as she points to them on the collage.

"For your self-portrait, you glued shapes. I wonder how you could make those shapes with finger paints instead," Ms. Demchak scaffolds Jedda's transfer.

"I could do this. And this. And then this," Jedda makes circles, ovals, and lines in the air with her fingers.

"You've decided to make your mom and you know how to make her body with finger paints!" Ms. Demchak says with excitement. Jedda begins painting shapes for her mom.

Meanwhile, Noah is making hair by tearing tissue paper with his hands and balling it up to glue. Illarah is gripping a paintbrush to paint a body using a vertical easel. Thomas is cutting shapes out of a stack of fabric, sandpaper, and foil to create his collage of clothing for his grandfather's portrait.

EFFECT SIZE FOR DELIBERATE PRACTICE = 0.79

Ms. Demchak remains for a couple more minutes asking questions about Jedda's mom's hair and the shape of her mouth to show she is singing. Ms. Demchak uses hand-over-hand to adjust Jedda's finger direction as she makes circles and ovals to reflect the letter formations for O and Q, which they are also currently learning.

Ms. Demchak records Jedda's narration on her chart. Later, she will type each child's narration and post it next to their portraits.

TEACHING FOR CLARITY AT THE CLOSE

"So many of you have finished your self-portraits. A few people are still working on theirs. Others are working on portraits of family members. Today, for our share, I want you to think about a big question: What does it feel like to be you?" Ms. Demchak pauses, allowing for think time. She then repeats her question, "What does it feel like to be you? When artists create their self-portraits, they try to show with their artwork how it feels to be them. You are artists. We've talked about a lot of emotion words. So, now think for a moment: what does it feel like to be you?"

EFFECT SIZE FOR SELF-REGULATION STRATEGIES = 0.54

The children turn knee-to-knee, eye-to-eye with their talking partners and share. Ms. Demchak hears words like *jumpy, excited,* and *happy.*

Ms. Demchak places an array of textiles in different colors, shapes, and textures in the middle of the circle. "Look for a piece of material that looks the way it feels to be you." Ms. Demchak gives the children time to stand up and feel the materials and choose one. The children again turn to their talking partners to explain why they chose the material. Some children are thinking about the analogy Ms. Demchak has presented, and some children have found material they are attracted to but are unsure how it connects to the question. Ms. Demchak listens to partner conversations.

"This is bumpy and I'm always bumping and jumping and hopping," says Bindi with excitement.

"This is like my blanket. It's soft and blue and shines," Oliver says adding, "I love my blanket."

"Do you ever feel like your blanket, Oliver? Do you ever feel soft and blue and shiny?" Ms. Demchak interjects, supporting Oliver's sense-making of the question.

"Yeah, when I climb in my cot and I'm tired and happy," Oliver replies.

"So at naptime, it feels soft and blue and shiny to be you because you're tired and happy," Ms. Demchak makes the connection explicit with her language.

After a couple of minutes, Ms. Demchak directs the whole group to look at one child's self-portrait to make the abstract question more concrete. "I notice in Bindi's self-portrait, she is hopping on wiggle spots. She used colorful puffy paint to make her body. And today, Bindi chose a bumpy, colorful piece of material to show what it feels like to be Bindi. What does this tell you about Bindi?"

"She loves to jump and climb and bounce," says Mia.

"Bindi makes hopping paths for us," adds Noah.

EFFECT SIZE FOR CLASSROOM DISCUSSION = 0.82

"She likes to roll down the hill. Bump! Bump! Bump!" exclaims Liam.

"Bindi, what do you think of their descriptions of you?" Ms. Demchak asks.

EFFECT SIZE FOR PEER- AND SELF- FEEDBACK = 0.42

"Yup, that's me!" Bindi confirms.

"Bindi, you made decisions about which materials to use, where you are, and what you're doing to show who you are and what it feels like to be you. I love hearing and seeing what it feels like to be you! As you work on your portraits, keep thinking about all the ways you can show what it feels like to be the person you are creating." Ms. Demchak brings the lesson to a close.

The children have returned to their social-emotional work with identifying emotions and celebrating their individual identities; they are practicing fine motor skills through painting, cutting with scissors, tearing paper, gluing, and drawing; they are planning who, where, and what for portraits and later for storytelling; and they are developing language through their conversations about decision making and narration of their processes and products.

MS. BULLOCK AND STORYTELLING

Storytelling is a central feature of Ms. Bullock's 3-year-old class. True stories, pretend stories, stories from books, family stories, stories from shared experiences—her classroom is rich with oral stories. Ms. Bullock knows that the more her children have opportunities to hear, retell, reenact, and create stories, the more their language will grow. In her classroom and in the community, storytelling is a multisensory experience, full of music and dance.

Ms. Bullock wants her children to explicitly know there are many ways to tell a story, which builds on their community's rich traditions and integrates learning meaningfully. The children have reenacted many familiar stories through combinations of movement and music. They have painted to music and storytelling songs from around the world. They have created movement routines with combinations of jumping and balancing. They have shared their own stories with a rhythmic pattern beat. They have reenacted stories through yoga storytelling poses. Today, Ms. Bullock wants to transfer their oral storytelling to written representations of their stories.

> EFFECT SIZE FOR WRITING PROGRAMS = 0.57

LEARNING INTENTIONS AND SUCCESS CRITERIA

Ms. Bullock begins planning by looking at the Illinois Early Learning and Development Standards (Illinois State Board of Education, 2013). She looks across content areas for meaningful connections and integration.

> EFFECT SIZE FOR INTEGRATED CURRICULA = 0.40

For her storytelling unit, she has identified four guiding standards:

The Arts 26.A&B: Understand processes, traditional tools, and modern technologies used in the arts. Understand ways to express meaning through the arts.

Language Arts 2.C.ECa: Interact with a variety of types of texts (e.g., storybooks, poems, rhymes, songs).

> **Language Arts 5.B.ECc:** With teacher assistance, use a combination of drawing, dictating, or writing to narrate a single event and provide a reaction to what happened.
>
> **Mathematics 8.A.ECb:** Recognize, duplicate, extend, and create simple patterns in various formats.

Next, Ms. Bullock uses these standards to create the following learning intentions and success criteria for her whole unit:

> **Unit Content Learning Intention:** We are learning there are many ways to tell a story.
>
> **Unit Language Learning Intention:** We are learning about sequencing language for storytelling.
>
> **Unit Social Learning Intention:** We are learning to ask questions and give compliments about a friend's story.
>
> ## Unit Success Criteria
>
> - We can use movement, musical instruments, singing, painting, or drawing to tell a story.
> - We can tell a story with a beginning, middle, and end.
> - We can record our story to retell it later.

Keeping the big picture and end in mind, she plans individual lessons using a mixture of deliberate and inquiry-based instruction. Each lesson also has learning intentions and success criteria that unpack the unit's goals into accessible pieces.

> EFFECT SIZE FOR CLASSROOM COHESION = 0.53

This scaffolds children's learning and allows them to gradually master the unit learning intentions and success criteria. Today's lesson is focused on the fourth and final unit success criteria:

> **Today's Content Learning Intention:** We are learning to record our story to retell it later.
>
> **Today's Language Learning Intention:** We are learning to connect pictures, actions, and words to record a story.
>
> **Today's Social Learning Intention:** We are learning about ways to combine ideas with a friend to record one story together.
>
> ## Today's Lesson Success Criteria
>
> - We can use pictures to represent movements or action in a story.
> - We can repeat pictures to show a repeating pattern from a story.
> - We can read our recorded story.
> - We can act out our recorded story.

The majority of her learners are ready to make this transfer; however, Ms. Bullock has planned differentiated supports to make sure every learner moves forward. Ms. Bullock's mini-lesson will activate their prior knowledge and her language-based interactions will scaffold, extend, and assess their thinking.

ACTIVATING PRIOR KNOWLEDGE

"And Tortoise wins!"

"Hare lost!"

The children have just retold a class favorite, *The Tortoise and the Hare* (Pinkney, 2013), with two children pretending to be the main characters racing around the circle.

"Just like when we play musical instruments for our oral count, we're going to play musical instruments to tell the story of Tortoise and Hare's race," Ms. Bullock says.

EFFECT SIZE FOR STRATEGIES TO INTEGRATE WITH PRIOR KNOWLEDGE = 0.93

Ms. Bullock explains their work for today: "We're going to make a repeating rhythm pattern for Tortoise and a repeating rhythm pattern for Hare. Then we can adjust them to make them fast or slow as we tell what Tortoise and Hare are doing. And, we're going to record our pattern so that we can retell and replay the story later." This is the first time the class will record a physical movement with an image together; however, individuals have begun experimenting with recording movement, like wind blowing, waves, and jumping, so Ms. Bullock knows they are ready for a deliberate lesson that will create a model for future reference.

EFFECT SIZE FOR DELIBERATE PRACTICE = 0.79

Everyone chooses an instrument from the center of the circle—some are prepared instruments (rain stick, maracas, triangle) and others are found (dried seed pods, stick and shell rattles) or created by the children (balloon-covered can drums, paper plate and bell tambourine, bottle top castanets, jar lid and rubber band banjo). Ms. Bullock puts out pictures of different rhythm movements—tap, shake, clap, stomp. She asks the class, "Think about what Tortoise sounds like as he moves to the finish line. What might he sound like?"

"He's quiet and slow," says Jaedyn.

"I think he sounds like . . . ," Kadisha says and carefully lifts her hands and legs as she crawls slowly across the floor.

Repeating Kadisha but making a small change to his movements so his hands and legs drag, Alex says, "I think he sounds like . . ."

"So we need a quiet, slow, pat or scratch sound to represent Tortoise. Let's see which rhythm movements sound like Tortoise when I play them quiet and slow," Ms. Bullock lightly and slowly taps her rain stick with her finger, saying, "This is a tap," and she shows the image representing tap. Next, she slowly shakes her rain stick, saying, "This is a shake," and she shows the image representing shake. "I can't clap with my instrument, so I'll do this one with my hands. I can clap my hands together or I can clap my hand on my rain stick. This is a clap," Ms. Bullock quietly claps her hands and then shows the image representing clap. "I can stomp with my instrument by bumping it on the ground. Or I can stomp with my feet. This is a stomp," Ms. Bullock quietly bumps the bottom of the rain stick on the ground and shows the corresponding image.

"Which rhythm movements sound like Tortoise?" Ms. Bullock repeats each one.

Several children share their ideas and they decide that the tap sounds like Kadisha's movement and the shake sounds like Alex's movement. Next, a few children share examples of how they could combine taps and shakes. The class particularly likes Dayquan's idea—tap tap shake shake—with long pauses between each.

Ms. Bullock glues the first tap on a big piece of paper and then asks, "How can I show you that we need a long pause before we play tap again? Where could I glue the next tap to remind us to wait?" Carmen points to a place that leaves a wide gap between the first tap and the second. "I see. We can leave a lot of space between the taps so we know to pause and wait because Tortoise moves so slowly," Ms. Bullock says.

Ms. Bullock glues images of tap tap shake shake with large gaps between each and then asks, "What comes next?"

Briera picks up the next images for tap tap shake shake and gives them to Ms. Bullock, saying, "Tap tap shake shake again."

Ms. Bullock makes this explicit as she glues down more images, "We repeat tap tap shake shake over and over because Tortoise always moves this way through the whole story."

Next, she uses their co-created recording to exemplify the success criteria:

> We can use pictures to represent movements or action in a story. We used tap tap shake shake to represent Tortoise's movement. We can repeat pictures to show a repeating pattern from a story. We repeated tap tap

shake shake many times because Tortoise's movement stays the same. Can we read our recorded story? Let's try.

Ms. Bullock points to the pictures as the class says slowly, quietly, and repeatedly, "Tap tap shake shake."

"Now we need to act out our recording. And since our recording is for our musical instruments, acting it out means playing our instruments together. Let's do it!" Ms. Bullock and the children play their instruments slowly, quietly, and repeatedly.

Ms. Bullock celebrates with the class and reminds them of the work left to do: "Wow! We did it! Now there's another character in our story that we need to represent. Who is the other character?"

Many children shout out, "Hare!"

"Tomorrow, we'll work as a team to represent Hare's movements. If you want to try ideas for this during our work time, you can!" Ms. Bullock reviews the unit's success criteria:

> During work time, you might tell a story with movement, musical instruments, singing, painting, or drawing. Remember to make sure your story has a beginning, middle, and end. Then see if you can record your story using pictures and repeating patterns so you can share it and retell it during sharing.

The children make and share their work plans and then move to centers. Ms. Bullock has four children she plans to interact with so she can check in on their mastery of both the unit and lesson success criteria so far.

SCAFFOLDING, EXTENDING, AND ASSESSING THINKING

Kayvion and Machele are balancing on one foot. Machele is singing, "Un elefante se balanceaba sobre la tela de una araña," a favorite counting song about more and more elephants balancing on a spiderweb until it breaks. It is a song that she and her dad taught to the class when he came to visit. As Machele sings, they switch legs and continue balancing. Then Machele sings, "Dos elefantes!" and they both jump two times before returning to their alternating one-leg balances. These are the movements the class has practiced each time they sing the song.

Ms. Bullock joins them and says, "I notice you're moving and singing about those silly elephants! I wonder if you could record the dance that tells the story so we can all teach it to our families, just like Machele and her dad taught us." Kayvion and Machele are eager to teach others and agree to the challenge.

"What do we need to record the story?" Ms. Bullock prompts.

"Pictures," Machele replies.

"What pictures would match your movements?" Ms. Bullock asks.

Kayvion does the three actions—balancing on one foot, switching to the other foot, and then jumping.

"Balance, balance, jump," Ms. Bullock narrates. "Let's see if we can find pictures to match." She pulls out a tray of images and they start to look through the pictures. Kayvion finds a jumping picture and Machele finds a balancing picture. They gather several of each.

"Now what?" Ms. Bullock asks.

"Glue them," Kayvion directs.

Together, they sing and move and then pause to find the matching picture. Each time, they glue it down and then return to singing and moving.

When they finish the first verse, they have glued down: jump, balance, balance, balance, balance.

"Let's read our story as we act it out this time!" They say the image words and do the corresponding actions, and then Ms. Bullock asks, "What happens next?"

"Dos elefantes!" Machele exclaims as she and Kayvion jump twice.

"I see. You say 'dos elefantes' and you go jump jump! How many jumps is that?" Ms. Bullock connects the song, actions, and representations.

"One, two," says Kayvion, and Machele holds up two fingers.

"Two jumps for two elephants! Now we need to get the pictures for those actions. What should we glue for this part of the story?" Ms. Bullock is breaking down the lesson success criteria into scaffolded questions as she supports Kayvion and Machele's movement from deep to transfer learning.

Machele sings while looking for two jump images. Kayvion jumps twice and then starts balancing on his leg. "Then balance, balance, balance, balance," he says as he acts it out.

EFFECT SIZE FOR QUESTIONING = 0.48

EFFECT SIZE FOR COLLABORATIVE LEARNING = 0.39

EFFECT SIZE FOR COGNITIVE TASK ANALYSIS = 1.29

He stops and looks for four balance images. They glue these down and then Kayvion rereads the story while Machele acts it out. They repeat this work for three elephants and four elephants.

"I notice some parts of your story are repeating and some are growing. Can you see the part that repeats?" Ms. Bullock is connecting their representations and story to the concept of patterns, the second lesson success criterion.

EFFECT SIZE FOR SELF-JUDGMENT AND REFLECTION = 0.75

"We go . . . ," Kayvion says and acts out balancing on his legs over and over. Machele points to the four balance pictures in a row.

"Every time, you balance on your legs four times. That's the repeating part of your story. Balance, balance, balance, balance. Can you see the part that grows—there are more and more and more?" Ms. Bullock asks rephrasing the word "grows" within her question.

"We jump one. We jump two. We jump three. We jump four," Machele says as she holds up fingers. Kayvion jumps and says the number words, "One, two, three, four."

"Yes! That is the growing part of your story. Where is that in your pictures?" Ms. Bullock again makes the connection to reading their representation. Machele and Kayvion both point to the jumping pictures. Ms. Bullock says, "You used pictures to represent movements in your story, you repeated the balance pattern, you read your story, and you acted it out! I see the beginning of your story has just one elephant and the middle of your story has four elephants."

EFFECT SIZE FOR FEEDBACK = 0.62

"What happens at the end of the story?" Ms. Bullock asks, as she shows the children how they met the success criteria for today's lesson in their work and extends their thinking back to the unit's success criteria to help them plan next steps.

"It goes 1, 2, 3, 4, 5, 6, 7, 8, 9, 10 elephants!" counts Kayvion.

"Y se rompio!" adds Machele.

"Yes! Ten elephants balance on the spiderweb and then it breaks! That is the end of the story, so you still have more to record." As she documents their work, Ms. Bullock notices Zakeisha, Ethan, and Carmen singing "Going on a Bear Hunt" as they paint. Ms. Bullock had planned to confer with two of those children today, so she joins their work to see how they are representing the story with paint.

TEACHING FOR CLARITY AT THE CLOSE

After work time, Ms. Bullock selects three groups of children to share their recordings. Kayvion and Machele share *Un Elephante* with picture images arranged in a repeating and growing pattern. Alaysia and Briera share a clapping and stomping repeating pattern based on their older sisters' step routines. Alex and Dayquan share *The Lion and the Mouse* (Pinkney, 2009) represented by a rhythmic repeating pattern they recorded for their drums. Each group shows their recording, reads it, and then teaches the class how to act it out.

To bring closure, Ms. Bullock plays a version of *Simon Says* to practice executive function skills, repeating patterns, and reading representations.

EFFECT SIZE FOR DELIBERATE PRACTICE = 0.79

She shows the children a repeating rhythm pattern represented with pictures. When she says, "Simon says" and then says and acts out the pattern, the class should do the same. But if she does not say "Simon says" before saying and acting out the pattern, the children should stay still. The class is beginning their transfer of movements and stories to pictorial representations.

Ms. Davis and Distance Learning in Art, Music, and Motor Skills

Ms. Davis believes the key to each effective lesson is her partnership with families; this is especially true in distance learning.

Ms. Davis has sent home a variety of art supplies, including playdough and supplies to make slime. She talked with families in advance to confirm they were comfortable with the supplies; in fact, one family had requested slime, which quickly became a favorite.

EFFECT SIZE FOR FAMILY INVOLVEMENT = 0.42

In small groups, the children engaged in several lessons balancing inquiry and deliberate instruction. They rolled playdough to create the letters in their names and playdough balls onto ten-frames to show number values. They worked with both slime and playdough while listening to music from around the world, moving their hands and fingers to the music. They asked questions like, "What would happen if . . . ?" They also discovered that slime does not keep its shape but playdough does, objects can be hidden in both slime

(Continued)

(Continued)

and playdough, and slime stretches while playdough stretches and then breaks.

Today, Ms. Davis wants to focus on the relationship between visual arts and spatial reasoning while practicing fine motor skills.

She will address four of Virginia's Early Learning and Development Standards (Virginia Department of Education, 2021):

> **Fine Arts:** Begins to describe art and the story it tells.
>
> **Fine Motor:** Uses tools that require strength, control, and skills of small muscles.
>
> **Mathematics:** Uses smaller shapes to compose larger and different shapes. Describes attributes of two and three dimensional shapes.
>
> **Emotional Competence:** Seeks and accepts help when needed.

Ms. Davis creates learning intentions and success criteria that she will communicate during her mini-lesson using visuals, modeling, and a think-aloud. She will continue to connect back to the learning intentions and success criteria through her language facilitation as the children work and share.

> **Content Learning Intention:** We are learning ways smaller shapes make larger shapes.
>
> **Language Learning Intention:** We are learning to express our thinking process with words.
>
> **Social Learning Intention:** We are learning to ask friends for help when we are stuck.
>
> ## Success Criteria
>
> - I can see smaller shapes within a larger shape.
> - I can make similar shapes with playdough or slime.
> - I can describe how I created my replica and what worked and didn't work.

Now, Ms. Davis is taking the familiar "Can You Build It?" routine and transferring it to the art medium of sculpture or statue. During the routine, Ms. Davis shares the image of a famous sculpture or statue, tells a brief story about it, describes the real material each is made of, asks questions, and even plays *I Spy*. Then, she challenges the class to make a replica of the sculpture or statue using either playdough or slime. As the children construct, Ms. Davis engages in conversations about their process, what is working and what is not, and what parts of the sculpture or statue they notice.

EFFECT SIZE FOR CLASSROOM DISCUSSION = 0.82

Finally, the children hold up their finished products for everyone to see. They have made Spider, Spoon and Cherry, the Statue of Liberty, and the Great Sphinx.

Their sculpture/statue work over time integrates fine motor skills, visual arts, music, science, and spatial reasoning. Today, as they view the art, create their replicas, and share their processes and products, the children are constantly talking. Ms. Davis also sends home the art supplies as well as "what if" and "how to" art videos using the supplies, thus creating extended opportunities for exploration and deliberate practice that are multisensory.

EFFECT SIZE FOR DELIBERATE PRACTICE = 0.79

ARTS AND MOTOR DEVELOPMENT IN PLAYFUL LEARNING

Like each of the previous content areas, the arts and motor skills can be the content of playful learning. As you have seen, they are also powerful integration tools to experience meaning-making across domains. To plan for playful learning within the arts and motor skills, consider the materials, contexts, and language that you will leverage:

- For our young learners, the creative arts are a critical means by which learners express their thoughts, ideas, and feelings. For many learning tasks, we can purposefully integrate an arts component into the experience. Encourage learners to describe and talk about their work as a means for integrating language development into learning.

- Integrate the creative arts into all aspects of social-emotional learning by using music, creative movement, dance, drama-based pedagogy, and the visual arts into class meetings.

- The creative arts offer a pathway for promoting inclusion and culturally responsive pedagogy. The arts allow learners to express, communicate, and engage in critical dialogue about their culture, language, family, community, and history.

- Balance learning experiences in the creative arts by utilizing both product art and process art. Product art involves samples, patterns, or models that require learners to follow specific directions. The product is specific and completed by following the directions (e.g., cutouts of the solar system, creating penguins for a class bulletin board on the environment, or using fruit to stamp out numbers). In process art, learners have a multitude of options and the freedom to create an original piece of artwork. In process art, there are no samples, patterns, or models. Each piece of art is unique (e.g., finger painting, creating a story board to tell an individual story, salt painting, or the mixing of colors in science).

- Find ways to get learners physically active during the day. This should come from a variety of activities. However, be sure to explicitly teach specific movements and experiences to avoid injury.

- Unfortunately, physical activity is often used as a form of punishment. This is NEVER okay. Use physical activity as a way to engage in playful learning and an opportunity for social interaction.

- Ensure that the physical activity is developmentally appropriate and focuses on cognitive, affective, and psychomotor learning outcomes (e.g., rather than jumping into a game, explicitly teach operating in a safe space, basic movements, and then overhand throwing).

- Like every other aspect of teaching and learning, plan ahead to ensure the environment and materials are conducive to physical activity and education (e.g., make sure the space is safe and that there are a variety of materials for learners of different levels of readiness).

- Finally, for both the creative arts and physical activity, make time! Plan for these aspects of the early childhood classroom. Do not let this time be considered a fringe benefit, but an essential part of teaching and learning.

CHAPTER 8

Knowing Your Impact
Evaluating Learning Progress

We began with a vision for early childhood education as a place where we maximize the impact of our teaching and learning. Along our journey together, we have seen early childhood educators striving to implement the Visible Learning research in their classrooms. Let us return to the three guiding principles that lay the foundation for our application of the Visible Learning research in early childhood education. First, our ultimate goal is to grow learners who have the efficacy to be active decision makers about their learning journeys. Second, we can meet this goal by ensuring that both educators and learners clearly and intentionally make sense of what they are learning, why they are learning it, and how they will know they are successful. Third, we can support our class as a whole and each individual learner in reaching this goal by using the right instructional strategy at the right time. These three principles are the heart of the visible learner. How did these principles guide the instructional decisions of Ms. Demchak, Ms. Bullock, Mr. Heaton, and Ms. Davis? In this chapter, we will unpack their intentional decisions as they communicate learning intentions and success criteria, create rigorous and engaging tasks, and use formative evaluations to drive instruction and feedback. We will refer back to the vignettes from Chapters 2–7 to highlight examples of these decision points.

VISIBLE LEARNERS

Can children at ages 3, 4, 5, and 6 years be active decision makers as learners? For many, this goal seems out of reach and developmentally inappropriate. But for those of us who spend each day with children, we know they already are active decision makers. They want to make the choices and do the tasks themselves. They are often excited and generous teachers of themselves and others, who prefer to do most of the work in classrooms rather than watch the teacher do it. As early childhood educators, we are responsible for funneling this drive for independence to efficacy as learners.

Our goal is to grow visible learners who see themselves as learners and can make their learning visible to others. Recall from Chapter 1 the six characteristics of visible learners (Frey et al., 2018):

- Know their current level of understanding; they can communicate what they do and do not yet know,

- Know where they are going next in their learning and are ready to take on the challenge,

- Select tools to move their learning forward,

- Seek feedback about their learning and recognize errors as opportunities to learn,

- Monitor their learning and make adjustments when necessary, and

- Recognize when they have learned something and serve as a teacher to others.

This is our vision for our young learners. Each day, we make intentional decisions to meet this goal: we effectively communicate our learning intentions and success criteria, we create engaging and rigorous tasks, we use formative evaluations to drive instruction and feedback, and we use feedback to close the gap between where learners are and where they are going.

 # EFFECTIVELY COMMUNICATING CLARITY FOR VISIBLE LEARNING

In order for learners to have the knowledge, understanding, and confidence of visible learners, early childhood educators must communicate clarity.

Communicating the what, why, and how of learning is teacher clarity (0.75). But how do we effectively communicate clarity to our young learners when they cannot yet read and when they are simultaneously working on a complex network of learning outcomes? In Chapter 1, we first introduced the four essentials of communicating clarity in the early childhood classroom (Thunder et al., 2021):

1. Use visuals alongside academic vocabulary in the context of learning. Have learners articulate what they are learning and connect multiple representations with academic vocabulary.

2. Demonstrate the higher-order thinking skills and processes by modeling (i.e., thinking aloud) the connections between what they are learning and why.

3. Explicitly teach meta-cognitive skills through listening and questioning so that learners are guided to think about their own learning.

4. Finally, provide visual rubrics, checklists, exemplars, and models to support learners as they begin to monitor their learning progress and know what success looks like.

> EFFECT SIZE FOR IMAGERY = 0.51

> EFFECT SIZE FOR SELF-VERBALIZATION AND SELF-QUESTIONING = 0.59

> EFFECT SIZE FOR META-COGNITIVE STRATEGIES = 0.60

> EFFECT SIZE FOR STRATEGY MONITORING = 0.58

In each of the subsequent chapters, we saw early childhood educators partner with young learners to intentionally communicate and make sense of learning intentions and success criteria. Let's return to unpack and understand those educators' decision points as they communicated clarity.

MR. HEATON COMMUNICATES CLARITY

In Chapter 3, we joined Mr. Heaton's mixed-age class as the majority of the class entered the transfer phase of learning about composing and decomposing shapes. Based on cross-curricular standards, Mr. Heaton created the following student-facing goals for his lesson, with one additional success criterion (denoted with an asterisk) only for his afternoon 4-year-old learners:

Content Learning Intention: We are learning to use what we know about shapes to create and build with shapes.

Language Learning Intention: We are learning to use number words to talk about shapes.

Social Learning Intention: We are learning the importance of solving problems by learning from each other.

Success Criteria

- I can create and build with shapes.
- I can describe my creations using shape and number words.
- *I can explain how I composed and decomposed shapes in my creations.

He planned to communicate, engage the children in making sense of, and facilitate self-evaluation based on the learning intentions and success criteria during three parts of his lesson— the mini-lesson, the work time, and the sharing and closing.

Mr. Heaton intentionally began his mini-lesson by activating the specific geometric prior knowledge the children would be transferring through a shape song. He used a combination of his academic vocabulary and an anchor chart of images about shapes to remind them of previous, related learning.

To communicate the learning intentions and success criteria, Mr. Heaton used a think-aloud paired with modeling to demonstrate using what he knew about shapes to build a replica of the Parthenon.

His mini-lesson provided the children with a representation of what success looks and sounds like as well as an example of one decision pathway to success.

Throughout his think-aloud and modeling, Mr. Heaton used the mathematically precise language of composing and decomposing shapes to describe what he visualized, built, and why. He used the language of the success criteria to summarize his process: "I built the Parthenon with shapes (Success Criterion 1) and I can describe my structure (Success Criterion 2). The roof is made of two triangular prisms, the sides are rectangular prisms and cylinders."

During work time, Mr. Heaton conferred with the children in order to explicitly connect their work and thinking to the learning intentions and success criteria. On this day, Mr. Heaton began by conferring with two children who needed help getting started—Amare and Bahar. Mr. Heaton engaged two peers, Evelyn and Freddie, working on similar tasks to help them "get unstuck."

Evelyn is a 4-year-old who stays for the afternoon session and Freddie is a 3-year-old. By engaging them as the teachers, Mr. Heaton differentiates and both practice Success Criterion 3.

Mr. Heaton asked Evelyn and Freddie questions that he planned in advance based on the learning intentions and success criteria.

The questions range from recall questions to more abstract and meta-cognitive questions:

> What shape is ____? What shape will you start with? How many ___ will you need? What shapes do you need? What parts are you creating? How are you using shapes?

Mr. Heaton uses feedback phrases that he also planned in advance in order to model using the learning intentions and success criteria to progress monitor:

> You are creating ____ using shapes (Success Criterion 1). You are describing ____ with shape and numbers words (Success Criterion 2). You are visualizing; you know what you want __ to look like and you're thinking about each part (Success Criterion 3).

EFFECT SIZE FOR FEEDBACK = 0.62

Throughout these conferences, Amare and Bahar were able to see and hear Evelyn and Freddie at work in the context of learning. Evelyn and Freddie's explanations connected the academic vocabulary of the learning intentions and success criteria with multiple visual representations. Evelyn and Freddie's work became examples of new ways to demonstrate the success criteria, which allowed Amare and Bahar to access the learning intentions and success criteria.

During the final part of the lesson, the sharing and closing, Mr. Heaton asked one learner to share her progress on a different task than the one he modeled during the mini-lesson. This allows the children to see yet another model of the learning intentions and success criteria and to practice using them to progress monitor and self-evaluate.

EFFECT SIZE FOR SELF-JUDGMENT AND REFLECTION = 0.75

For a multiday lesson, Mr. Heaton knows this additional model is particularly important. He conferred with Croydon about her number puzzle during worktime so he was ready to facilitate her share with meta-cognitive questions. He intentionally selected her to share because her work would visually represent the learning intentions and success criteria in a different yet accurate way. Finally, Mr. Heaton closes his lesson with a verbal summary of the learning intentions and success criteria. Mr. Heaton may communicate the learning intentions and success criteria using different strategies depending on the learning intentions, success criteria, and tasks, but he is always certain to communicate clarity.

MORE EXAMPLES OF COMMUNICATING CLARITY

Each of the lessons from Ms. Demchak, Ms. Bullock, Mr. Heaton, and Ms. Davis's classrooms present additional ways to communicate clarity:

*   In Chapters 2 and 6, Ms. Bullock and Mr. Heaton take photos of children demonstrating the success criteria in the context of learning.

- In Chapters 6 and 7, Ms. Demchak uses think-alouds and class discussion based on read-alouds to facilitate children's meaning-making of the learning intentions and success criteria.

- In Chapters 4 and 7, Ms. Bullock co-creates exemplars with her class to model both possible processes and products for demonstrating the success criteria. In Chapter 3, Ms. Davis also co-creates exemplars, but in the distance learning classroom, this involves parallel modeling where she and the learners build simultaneously.

- In Chapters 2 and 4, Mr. Heaton pairs thinking aloud with drawing to model decisions and his reasoning related to the learning intentions and success criteria.

- In Chapters 2 and 3, Ms. Bullock and Ms. Demchak have children model the learning intentions and success criteria by acting them out and narrating with academic language. In Chapter 6, Ms. Davis uses a puppet to act out and model while in distance learning.

- In Chapters 2 and 3, Ms. Demchak, Ms. Bullock, and Mr. Heaton use anchor charts to visually represent the learning intentions and success criteria and to provide visual progress monitoring tools.

- In Chapter 5, Ms. Demchak creates a visual checklist of the success criteria for the children to use for self-monitoring, while Ms. Bullock and Mr. Heaton think aloud and model with concrete materials to demonstrate the meaning of the learning intentions and success criteria.

There are countless ways to communicate clarity but, most importantly, each of these reflects the four essentials of communicating clarity in the early childhood classroom.

ENGAGING AND RIGOROUS TASKS FOR VISIBLE LEARNING

Visible learners select tools to guide their learning. In order for learners to make meaningful and appropriate selections, they must lean on their understanding of where they are going and their confidence to take on the challenge. Learners need quality choices for tasks, tools, materials, language, and interactions, which are created and implemented by early childhood educators. The educators' selection and implementation of tasks determines the quality of and the opportunities for response that learners can create.

In other words, to grow visible learners, the tasks matter. Tasks for Visible Learning make learner thinking visible and allow both educators and learners to observe the learning process. They are also aligned to the learning intentions and success criteria. There are eight qualities of engaging and rigorous tasks: personal response, clear and modeled expectations, sense of audience, social interaction, emotional safety, choice, novelty, and authenticity (Antonetti & Garver, 2015).

To promote equity, quality tasks must be situated within children's prior knowledge, promote positive identity, grow agency, position all learners as competent, and share authority for learning with learners (Berry & Thunder, 2012).

How can early childhood educators use these qualities to select and implement tasks aligned to learning intentions and success criteria? Let's examine tasks from the classrooms of Ms. Demchak, Ms. Bullock, Mr. Heaton, and Ms. Davis as well as their decision-making processes for selecting and implementing the tasks.

MS. DEMCHAK SELECTS ENGAGING AND RIGOROUS TASKS

In Chapter 2, Ms. Demchak's prekindergarten class was noticing, naming, and sorting objects by attributes. She had noticed that her learners intuitively and nonverbally sorted but did not attach language to their sorts. Ms. Demchak could have chosen any objects with a variety of attributes for sorting; her choice of objects is always based on her learners' interests.

In fact, her learning intentions and success criteria are purposefully broad in the use of the terms "objects" and "attributes" to allow for these to change and yet still align with the same goals:

EFFECT SIZE FOR TASK VALUE = 0.46

EFFECT SIZE FOR COLLABORATIVE LEARNING = 0.39

EFFECT SIZE FOR CONCENTRATION/ PERSISTENCE/ ENGAGEMENT = 0.54

EFFECT SIZE FOR TEACHER CLARITY = 0.84

EFFECT SIZE FOR STRATEGIES TO INTEGRATE WITH PRIOR KNOWLEDGE = 0.93

EFFECT SIZE FOR SELF- CONCEPT = 0.47

EFFECT SIZE FOR SELF- EFFICACY = 0.66

EFFECT SIZE FOR CONCENTRATION/ PERSISTENCE/ ENGAGEMENT = 0.54

Content Learning Intention: We are learning to notice and sort objects by attributes.

Language Learning Intention: We are learning to name objects by attributes.

Social Learning Intention: We are learning to actively listen.

Success Criteria

- We can sort the same objects by different attributes.
- We can describe sorts using words.
- We can listen to and respond to each other's sorting strategies.

In previous years, her class focused their sorts on weather, animals, food, and superheroes and magical creatures. This year, she noticed every child—boys, girls, children with and without disabilities, English language learners, children who are shy and outgoing—loved to use vehicles, which can be sorted and resorted by different attributes. Her English language learners spoke in their home languages about vehicles, and her quiet children used vehicles with confidence and joy. By focusing her learning intentions and success criteria on the big concepts and skills of sorting rather than particular objects, Ms. Demchak was able to emphasize the language of sorting with vehicles and other objects of children's interest. By selecting objects that were familiar and positive, Ms. Demchak was able to *situate tasks within children's prior knowledge* and *position all learners as competent.*

EFFECT SIZE FOR STRATEGIES TO INTEGRATE WITH PRIOR KNOWLEDGE = 0.93

EFFECT SIZE FOR TEACHER EXPECTATIONS = 0.42

Ms. Demchak also used her noticing of her children's interests to place vehicles and vehicle-related materials in every center. In Art Area, Ms. Demchak noticed stickers, ink stamps, play-dough, and "how-to" drawing directions were popular choices of her learners; she put vehicle versions of each material in Art Area in order to maintain a balance between familiarity and *novelty* as well as allow for *choice* and maximize opportunities for *social interaction* with vehicles (Antonetti & Garver, 2015). In Costumes Area, the children regularly dressed up and created real-life scenarios to act out together, so she placed costumes for vehicle drivers—construction worker, firefighter, pilot, astronaut, and so on—and parts of vehicles for pretending, such as a steering wheel and walkie talkies.

EFFECT SIZE FOR COLLABORATIVE LEARNING = 0.39

Again, the vehicle materials allowed for *choice, novelty,* and *authenticity* as children reenacted familiar vehicle-related situations, again *situating tasks within their prior knowledge.* Spread around the other centers were tubs of miniature vehicles and vehicles to be put together and taken apart with real-life tools, thus promoting *choice, authenticity,* and *social interaction* during playful learning. Each of the materials offered opportunities to demonstrate the success criteria.

After creating spaces with tools and materials for sorting vehicles in playful learning, Ms. Demchak planned a mini-lesson task, interactions and language for supporting children's choice of tasks in playful learning, and a sharing task to close that were aligned with the learning intentions and success criteria. Because the children were all familiar with vehicles, Ms. Demchak chose a collaborative model and discussion for the mini-lesson, where the class collaborated to sort vehicles by where the vehicle travels. This allowed for each individual to contribute a *personal response* with a *sense of audience,* communicated *clear and modeled expectations* (the learning intentions and success criteria), grew their *agency as sorters and problem solvers, positioned all learners as competent,* and *shared authority for learning with learners.* Through rich class discussion with physical models and visual representations, the class built on each other's ideas and language.

EFFECT SIZE FOR CLASSROOM DISCUSSION = 0.82

During planning with her vertical professional learning community, Ms. Demchak had specifically selected vehicles for the mini-lesson that she anticipated would spark debate. Therefore, specific vocabulary would be needed, such as submarines, which sink and float in water, and race cars, tractors, dirt bikes, and trains, which all travel on land but on roads, tracks, or grass.

During centers, Ms. Demchak wanted to encourage *social interactions* around sorting vehicles but allow for *choice* with familiar objects, which would support *emotional safety.* Rather than tell the children what to sort or how to use the vehicles in each center, Ms. Demchak conferred with them as they worked, asking questions, facilitating language, and engaging as a conversational partner while constantly connecting back to the learning intentions and success criteria.

EFFECT SIZE FOR QUESTIONING = 0.48

In Chapter 2, we followed Ms. Demchak as she conferred with Noah, a quiet learner at school but a verbose vehicle expert at home. Ms. Demchak used her knowledge of Noah to *position him as competent* and to create an *emotionally safe* space for him to take vocal risks as a learner and friend.

EFFECT SIZE FOR TEACHER–STUDENT RELATIONSHIPS = 0.47

Throughout the lesson and the unit, Ms. Demchak noticed Noah talking more often in whole group and interacting with peers more during playful learning. Noah grew in his comfort and confidence at school, talking more and beginning to see himself as the vehicle expert he was. Sorting vehicles was a task that *promoted his positive identity* and *grew his agency* as a learner, speaker, and friend.

EFFECT SIZE FOR SELF-CONCEPT = 0.47

When planning her lesson, Ms. Demchak knew she would select learners to share who sorted vehicles in a new way (the first success criterion), thus *sharing authority for learning with her learners.* As she interacted with the children during work time, she noted who sorted vehicles in a new way, and she asked Illarah and Liam to share their vehicle stamp and sticker sort in which they sorted by type of vehicle.

EFFECT SIZE FOR PROVIDING FORMATIVE EVALUATION = 0.40

This gave Illarah and Liam a *sense of audience* for their work. Ms. Demchak planned questions to facilitate the class discussion around Illarah and Liam's sharing, moving from recall and descriptive questions to meta-cognitive and abstract questions. The *novelty* of their sort combined with the *social interaction* of the class discussion led to more specific language being practiced and learned. Ms. Demchak's selection and implementation of her vehicle sorting tasks contributed to the quality of the children's responses and the movement of all learners forward toward mastery of the learning intention.

MORE EXAMPLES OF ENGAGING AND RIGOROUS TASKS

The lessons from Ms. Demchak, Ms. Bullock, Mr. Heaton, and Ms. Davis's classrooms present additional examples of engaging and rigorous tasks as well as the decision-making processes around selecting and implementing those tasks:

- In Chapter 2, Ms. Bullock's children pretend to have jobs within a miniature-sized community. Mr. Heaton's children build a foxes' den and then pretend to be animals living in the habitat. Ms. Davis's families create a digital library of each child reading their own *All About Me* book.

- In Chapter 3, Ms. Demchak's class builds sets using materials found in nature and their playful learning centers, including building sets of matchbox cars on five-frame parking lots. Ms. Bullock's class experiments with a variety of measuring tools, including scales. Mr. Heaton's class chooses a challenge to create structures, stories, tiling, and number charts using their shape knowledge. Ms. Davis's class builds and describes multilink cube animals.

- In Chapter 4, Ms. Demchak's learners make and compare their names. Ms. Bullock's learners read and write lists. Mr. Heaton's learners create their own *Anansi* stories. Ms. Davis's learners make puppets to retell stories.

- In Chapter 5, Ms. Demchak's class is challenged with designing and constructing the three little pigs' new house that can withstand the Big Bad Wolf. Mr. Heaton's class is translating a three-dimensional miniature town into a two-dimensional map. Ms. Davis's class is co-creating videos with their families about their family histories and family walks.

- In Chapter 6, Ms. Demchak's prekindergarteners consider different perspectives through favorite read-alouds and dollhouse and puppet play. Mr. Heaton's mixed-aged class sets goals for outdoor learning. Ms. Davis's 4-year-olds play emotions *Charades* with a favorite class puppet.

- In Chapter 7, Ms. Demchak's learners create family portraits. Ms. Bullock's learners record their storytelling through song, movement, and painting. Ms. Davis's learners build slime and playdough sculptures.

Each educator's selection and implementation of these tasks is guided by the characteristics of quality tasks as well as the learning intentions and success criteria. By selecting and implementing high-quality tasks, their learners have the opportunity to create high-quality responses.

FORMATIVE EVALUATION FOR VISIBLE LEARNING

Formative evaluation is early childhood educators' tool for making the characteristics of visible learners actionable and achievable by learners.

Each of the early childhood educators in this book uses formative evaluations in ways that reflect the five key elements of the formative evaluation process (Leahy et al., 2005):

- Clarify, communicate, and understand learning intentions and success criteria,
- Orchestrate discussions and tasks to elicit evidence of learning,
- Provide feedback to move learning forward,
- Activate learners as resources for each other, and
- Activate learners as owners of their own learning.

They use conferences, language-based interactions, and children's work as formative evaluations. Every day, they document these formative evaluations and analyze trends in order to make instructional decisions. Their formative evaluations are aligned with the learning intentions and success criteria and create opportunities to communicate these to learners. These educators use formative evaluations to drive class discussions, peer discourse, and teacher questioning.

They analyze the formative evaluations to make plans for next instructional steps and differentiating tasks. They rely on formative evaluations to inform their feedback and to engage children in peer and self-feedback.

FORMATIVE EVALUATION AND CLASSROOM DISCOURSE

Formative evaluations help these educators learn about and leverage children's interests and experiences to facilitate classroom discourse. Let's look closer at the ways Ms. Demchak, Ms. Bullock, Mr. Heaton, and Ms. Davis use formative evaluation to drive rich talk in their classrooms.

EFFECT SIZE FOR PROVIDING FORMATIVE EVALUATION = 0.40

EFFECT SIZE FOR TEACHER CLARITY = 0.84

EFFECT SIZE FOR CLASSROOM DISCUSSION = 0.82

EFFECT SIZE FOR FEEDBACK = 0.62

EFFECT SIZE FOR HELP SEEKING = 0.72

EFFECT SIZE FOR SELF-EFFICACY = 0.66

EFFECT SIZE FOR CLASSROOM COHESION = 0.53

In Chapter 4, Ms. Bullock used her ongoing observational and interactional formative evaluations to note and then capitalize on her children's playful learning. Ms. Bullock launched a genre study of lists because she noticed Alaysia announcing she made a grocery list like her mom, which then inspired many of the 3-year-olds to make scribbles on small pieces of paper and call them lists. On the day we visit Ms. Bullock's class, they are working toward these learning intentions and success criteria:

> **Content Learning Intention:** We are learning about a type of writing called lists.
>
> **Language Learning Intention:** We are learning that lists help us to communicate our message to others.
>
> **Social Learning Intention:** We are learning about taking turns talking with classmates.
>
> ## Success Criteria
>
> - We can read and write a list to do our job.
> - We can talk about our lists.

During the mini-lesson, Ms. Bullock had Alaysia share her grocery list, used her share to activate the other children's prior knowledge, and modeled writing and reading a list. Because Ms. Bullock has documented the children's interactions, language, and experiences as formative evaluation data, she was able to plan questions to activate their prior knowledge: "When have you seen people make a list? When have you made a list?" She was also able to use these notes to anticipate the children's connections to common experiences outside of school as well as their study of occupations.

EFFECT SIZE FOR STRATEGIES TO INTEGRATE WITH PRIOR KNOWLEDGE = 0.93

Then Ms. Bullock identified important new vocabulary to model and practice, such as prescriptions, appointments, and food orders. Her anticipation based on formative evaluations also enabled Ms. Bullock to prepare list-making supplies for each center; she knew the children had already experimented with grocery lists so she put out food pictures and she had images from familiar songs and books as well as animals.

EFFECT SIZE FOR QUESTIONING = 0.48

While the children worked in centers, Ms. Bullock interacted with them and documented her interactions.

She planned to note new ways the children were trying to use lists so that they could share and teach the other children and so that she could provide materials to support their attempts. For example, Ms. Bullock noticed Kadisha making phone calls on the pretend phone and writing, so she joined her and asked, "What are you writing?"

"I'm making lists. That say 'Dayquan.' I call his house," Kadisha explains.

"Why do you need a list?" Ms. Bullock probes.

"So I know who next," Kadisha responds. She turns to the pages in the class phone book and stops at Machele. "Machele."

"How will you know when you've called everyone in our class?" Ms. Bullock wonders.

"They be on the list," Kadisha points to her list.

"You're writing a list of names to keep track of who to call about Family Play Day. I should do that when I call families too. Thank you for the great idea. I wonder how many names will be on your list when you've called everyone."

"Maybe 20 or 100," Kadisha starts dialing Machele's number.

Ms. Bullock realized during this interaction that she could support list writing and reading by putting out a list of children's names and she could ask Kadisha to model for the class one way to use the class list. She documented this in the moment. She also documented other children she would select to share with the whole class as well as to note other child-inspired ideas for lists:

- Alaysia, Zakeisha, and Alex calling sick patients to make appointments—another opportunity to use a class list,

- Ethan and Dayquan watching geese outside, which inspired her to make an image list of things to spy outside that could be taped to the window (another type of list), and

- Carmen and Briera making a list of words that rhyme (a list to show what they know).

Ms. Bullock relied on her formative evaluation to intentionally select children to share, to plan her teacher questions, and to identify significant language to model and practice as she facilitated language with class discussions and peer discourse.

MORE EXAMPLES OF FORMATIVE EVALUATION AND CLASSROOM DISCOURSE

There are many more examples of each of the early childhood educators using formative evaluation to drive the rich talk in their classrooms—talk that is aligned to the learning intentions and success criteria:

- In Chapter 2, Ms. Bullock takes photos of children demonstrating the success criteria in the context of learning and uses this formative evaluation documentation to drive a class discussion.

- In Chapter 2, Ms. Davis uses formative evaluation through family-recorded *All About Me* books to plan for playful learning experiences with materials of interest and prompts, questions, and modeling that move learning forward.

- In Chapters 3 and 7, Ms. Bullock uses her formative evaluation documentation during work time to identify which children would share and help introduce significant language and representations.

- In Chapter 5, Ms. Bullock notes the types of questions the children are already asking, what connections they are making, what language they are using, and what investigations would be appropriate next steps.

- In Chapter 6, Mr. Heaton relies on his formative evaluation documentation to select children he conferred with during outdoor choice time to share their new goals with the class and to facilitate their sharing.

FORMATIVE EVALUATION, INSTRUCTIONAL STRATEGIES, AND DIFFERENTIATION

EFFECT SIZE FOR APPROPRIATELY CHALLENGING GOALS = 0.59

Ms. Demchak, Ms. Bullock, Mr. Heaton, and Ms. Davis use formative evaluation to drive their decisions about next instructional steps. By analyzing their formative evaluations, they are able to identify which phase of learning children are in and select the right strategy at the right time to match their needs. They also use formative evaluation to differentiate tasks based on developmentally appropriate levels of challenge.

EFFECT SIZE FOR TEACHER EXPECTATIONS = 0.42

In Chapter 7, Ms. Demchak used formative evaluation to determine that learners in her class span each phase of learning (surface, deep, and transfer) related to the learning intentions, so she creates success criteria accessible to all the children regardless of learning phase.

Content Learning Intention: We are learning to represent who we are and our families.

Language Learning Intention: We are learning that portraits are a way to communicate a message about what it feels like to be that person.

Social Learning Intention: We are learning to listen and respond with what we notice and wonder.

Success Criteria

- I can create recognizable people using shapes.
- I can tell about each person in my family: who they are, where they are, and what they're doing.
- I can explain my decisions about how to make each person in my family.

Ms. Demchak used her formative evaluation documentation to track who completed self- and family portraits with transcribed narrations. This drove her decisions of who to intentionally interact with during work time. Jedda finished her self-portrait and was ready to work at the transfer phase of learning in two ways: she was ready to transfer what she learned about portrait making while creating her self-portrait in order to create her mom's portrait, and she was ready to apply what she learned from exploring multimedia materials to making decisions about how to represent her mom. Simultaneously, Jedda was in the surface phase of learning, just learning to make circles and ovals.

Knowing this, Ms. Demchak was able to select the right strategy at the right time to support Jedda and move her learning forward. She engaged Jedda in identifying similarities and differences between her self-portrait and her mom's portrait:

> EFFECT SIZE FOR TRANSFER STRATEGIES = 0.86

> I know you made your self-portrait. Let's see if looking at that can help us. How did you make yourself? . . . I wonder what would be the same about making you and making your mom. . . . For your self-portrait, you glued shapes. I wonder how you could make those shapes with finger paints instead.

Ms. Demchak also asked Jedda cognitive task analysis questions to scaffold her transfer: What do you need to decide next? What material could you use to make your mom? What is your mom doing?

> EFFECT SIZE FOR COGNITIVE TASK ANALYSIS = 1.29

She paired these with reflective reasoning questions: Why do you want to use finger paints to make your mom? Why would your mom be on white paper? What's something that you want people to know about your mom?

When Jedda tried to make circles and ovals, Ms. Demchak used deliberate instruction by modeling hand-over-hand.

Ms. Demchak then used this interaction as a formative evaluation as well as Jedda's transcribed narration. Each day, these formative evaluations drive her next-day instructional decisions.

MORE EXAMPLES OF FORMATIVE EVALUATION, INSTRUCTIONAL STRATEGIES, AND DIFFERENTIATION

Examples of the ways formative evaluation can drive differentiation, selecting the right strategy at the right time, and planning next-day instruction are present in every classroom we visit in this book:

- In Chapters 2 and 6, Ms. Bullock and Mr. Heaton use formative evaluation to document who is meeting which success criteria and to plan their next-day mini-lesson and interactions.

- In Chapters 3 and 4, Ms. Demchak uses formative evaluation to differentiate the task boxes that children work on while making sure they all work toward the same learning intentions and success criteria.

- In Chapter 3, Mr. Heaton uses formative evaluation to adjust Evelyn's task by increasing the difficulty and maintaining the complexity.

- In Chapter 4, Ms. Davis uses formative evaluation to select the right strategies at the right time to use in her one-on-one sessions.

- In Chapter 5, Ms. Bullock uses formative evaluation to identify a high-interest topic to use as the context to deliberately learn and practice asking questions and problem solving.

- In Chapter 6, Ms. Demchak engages the children in a thumbs-up/down/sideways formative evaluation to practice self-evaluation and meta-cognition. She documents how each child responded so she can follow up with them.

FORMATIVE EVALUATION AND FEEDBACK

Feedback is an essential component of the formative evaluation process.

Our early childhood educators use formative evaluation to drive feedback for individual learners as well as for themselves to evaluate the effectiveness of their instructional decisions. We will examine this critical part of Visible Learning more deeply in the next section.

> EFFECT SIZE FOR FEEDBACK = 0.62

FEEDBACK FOR VISIBLE LEARNING

In the early childhood classroom, where language is the heart of learning, feedback is the content of the language. Early childhood educators are constantly providing feedback when they interact with children as conversational partners and as language facilitators. In order for this feedback to be effective for learning and maximize learning opportunities, we need to be intentional in our language choices.

Too often, feedback is considered from the teacher's perspective and there are debates about the quantity, frequency, type, and form of feedback. Yes, these are all interesting questions, but the critical piece is understanding feedback from the learner's perspective. Effective feedback is "just-in-time, just-for-me information delivered when and where it can do the most good" (Brookhart, 2008, p. 1). It needs to be heard, understood, and actionable. If feedback is not actioned, it is not effective! Feedback closes the gap between where learners are and where they are going by aligning with the language and content of the learning intentions and success criteria. Similarly, by making the success criteria transparent and fitting the Goldilocks principle (not too hard, not too easy, and not too boring), feedback is often more effective as the learner appreciates the purpose and value of closing the gap between where they are and the success criteria.

> Feedback closes the gap between where learners are and where they are going by aligning with the language and content of the learning intentions and success criteria.

Effective feedback is timely, specific, and constructive. Timely feedback means learners have opportunities to respond within close proximity to engaging in the content. Feedback should be immediate when it is about the task, the content, or the vocabulary (the surface-level aspects of learning) and when children are in the midst of deliberate practice and making sense of knowledge-based or factual information (surface consolidating). Feedback can be delayed if children are engaging in error analysis or making sense of mistakes (the deeper-level aspects of learning). Timely feedback also means there need to be opportunities for the feedback to be actioned—there is time to act on the feedback within the lesson and the unit of study.

Specific feedback means the amount is a bite-sized, consumable chunk of information and the content is aligned with the learning intentions and success criteria. Relying on the language of the learning intentions and success criteria helps to communicate where the individual learner is going related to the goals, how the learner is going, and where the learner needs to go next. In other words, the specific feedback helps the learner see their own work within the learning intentions and success criteria and envision what to do next to move forward. This alignment should also support making sure the language and content of the feedback is understandable to the individual learner.

Constructive feedback means the feedback is not about the individual person but rather it is focused on the learning journey. Constructive feedback can address the task, the process, or the learner's self-regulation.

There is everything right about praise, but so often the power of the feedback is diluted when praise is sandwiched into the feedback about the surface or deeper learning—as the learner hears and recalls more of the praise feedback. Praise young children (it is the essence of relationships) but do not mix praise about the person when you provide feedback about the task or learning intentions.

Effective feedback can come from the teacher, peers, and the learners themselves.

In order for feedback to be intentional, we must plan our interactions and language for teacher feedback, teach and practice peer feedback, and teach and practice self-feedback. There are three types of self-feedback: self-monitoring, self-reflecting, and self-evaluating.

Self-monitoring involves keeping a mental or physical record of the learning journey and using that record to make adjustments to learning tasks, processes, or self-regulation when necessary. Self-reflecting is making sense of the record of the learning journey and asking oneself: Where am I going? How am I going? Where do I go next? Self-evaluating is analyzing the learning journey record compared to the success criteria and determining where the learner is relative to the learning intention.

Each of these types of self-feedback can and should be taught and practiced in the early childhood classroom. Providing opportunities for these self-notions to be said aloud is powerful not only because you can hear "learners thinking," but it also allows other children to hear possibly alternative ways of thinking and processing—and helps all develop a language of learning.

Feedback and formative evaluation go hand-in-hand in the Visible Learning classroom. Formative evaluation drives feedback and feedback moves learning forward through language-based interaction. The visible learner seeks feedback and self-monitors, then uses this feedback to self-reflect, self-evaluate, make adjustments and selections, and teach others. The educator in a Visible Learning classroom uses formative evaluation as feedback to themselves about how effective their instructional decisions were for each learner and makes adjustments based on this feedback.

The early childhood educators in this book know each of their interactions is feedback and therefore needs to be intentional in order for the feedback to be an opportunity to move learning forward. This is in-the-moment feedback. The educators also use significant learning junctures throughout the year as opportunities to teach and deliberately practice effective feedback.

They create routines and structures that support and intentionally develop effective feedback practices by teachers, peers, and the learners themselves. They make decisions about what formative evaluations and feedback to share, when to share it, and how to share it. Let's look more closely at Ms. Demchak, Ms. Bullock, Mr. Heaton, and Ms. Davis's feedback practices.

> EFFECT SIZE FOR PROVIDING FORMATIVE EVALUATION = 0.40

MR. HEATON AND IN-THE-MOMENT FEEDBACK FOR LEARNERS

In Chapter 6, Mr. Heaton introduced the concept and process of goal setting to his learners. He spent their outdoor time intentionally interacting with individuals to coach them in setting a goal and making a plan to attain it.

The class was working toward these learning intentions and success criteria:

> EFFECT SIZE FOR GOAL COMMITMENT = 0.40

Content Learning Intention: We are learning that setting and working toward goals is one way to learn.

Language Learning Intention: We are learning about ways to talk about and reflect on our goals.

Social Learning Intention: We are learning to encourage our friends as they work on goals.

Success Criteria

- I can think about what I can do and what I can't do yet and set a goal to learn something new.
- I can make a plan to work toward my goal at home and school.

By interacting with Arthur for about 10 minutes, Mr. Heaton was able to give just-for-Arthur, just-in-time feedback. It was timely, specific, and constructive. Mr. Heaton's first piece of feedback was aligned with the first success criterion.

"Arthur, what is something that you want to try outside but it's hard?" Mr. Heaton asked.

"I can't do the pole," Arthur responds.

"The pole is hard," Mr. Heaton commiserates. "But it's something you can learn to do with practice. Would you like to learn how to slide down the pole?"

"Yes!" Arthur says excitedly.

"What a great goal! Your goal is to slide down the pole."

The majority of Mr. Heaton's feedback was focused on the second success criterion.

When Arthur said he was watching in order to learn about his goal, Mr. Heaton responded about the process: "Watching someone else is a great way to notice how they do something. What have you noticed?" He affirmed that watching is an effective strategy but pushed for more information about how it was actually helping Arthur learn.

Mr. Heaton also facilitated peer feedback from Aurora to Arthur: "Let's go over and ask Aurora to tell us how she slides down the pole."

When it's Aurora's turn, she narrates as she quickly holds onto the pole and slides down, "Hands on. Legs on. Slide down!"

Mr. Heaton helped Arthur further analyze the task by giving task feedback when Arthur ran into a problem: "Let's remember Aurora's advice. Hands on. You've got your hands on. What's next?"

"Legs on. Slide down." Arthur remembers the chant. "I can't put my legs on. It's too high."

"Let's try one leg at a time. I'll help. I won't let you fall," Mr. Heaton holds his arms out. Arthur slowly puts one leg out and Mr. Heaton directs, "One leg on—wrap your leg around the pole like a snake. Put your foot around to the other side." Arthur tries. Mr. Heaton then says, "Now two legs on—pull your body up to hold onto the pole. I'll hold your shoulders for extra help." Mr. Heaton breaks down Aurora's advice in the spot that is challenging to Arthur.

Mr. Heaton gave process feedback after Arthur's first successful slide down the pole: "Wow! Your goal is to slide down the pole! You watched kids do it. Then you asked Aurora for help. Then you tried her advice. And now you've slid down the pole!" This feedback modeled self-monitoring feedback to prepare Arthur for this next step in becoming a visible learner.

EFFECT SIZE FOR STRATEGY MONITORING = 0.58

When Arthur declares that he wants to do it by himself, Mr. Heaton gives him self-regulation feedback: "That means you'll need to practice. Get back in line and remember: Hands on. *One leg on. Two legs on.* Slide down!" Mr. Heaton emphasizes the part that Arthur needed the most help with.

EFFECT SIZE FOR SELF-REGULATION STRATEGIES = 0.54

Mr. Heaton gave Arthur a chance to immediately practice self-monitoring during the sharing that day and reminded his peers to give him timely, specific, and constructive feedback as well: "Arthur, you set a goal about the fire pole. What is your goal?" Mr. Heaton uses goal-setting language to emphasize the special thinking they did.

"To go down the fire pole by myself," he states.

"You started practicing already! What did you do today to practice your goal of going down the fire pole by yourself?" Mr. Heaton extends.

"I watched. Then Aurora told me how to do it. And Mr. Heaton helped. And I went down *three* times!" Arthur remembers.

"Do feel like you've met your goal or do you want to practice some more?" Mr. Heaton asks a question that engages Arthur in self-evaluation and progress monitoring.

"I'm gonna practice more. I want to be fast with no help!" Arthur moves his hand like it is sliding down the pole quickly.

"Working toward a goal is hard work and takes practice. If you see Arthur working on his goal of sliding down the fire pole, remember to encourage him!" Mr. Heaton gives Arthur feedback while building on their collaborative community.

Mr. Heaton documented his interaction with Arthur through notes and a photograph, which serve as formative evaluation documentation. He connected this work with Arthur's family so that they could also support Arthur and provide feedback. Mr. Heaton sent the photo home to Arthur's family with a brief note about his goal.

EFFECT SIZE FOR FAMILY INVOLVEMENT = 0.42

Through effective feedback paired with formative evaluation, Mr. Heaton was able to close the gap between where Arthur was and where he both needed and wanted to go.

MORE EXAMPLES OF IN-THE-MOMENT FEEDBACK FOR VISIBLE LEARNING

In early childhood, teacher and peer feedback occur at the same time as being a conversational partner and language facilitator. This language-based interaction is what makes playful learning effective. These forms of feedback serve as models for self-feedback while teacher and peer questioning can serve as the scaffolds or coaching to practice self-feedback. There are many powerful examples of timely, specific, and constructive feedback that close the gap between the learners and the learning intentions:

- In Chapter 2, Mr. Heaton's feedback during playful learning modeled language, extended ideas, and reminded the children to be active decision makers.

- In Chapter 3, Ms. Demchak balances feedback for the whole class during the mini-lesson and closing share with feedback for individuals and partners during work time. To model frames for feedback, she uses phrases like "I notice" and "I wonder."

- In Chapters 4 and 7, Mr. Heaton and Ms. Bullock use sharing to practice peer feedback and model self-monitoring, self-reflecting, and self-evaluation using the success criteria.

- In Chapter 5, Ms. Demchak and Mr. Heaton provide feedback by facilitating language, asking guiding questions, and reminding the children of familiar models to transfer to a new problem-solving situation.

- In Chapters 4 and 6, Ms. Davis uses class puppets to model giving feedback aligned with the success criteria.

MS. BULLOCK AND FEEDBACK FROM LEARNERS

When learning is visible, learners become teachers and teachers become learners. Early childhood educators can use formative evaluation as feedback from learners to determine whether and how effective their instructional decisions were for the children. In Chapter 5, Ms. Bullock intentionally uses feedback from her learners to determine ways to revise and refine her instruction.

This first day of engaging with the exploration trays is also a first day of intentional learning about scientific concepts, practice, and a distinct way of knowing. The class works toward these learning intentions and success criteria:

Content Learning Intention: We are learning that scientists ask questions and investigate answers.

Language Learning Intention: We are learning to communicate our questions and answers using words and actions.

Social Learning Intention: We are learning to think about what friends are saying.

Success Criteria

- I can ask BIG questions.
- I can try different ways to answer my questions.
- I can show and tell my questions and answers.
- I can think about friends' words when they share.

Ms. Bullock plans to use her formative evaluation as feedback from the learners to herself. She takes an asset-focused stance, acknowledging the wealth of scientific knowledge her children bring, as she documents which exploration trays they choose, what connections they make, what language they use, and what types of questions they ask. Before teaching, Ms. Bullock creates an observation/conference chart based on what data she wants to collect (see Figure 5.3 in Chapter 5, which is reproduced on the next page).

Then, Ms. Bullock plans each component of her lesson. In her mini-lesson, Ms. Bullock models one way to engage with the materials in one exploration tray and thinks aloud as she works. During work time, Ms. Bullock interacts with the children, scaffolding, extending, and assessing their scientific thinking through her language. Her formative evaluation documentation helps Ms. Bullock facilitate the children's sharing about their exploration trays as she records their discoveries.

After the lesson, Ms. Bullock analyzes her formative evaluation documentation for feedback from the learners. Ms. Bullock notices that the magnet trays are the most popular. For some children, like Kayvion, this is their first time using magnets; even though they do not know the names of the materials, they are invested in experimenting with them. For other children, like Sabina, magnets are a familiar tool but they are used and look differently at home than at school. At home, Sabina's magnets are letters and her mom uses them to display her work on the refrigerator. At school, there are magnet wands and magnet balls that can be used to pick up paperclips and move washers. Magnets are a high-interest topic to dive deeply into next, and there are children at the surface and deep phases of magnet learning.

EFFECT SIZE FOR CLASSROOM COHESION = 0.53

FIGURE 8.1 ● Observation/Conference Chart

Date _____

NAME	EXPLORATION TRAY	CONNECTIONS	LANGUAGE	QUESTIONS	NOTES

Content Learning Intention:

We are learning scientists ask questions and investigate answers.

Language Learning Intention:

We are learning to communicate our questions and answers using words and actions.

Social Learning Intention: We are learning to think about what friends are saying.

Success Criteria:

- I can ask BIG questions.
- I can try different ways to answer my questions.
- I can show and tell my questions and answers.
- I can think about friends' words when they share.

Anticipated BIG Questions:

- How does this work?
- How is this made?
- How is this the same or different?
- Why?
- What would happen if…?
- Will it always work?

online resources ⚓ Available for download at **resources.corwin.com/VLforEarlyChildhood**

Ms. Bullock's choice of task, the exploration trays, and her observation/conference chart were effective for her initial evaluation of children's language, questions, and connections. However, the exploration trays were ineffective for some of her learners to meet the learning intentions and success criteria today. Some children try the same strategy—stacking—regardless of the materials. Some children only ask questions about objects' names, while some do not ask any questions and instead simply tell about the materials.

Ms. Bullock realizes this is one lesson, the first lesson, and her learners need multiple opportunities and she needs to use a variety of instructional strategies in order for her learners to be successful. At the same time, the feedback from the learners reminds her that she needs to use the right strategies at the right time for learners at the surface phase of questioning and problem solving. This means that tomorrow she will use deliberate instruction and practice, modeling, guiding questions, and direct vocabulary instruction as they continue learning to ask BIG questions and problem solve.

> EFFECT SIZE FOR DELIBERATE PRACTICE = 0.79

Tomorrow, the learning intentions and success criteria will emphasize scientific communication and problem solving with magnets:

> EFFECT SIZE FOR VOCABULARY INSTRUCTION = 0.63

Content Learning Intention: Today, we are learning that magnets make things move.

Language Learning Intention: We are learning ways to describe movement with words and actions.

Social Learning Intention: We are learning to work together to try many strategies to solve a problem.

Success Criteria

We'll know we have it when . . .

- We can answer the question "How do magnets make things move?" with words and actions.
- We can show different ways magnets make things move.

Tomorrow, the children will work as teams of scientists to deliberately practice using multiple different strategies to problem solve.

> EFFECT SIZE FOR EXPLICIT TEACHING STRATEGIES = 0.57

In teams, the children will be able to engage in rich conversation, which Ms. Bullock hopes will ignite more BIG questions. Because of Ms. Bullock's clarity throughout planning and implementation, her lesson was full of opportunities for feedback— feedback for her learners and feedback for herself.

MS. DAVIS AND STUDENT-LED FAMILY CONFERENCES

It is the end of the school year and time for student-led conferences in Ms. Davis's prekindergarten classroom.

Armoni walks in with his family. Ms. Davis hands him his plan and Armoni begins with a classroom tour. "This is my lunch choice. This is my cubby. Then I answer the Question of the Day. Let's do it together. I'll point and read. You can help me. 'Which do you like more?'" He points to the images of two book covers from the *Who Would Win?* series (Pallotta, 2016) and 'reads' them, "'*Komodo Dragon vs. King Cobra* or *Tarantula vs. Scorpion?*' *Tarantula vs. Scorpion!*" As he puts his name under his answer, Armoni explains why he liked that book more. His sisters have read the series too and a discussion ensues.

The classroom tour ends when Armoni reaches a tray of work he has laid out. "This is puzzle work and it is my favorite! I find the corners first. Do you want to make it with me? I'll show you how I find the corners." His family works together to assemble the puzzle with direction from Armoni.

Next on Armoni's plan is the Costumes Area—his favorite center. "In Costumes Area, you can wear a costume, cook, drive a bus, call on the walkie-talkie, sword fight—whatever you imagine! What do you want to pretend?" Armoni introduces the center and makes a plan with his family. They ride in a spaceship to Saturn with Armoni as the pilot.

When they "land," Armoni checks his plan. "Let's clean up and next I'll teach you to play *Memory*." The family follows Armoni to an empty table. Armoni gets a deck of numeral cards and begins teaching, "First, I put out three cards and three cards and three cards," Armoni makes an array of cards facing down. "We take turns. Dad, you go first. Turn over two cards and see if they match."

Armoni's family plays *Memory* by matching numeral cards. They are laughing and talking, asking questions and debating.

The final item on Armoni's plan is his goal portfolio. His family gathers around as he shows them what he could do at the beginning of the year, mid-year, and now at the end of the year for a variety of concepts and skills. Each concept or skill has a learning intention and success criteria at the top of the page inside a sheet protector. Then written, drawn, or glued to the page with photographs or other objects placed inside the sheet protector are proof of Armoni's progress toward meeting the learning intention and success criteria. His work from each learning juncture is labeled with a different color to show progress over time.

Ms. Davis chose some learning intentions for all prekindergartners to share (such as ones related to oral counting, set building, subitizing, name writing, letter-sound skills, phoneme segmentation, and storytelling). Armoni shows with immense pride what he knew when school began and how much he can do now. His family video records as he counts to 300. His sister challenges him to delete the first phoneme in *pool*. "OOL!" Armoni shouts, "That's easy. I need something harder!"

Each family also chose some learning intentions to work toward together during earlier student-led family conferences. Armoni's family set goals for him to tie his shoes and memorize his dad's phone number.

> EFFECT SIZE FOR FAMILY INVOLVEMENT = 0.42

He demonstrates for everyone that he has mastered these skills and they all high-five him. Three learning intentions were selected by Armoni for himself: I am learning to read a book, I am learning to draw a Minion, and I am learning to dribble two basketballs at the same time. Armoni and Ms. Davis worked together to establish the success criteria for these three goals, and Armoni was in charge of collecting the proof.

> EFFECT SIZE FOR GOAL COMMITMENT = 0.40

He has a predictable text about colors that he points and reads to his family. They clap and cheer. Next, Armoni reads a story he created with detailed, colorful drawings of Minions on each page. His family knows Armoni has been working on this story because he has taught them all how to draw Minions at home. Finally, he shows them a picture of him dribbling two basketballs simultaneously and says, "That's the day I met my goal. I dribbled three times—bounce, bounce, bounce! I can show you now outside."

> EFFECT SIZE FOR SELF-JUDGMENT AND REFLECTION = 0.62

> EFFECT SIZE FOR SELF-VERBALIZATION AND SELF-QUESTIONING = 0.75

It is clear to Ms. Davis, the family, and Armoni himself that Armoni

- Knows his current level of understanding; communicates what he does and does not yet know,
- Knows where he is going next in his learning and is ready to take on the challenge,
- Selects tools to move his learning forward,
- Seeks feedback about his learning and recognizes errors as opportunities to learn,
- Monitors his learning and makes adjustments when necessary, and
- Recognizes when he has learned something and serves as a teacher to others.

Armoni is a visible learner ready to continue this growth next year.

Ms. Davis and Student-Led Conferences in Distance Learning

This year, Ms. Davis still wants to hold student-led conferences at important learning junctures throughout the year, but her class is engaged in distance learning. Ms. Davis is rethinking how to make student-led conferences happen. With video conferencing platforms, she can still meet with families and have the children take the lead in showing and teaching their family members. Through digital classroom management programs, Ms. Davis can create digital portfolios for her learners. In fact, she can partner with her families so they can also document their children's progress through videos and photos. And she can continue using goal portfolios containing a mixture of common, family-selected, and child-selected learning intentions and success criteria. Ms. Davis needs to teach both families and children how to track progress in the goal portfolios using different colors for each learning juncture, but this does not feel like extra work. Rather it feels like the right work to truly partner with families to grow visible learners with families who can advocate for their learners.

 ## CONCLUSION

When we began this learning journey together, we shared a vision of visible learners. Throughout the research and vignettes, we have kept our eyes on the development of visible learners because this is our ultimate goal: to grow learners who have the efficacy to be active decision makers about their learning. We have so much to learn about early childhood education and about our learners. There is no end in sight to the questions and new ideas and possibilities that arise through the connection of research and practice. The reality is that as early childhood educators, we also want to be visible learners. We want to

- Know our current level of understanding; communicate what we do and do not yet know,

- Know where we are going next in our learning and be ready to take on the challenge,

- Select tools to move our learning forward,

- Seek feedback about our learning and recognize errors as opportunities to learn,

- Monitor our learning and make adjustments when necessary, and

- Recognize when we have learned something and serve as a teacher to others.

We hope that you now have a clearer vision of your current level of understanding related to early childhood education as well as an enhanced vision of where you are going and the classroom you want to create. We hope you feel empowered to take on this challenge and make this vision a reality. We hope you have a full toolbox to select the right strategy at the right time for your learners. We hope you continue to seek feedback and recognize that trying something new and making mistakes are opportunities to learn and improve your practice. We hope you now have some guideposts to help you monitor your progress and make adjustments. We hope you reach out to your community of educators to collaborate and teach each other through modeling and sharing. And we hope you see visible learners in yourself and your children.

Appendix

Effect Sizes

Access the complete and most recent versions of the influence and effect size data at http://www.visiblelearningmetax.com/Influences

References

Adams, M. J. (2013). *ABC foundations for young children: A classroom curriculum.* Brookes.

American Speech-Language-Hearing Association. (n.d.). *How does your child hear and talk?* https://www.asha.org/public/speech/development/chart/

Antonetti, J. V., & Garver, J. R. (2015). *17,000 classroom visits can't be wrong: Strategies that engage students, promote active learning, and boost achievement.* ASCD.

August, D., & Shanahan, T. (Eds.) (2006). *Developing literacy in second language learners. Report of the national literacy panel on minority-language children and youth.* Lawrence Erlbaum.

Australian Government Department of Education and Training. (2019). *Early Years Learning Framework.* https://www.dese.gov.au/national-quality-framework-early-childhood-education-and-care-0/earlyyearslearningframework

Ausubel, D. P., Novak, J. D., & Hanesian, H. (1968). *Educational psychology: A cognitive view.* Rinehart & Winston.

Ball, D. L. (2020, July). *Get up, stand up: Fighting systemic injustice through teaching* [Presentation]. TeachingWorks 2020 Virtual Summer Institute Keynote Address.

Baroody, A. J. (2004). The role of psychological research in the development of early childhood mathematics standards. In D. H. Clements, J. Sarama, & A. DiBiase (Eds.), *Engaging young children in mathematics: Standards for pre-school and kindergarten mathematics education* (pp. 149–172). Lawrence Erlbaum.

Barrett, M. S., Flynn, L. M., & Welch, G. F. (2018). Music value and participation: An Australian case study of music provision and support in early childhood education. *Research Studies in Music Education, 40*(2), 226–243. https://doi.org/10.1177/1321103X18773098

Battelle for Kids. (2021, January). *Portrait of a graduate.* https://portraitofagraduate.org/

Bazyk, S., Michaud, P., Goodman, G., Papp, P., Hawkins, E., & Welch, M. A. (2009). Integrating occupational therapy services in a kindergarten curriculum: A look at the outcomes. *The American Journal of Occupational Therapy, 63*(2), 160–171. https://doi.org/10.5014/ajot.63.2.160

Beck, I. L., McKeown, M. G., & Kucan, L. (2013). *Bring words to life. Robust vocabulary instruction* (2nd ed). Guilford Press.

Bell, R. L. (2008). *Teaching the nature of science through process skills: Activities for Grades 3–8.* Allyn & Bacon/Longman.

Berry, R. Q., III, & Thunder, K. (2012). The promise of qualitative metasynthesis: Mathematics experiences of Black learners. *Journal of Mathematics Education at Teachers College, 3*(2), 43–55. https://doi.org/10.7916/jmetc.v3i2.757

Berry, R. Q., III, & Thunder, K. (2017). Concrete, representational, and abstract: Building fluency from conceptual understanding. *Virginia Mathematics Teacher, 43*(2), 28–32.

Bhatia, P., Davis, A., & Shamas-Brandt, E. (2015). Educational gymnastics: The effectiveness of Montessori practical life activities in developing fine motor skills in kindergarteners. *Early Education and Development, 26*(4), 594–607. https://doi.org/10.1080/10409289.2015.995454

Bishop, R. S. (1990). Mirrors, windows, and sliding glass doors. *Perspectives: Choosing and Using Books for the Classroom, 6*(3).

Brookhart, S. H. (2008). *How to give effective feedback to your students* (2nd ed.). ASCD.

Bronfenbrenner, U. (2005). *Ecological systems theory (1992).* In U. Bronfenbrenner (Ed.), *Making human beings human: Bioecological perspectives on human development* (pp. 106–173). Sage.

Brown, J., Sherrill, C., & Gench, B. (1981). Effects of an integrated physical education/music program in changing early childhood perceptual-motor performance. *Perceptual and Motor Skills, 53*(1), 151–154. https://doi.org/10.2466/pms.1981.53.1.151

Cameron, C. E., Murrah, W. M., Grissmer, D., Brock, L. L., Bell, L. H., Worzalla, S. L., & Morrison, F. J. (2012). Fine motor skills and executive function both contribute to kindergarten achievement. *Child Development, 83*(4), 1229–1244.https://doi.org/10.1111/j.1467-8624.2012.01768.x

Chawla, L. (2007). Childhood experiences associated with care for the natural world: A theoretical framework for empirical results. *Children, Youth and Environments, 17*(4), 144–170.

Civil, M. (1998). Bridging in-school mathematics and out-of-school mathematics: A reflection. *Annual Meeting AERA,* San Diego, CA (p. 1235). http://www.eric.ed.gov

Clements, D. H. (2004). Geometric and spatial thinking in early childhood education. In D. H. Clements, J. Sarama, & A. M. Di Biase (Eds.), *Engaging young children in mathematics: Standards for early childhood mathematics education* (pp. 267–298). Lawrence Erlbaum.

Clements, D. H., & Sarama, J. (2007). Early childhood mathematics learning. In F. K. Lester, Jr. (Ed.), *Second handbook of research on mathematics teaching and learning* (pp. 461–559). Information Age Publishing.

Collins, K., & Glover, M. (2015). *I am reading: Nurturing young children's meaning making and joyful engagement with any book.* Heinemann.

Cooper, H., Allen, A. B., & Patall, E. (2010). Effects of full-day kindergarten on academic achievement and social development. *Review of Educational Research, 80*(1), 34–70.

Dickinson, D. K. (2011). Teachers' language practices and academic outcomes of preschool children. *Science, 333*(6045), 964–967.https://doi.org/10.1126/science.1204526

Dickinson, D. K., Collins, M. F., Nesbitt, K., Toub, T. S., Hassinger-Das, B., Hadley, E. B. Hirsh-Pasek, K., & Golinkoff, R. M. (2019). Effects of teacher-delivered book reading and play on vocabulary learning and self-regulation among low-income preschool children. *Journal of Cognition and Development, 20*(2), 136–164. https://doi.org/10.1080/15248372.2018.1483373

Driver, R., Squires, A., Rushworth, P., & Wood-Robinson, V. (1994). *Making sense of secondary science: Research into children's ideas.* Routledge.

Duncan, G. J., Dowsett, C. J., Claessens, A., Magnuson, K., Huston, A., Klevanov, P., & Japell, C. (2007). School readiness and later achievement. *Developmental Psychology, 43*(6), 1428–1446. https://doi.org/10.1037/0012-1649.43.6.1428

Eckhoff, A. (2008). The importance of art viewing experiences in early childhood visual arts: The exploration of a master art teacher's strategies for meaningful early arts experiences. *Early Childhood Education Journal, 35*(5), 463–472. https://doi.org/10.1007/s10643-007-0216-1

Fendick, F. (1990). *The correlation between teacher clarity of communication and student achievement gain: A meta-analysis* (Doctoral dissertation, University of Florida).

Fisher, D., Frey, N., & Hattie, J. (2020). *The distance learning playbook, Grades K–12: Teaching for engagement and impact in any setting.* Corwin.

Frey, N., Hattie, J., & Fisher, D. (2018). *Developing assessment-capable visible learners, Grades K–12: Maximizing skill, will, and thrill.* Corwin.

Fuson, K. C. (2004). Pre-K to grade 2 goals and standards: Achieving 21st-century mastery for all. In D. H. Clements, J. Sarama, & A. DiBiase (Eds.), *Engaging young children in mathematics: Standards for pre-school and kindergarten* mathematics education (pp. 105–148). Lawrence Erlbaum.

Garner, P. W., Mahatmya, D., Brown, E. L., & Vesely, C. K. (2014). Promoting desirable outcomes among culturally and ethnically diverse children in social emotional learning programs: A multilevel heuristic model. *Educational Psychology Review*, 26(1), 165–189. https://psycnet.apa.org/doi/10.1007/s10648-014-9253-7

Gelman, R., & Brenneman, K. (2004). Science learning pathways for young children. *Early Childhood Research Quarterly*, 19(1), 150–158. https://doi.org/10.1016/j.ecresq.2004.01.009

Gelman, R., & Gallistel, C. R. (1978). *The child's understanding of number*. Harvard University Press.

Gilliam, W. S., & Zigler, E. F. (2000). A critical meta-analysis of all evaluations of state-funded preschool from 1977 to 1998: Implications for policy, service delivery and program evaluation. *Early Childhood Research Quarterly*, 15(4), 441–473. https://psycnet.apa.org/doi/10.1016/S0885-2006(01)00073-4

Ginsburg, H. P., & Golbeck, S. L. (2004). Thoughts on the future of research on mathematics and science learning and education. *Early Childhood Research Quarterly*, 19(1), 190–200. https://doi.org/10.1016/j.ecresq.2004.01.013

Goldstein, L. S. (2008). Teaching the standards is developmentally appropriate practice: Strategies for incorporating the sociopolitical dimension of DAP in early childhood teaching. *Early Childhood Education Journal*, 36(3), 253–260. https://doi.org/10.1007/s10643-008-0268-x

Gough, P., & Tunmer, W. (1986). Decoding, reading, and reading disability. *Remedial and Special Education*, 7(1), 6–10. https://doi.org/10.1177/074193258600700104

Graham, S., Kiuhara, S. A., & MacKay, M. (2020). The effects of writing on learning in science, social studies, and mathematics: A meta-analysis. *Review of Educational Research*, 90(2), 179–226. https://doi.org/10.3102/0034654320914744

Gross, D., & Grady, J. (2002). Group-based parent training for preventing mental health disorders in children. *Issues in Mental Health Nursing*, 23(4), 367–383. https://doi.org/10.1080/01612840290052578

Hadley, E. B., Dickinson, D. K., Hirsh-Pasek, K., & Golinkoff, R. M. (2018). Building semantic networks: The impact of a vocabulary intervention on preschools' depth of word knowledge. *Reading Research Quarterly*, 54(1), 41–61. https://doi.org/10.1002/rrq.225

Hammond, Z. (2015). *Culturally responsive teaching and the brain: Promoting authentic engagement and rigor among culturally and linguistically diverse students*. Corwin.

Hansen, J. (2001). *When writers read*. Heinemann.

Hattie, J., Bustamante, V., Almarode, J., Fisher, D., & Frey, N. (2021). *Great teaching, by design. From intention to implementation in the Visible Learning classroom*. Corwin.

Hattie, J., Fisher, D., Frey, N., Gojak, L.M., Delano Moore, S., & Mellman, W. (2017). *Visible learning for mathematics: What works best to optimize student learning, Grades K–12*. Corwin.

Hindman, A. H., Skibbe, L. E., Miller, A., & Zimmerman, M. (2010). Ecological contexts and early learning: Contributions of child, family, and classroom factors during Head Start to literacy and mathematics growth through first grade. *Early Childhood Research Quarterly*, 25(2), 235–250. https://doi.org/10.1016/j.ecresq.2009.11.003

Hirsh-Pasek, K., Golinkoff, R., Berk, L., & Singer, D. (2009). *A mandate for playful learning in preschool: Presenting the evidence*. Oxford University Press.

Horn, M., & Giacobbe, M. E. (2007). *Talking, drawing, writing: Lessons for our youngest writers*. Stenhouse.

Horst, J. S., Parsons, K. L., & Bryan, N. M. (2011). Get the story straight: Contextual repetition promotes word learning from storybooks. *Frontiers in Psychology*, 2, 17. https://dx.doi.org/10.3389/fpsyg.2011.00017

Husband, T., Jr. (2010). He's too young to learn about that stuff: Anti-racist pedagogy and early childhood social studies. *Social Studies Research and Practice, 5*(2), 61–75.

Illinois State Board of Education. (2013). *Illinois Early Learning and Development Standards.* https://illinoisearlylearning.org/ields/

Jasmin, E., Gauthier, A., Julien, M. & Hui, C. (2018). Occupational therapy in preschools: A synthesis of current knowledge. *Early Childhood Education Journal, 46*(1), 73–82. https://doi.org/10.1007/s10643-017-0840-3

Jennings, P. A., & Greenberg, M. T. (2009). The prosocial classroom: Teacher social and emotional competence in relation to student and classroom outcomes. *Review of Educational Research, 79*(1), 491–525. https://doi.org/10.3102/0034654308325693

Jeynes, W. H., & Littell, S. W. (2000). A meta-analysis of studies examining the effect of whole language instruction on literacy of low-SES students. *The Elementary School Journal, 101*(1), 21–33. https://doi.org/10.1086/499657

Jimenez, B., Browder, D., Spooner, F., & DiBiase, W. (2012). Inclusive inquiry science using peer-mediated embedded instruction for students with moderate intellectual disability. *Exceptional Children, 78*(3), 301–317. https://doi.org/10.1177/001440291207800303

Jones, C. D., Clark, S. K., & Reutzel, D. R. (2012). Enhancing alphabet knowledge instruction; Research implications and practical strategies for early childhood educators. *Early Childhood Education Journal, 41*(2), 81–89. https://doi.org/10.1007/s10643-012-0534-9

Jordan, N. C., & Levine, S. C. (2009). Socioeconomic variation, number competence, and mathematics learning difficulties in young children. *Development Disabilities Research Reviews, 15*, 60–68. https://doi.org/10.1002/ddrr.46

Jordan, N. C., Kaplan, D., Olah, L. N., & Locuinak, M. N. (2006). Number sense growth in kindergarten: A longitudinal investigation of children at risk for mathematics difficulties. *Child Development, 77*(1), 153–175. https://doi.org/10.1111/j.1467-8624.2006.00862.x

Kilpatrick, D. A. (2016). *Reading success: A comprehensive, step-by-step program for developing phonemic awareness and fluent word recognition.* Casey & Kirsch.

Kindler, A. M., & Darras, B. (1998). Culture and development of pictorial repertoires. *Studies in Art Education, 39*(2), 147–167. https://doi.org/10.2307/1320466

Leahy, S., Lyon, C. J., Thompson, M., & Wiliam, D. (2005). Classroom assessment: Minute by minute, day by day. *Educational Leadership: Assessment to Promote Learning, 63*(3), 19–24.

Lenhart, L. A., Roskos, K. A., Brueck, J., & Liang, X. (2019). Does play help children learn words?: Analysis of a book play approach using an adapted alternating treatments design. *Journal of Research in Childhood Education, 33*(2), 290–306. https://doi.org/10.1080/02568543.2019.1577776

Lillard, A. S., Lerner, M. D., Hopkins, E. J., Dore, R. A., Smith, E. D., & Palmquist, C. M. (2013). The impact of pretend play on children's development: A review of the evidence. *Psychological Bulletin, 139*(1), 1–34. https://doi.org/10.1037/a0029321

Massey, S. L. (2013). From the reading rug to the play center: Enhancing vocabulary and comprehensive language skills by connecting storybook reading and guided play. *Early Childhood Education Journal, 41*(2), 125–131. https://doi.org/10.1007/s10643-012-0524-y

Mindes, G. (2015). Preschool through Grade 3: Pushing up the social studies from early childhood education to the world. *Young Children, 70*(3), 10–15.

Morrow, L., Freitag, E., & Gambrell, L. (2009). *Using children's literature in preschool to develop comprehension: Understanding and enjoying books (preschool literacy collection)* (2nd ed.). International Reading Association.

Muhammad, G. (2020). *Cultivating genius: An equity framework for culturally and historically responsive literacy.* Scholastic.

Murano, D., Sawyer, J. E., & Lipnevich, A. A. (2020). A meta-analytic review of preschool social and emotional learning interventions. *Review of Educational Research, 90*(2), 227–263. https://doi.org/10.3102/0034654320914743

National Council for the Social Studies. (2019). *NCSS position statement: Early childhood in the social studies context*. Author.

National Council of Teachers of Mathematics. (2020). *Catalyzing change in early childhood and elementary mathematics*. Author.

National Governors Association Center for Best Practices, Council of Chief State School Officers. (2010). *Common Core State Standards for Mathematics*. Author.

National Research Council. (2009). *Mathematical learning in early childhood: Paths toward excellence and equity*. Committee on Early Childhood Mathematics. C. T. Cross, T. A. Woods, & H. Schweingruber (Eds.). National Academy Press.

National Science Teachers Association. (2014). *NSTA position statement: Early childhood science education*. Author.

Neill, T. & Patrick, L. (2016, July 19). *Turning it up: A framework for STEM education*. http://okmathteachers.com/stemframework/

Neuman, S. B., & Dwyer, J. (2011). Developing vocabulary and conceptual knowledge for low-income preschoolers: A design experiment. *Journal of Literacy Research*, 43(2), 103–129. https://doi.org/10.1177/1086296X11403089

Neuman, S. B., & Roskos, K. (1992). Literacy objects as cultural tools: Effects on children's literacy behaviors in play. *Reading Research Quarterly*, 27(3), 203–225. https://doi.org/10.2307/747792

Ozernov-Palchik, O., & Patel, A. D. (2018). Musical rhythm and reading development: Does beat processing matter? *Annals of the New York Academy of Sciences*, 1423(1), 166–175. https://doi.org/10.1111/nyas.13853

Pagani, L., Fitzpatrick, C., Archambault, I., & Janosz, M. (2010). School readiness and later achievement: A French Canadian replication and extension. *Developmental Psychology*, 46(5), 984–994. https://doi.org/10.1037/a0018881

Perry, B., & Dockett, S. (2008). Young children's access to powerful mathematical ideas. In L.D. English & D. Kirshner (Ed.), *Handbook of international research in mathematics education* (2nd ed.) (pp. 75–105). Lawrence Erlbaum.

Pianta, R., Downer, J., & Hamre, B. (2016). Quality in early education classrooms: Definitions, gaps, and systems. *The Future of Children*, 26(2), 119–137.

Piasta, S. B., Petscher, Y., & Justice, L. M. (2012). How many letters should preschoolers in public programs know? The diagnostic efficiency of various preschool letter-naming benchmarks for predicting first-grade literacy achievement. *Journal of Educational Psychology*, 104(4), 945–958. https://doi.org/10.1037/a0027757

Piasta, S. B., & Wagner, R.K. (2010). Developing early literacy skills: A meta-analysis of alphabetic learning and instruction. *Reading Research Quarterly*, 45(1), 8–38. https://doi.org/10.1598/RRQ.45.1.2

Rahayu, S., & Tytler, R. (1999). Progression in primary school children's conceptions of burning: Toward an understanding of the concept of substance. *Research in Science Education*, 29(3), 295–312. https://doi.org/10.1007/BF02461595

Raikes, H. H., White, L., Green, S., Burchinal, M., Kainz, K., Horm, D., Bingham, G., Cobo-Lewis, A., St. Clair, L., Greenfield, D., & Esteraich, J. (2019). Use of the home language in preschool classrooms and first- and second-language development among dual-language learners. *Early Childhood Research Quarterly*, 27(2), 145–158. https://doi.org/10.1016/j.ecresq.2018.06.012

Ramani, G. B., & Siegler, R. S. (2008). Promoting broad and stable improvements in low-income children's numerical knowledge through playing number board games. *Child Development*, 79(2), 375–394. https://doi.org/10.1111/j.1467-8624.2007.01131.x

Richards, R. D. (2018). Supporting young artists in making connections: Moving from mere recognition to perceptive art experiences. *The International Journal of Art and Design Education*, 37(1), 137–148. https://doi.org/10.1111/jade.12187

Riches, C., & Genesee, F. (2006). Cross-linguistic and cross-modal aspects of literacy development. In F. Genesee, K. Lindholm-Leary, W. Saunders, & D. Christian. *Educating English language* learners: A synthesis of research evidence (pp. 64–108). Cambridge University Press.

Rickards, F., Hattie, J., & Reid, C. (2021). *The turning point for the teaching profession. Growing expertise and evaluative thinking.* Routledge.

Roskos, K., & Neuman, S. (1998). Play as an opportunity for literacy. In O. N. Saracho & B. Spodek (Eds.), *Multiple perspectives on play in early childhood education* (pp. 100–115). SUNY Press.

Sarama, J., Lange, A., Clements, D., & Wolfe, C. (2012). The impacts of an early mathematics curriculum on oral language and literacy. *Early Childhood Research Quarterly, 27*(3), 489–502. https://doi .org/10.1016/j.ecresq.2011.12.002

Samarapungavan, A. (1992). Children's judgements in theory choice tasks: Scientific rationality in childhood. *Cognition, 45*(1), 1–32. https://doi .org/10.1016/0010-0277(92)90021-9

Scarborough, H. S. (2001). Connecting early language and literacy to later reading (dis)abilities: Evidence, theory, and practice. In S. Neuman & D. Dickinson (Eds.), *Handbook for research in early literacy* (pp. 97–110). Guilford Press.

Schulz, L. E., & Bonawitz, E. B. (2007). Serious fun: Preschoolers engage in more exploratory play when evidence is confounded. *Developmental Psychology, 43*(4), 1045–1050. https://doi .org/10.1037/0012-1649.43.4.1045

Shilling, W. A. (2002). Mathematics, music, and movement: Exploring concepts and connections. *Early Childhood Education Journal, 29*(3), 179–184. https:// doi.org/10.1023/A:1014536625850

Sodian, B., Zaitchik, D., & Carey, S. (1991). Young children's differentiation of hypothetical beliefs from evidence. *Child Development, 62*(4), 753–766. https://doi.org/10.2307/1131175

Sophian, C. (1999). Children's ways of knowing: Lessons from cognitive development research. In J. V. Copley (Ed.), *Mathematics in the early years* (pp. 11–20). NCTM.

Spooner, F., Knight, V., Browder, D. M., Jimenez, B., & DiBiase, W. (2011). Evaluating evidence-based practice in teaching science content to students with severe developmental disabilities. *Research and Practice for Persons With Severe Disabilities, 36*(1), 62–75. https:// doi.org/10.2511/rpsd.36.1-2.62

Stein, S. J., & McRobbie, C. J. (1997). Students' conceptions of science across the years of schooling. *Research in Science Education, 27,* 611–628. https://doi .org/10.1007/BF02461484

Stipek, D., Clements, D., Coburn, C., Franke, M., & Farran, D. (2017). PK–3: What does it mean for instruction? *Society for Research in Child Development, 30*(2), 1–23. https://doi .org/10.1002/j.2379-3988.2017.tb00087.x

Tai, R. H., Liu, C., Maltese, A. V., & Fan, X. (2006). Planning for early careers in science. *Science, 312*(5777), 1143–1144. https://doi.org/10.1126/science.1128690

Thunder, K. (2014, November 8). *Math foundation blocks.* [Professional Learning Workshop]. Training and Technical Assistance Center, Waynesboro, VA.

Thunder, K., Almarode, J., Fisher, D., & Frey, N. (2021). *Communicating clarity in the early childhood classroom* [Manuscript in preparation].

Thunder, K. & Demchak, A. (2017, November). *Student-centered assessment: Goal setting and young children* [Conference presentation]. National Association for the Education of Young Children Annual Conference, Atlanta, GA.

Thunder, K., & Demchak, A. (2020, March). *STEM challenges in early childhood classrooms* [Conference presentation]. Virginia Council of Teachers of Mathematics Annual Conference, Richmond, VA.

Tudge, J. R. H., & Doucet, F. (2004). Early mathematical experiences: Observing young Black and white children's everyday activities. *Early Childhood Research Quarterly, 19*(1), 21–39. https:// doi.org/10.1016/j.ecresq.2004.01.007

Tytler, R., & Peterson, S. (2003). Tracing young children's scientific reasoning. *Research in Science Education, 33*(4), 433–465. https://doi.org/10.1023/B:RISE .0000005250.04426.67

U.K. Department of Education. (2021). *Statutory framework for the Early Years*

Foundation Stage: Setting the standards for learning, development and care for children from birth to five. https://assets .publishing.service.gov.uk/government/ uploads/system/uploads/attachment_ data/file/974907/EYFS_framework_-_ March_2021.pdf

van der Fels, I. M. J., Te Wierike, S. C. M., Hartman. E., Elferink-Gemser, M. T., Smith, J., & Visscher, C. (2015). The relationship between motor skills and cognitive skills in 4-16 year old typically developing children: A systematic review. *Journal of Science and Medicine in Sport*, 18(6), 697–703. https://doi .org/10.1016/j.jsams.2014.09.007

Van de Walle, J. A., Karp, K. S., & Bay-Williams, J. M. (2019). *Elementary and middle school mathematics: Teaching developmentally* (10th ed.). Pearson.

Vélez-Ibáñez, C. G., & Greenberg, J. B. (1992). Formation and transformation of funds of knowledge. *Anthropology and Education Quarterly*, 23(4), 313–335.

Virginia Department of Education. (2012). *Practices for science investigation: Kindergarten-physics progression*. Author.

Virginia Department of Education. (2021). *Virginia's early learning and development standards (ELDS): Birth–five learning guidelines*. https://www.doe.virginia .gov/early-childhood/curriculum/va-elds-birth-5.pdf

Visible Learning Meta^X. (2021, February). https://www.visiblelearningmetax.com/

Wasik, B. A., & Jacobi-Vessels, J. L. (2017). Word play: Scaffolding language development through child-directed play. *Early Childhood Journal*, 45(6), 769–776. https:// doi.org/10.1007/s10643-016-0827-5

Wellman, H. M., & Liu, D. (2004). Scaling of theory-of-mind tasks. *Child Development*, 75(2), 523-541.

Wood Ray, K., & Glover, M. (2008). *Already ready: Nurturing writers in preschool and kindergarten*. Heinemann.

Zachopoulou, E., Tsapakidou, A., & Derri, V. (2004). The effects of a developmentally appropriate music movement program on motor performance. *Early Childhood Research Quarterly*, 19(4), 631–642. https://doi.org/10.1016/j.ecresq .2004.10.005

Zinsser, K. M., Christensen, C. G., & Torres, L. (2016). She's supporting them; who's supporting her? Preschool center-level social-emotional supports and teacher well-being. *Journal of School Psychology*, 59, 55–66. https://doi.org/10.1016/j.jsp .2016.09.001

CHILDREN'S LITERATURE

Aardema, V. (2000). *Anansi does the impossible!: An Ashanti tale*. Aladdin.

Adler, D. A. (2017). *Magnets push, magnets pull*. Holiday House.

Beaty, A. (2016). *Ada Twist, scientist*. Harry N. Abrams.

Carle, E. (1994). *The very hungry caterpillar*. Philomel Books.

Cherry, M. (2019). *Hair love*. Kokila.

Cronin, B. B. (2016). *The lost house*. Viking Books for Young Readers.

Dobkin, B. (2010). *Anansi and his children*. Teaching Strategies.

Kimmel, E. A. (2002). *Anansi and the magic stick*. Holiday House.

Lowell, S. (1992). *The three little javelinas*. Cooper Square Publishing, LLC.

Mora, O. (2019). *Saturday*. Little, Brown Books for Young Readers.

Pallotta, J. (2016). *Komodo dragon vs. King cobra (Who would win?)*. Scholastic Inc.

Pallotta, J. (2016). *Tarantula vs. Scorpion (Who would win?)*. Scholastic Inc.

Pinkney, J. (2009). *The lion and the mouse*. Little, Brown Books for Young Readers.

Pinkney, J. (2013). *The tortoise and the hare*. Little, Brown Books for Young Readers.

Willems, M. (2008). *Are you ready to play outside? (An elephant and piggie book)*. Hyperion Books for Children.

Willems, M. (2013). *A big guy took my ball! (An elephant and piggie book)*. Hyperion Books for Children.

Index

for classroom discussion, 25, 43, 52, 66, 98, 101, 111, 121, 127, 138, 185, 187, 195, 199, 205, 215, 217
for cognitive task analysis, 59, 85, 120, 136, 174, 193, 201, 210, 221
for collaborative learning, 114, 126, 201, 213, 214
for collective teacher efficacy, 30, 129, 162
for concentration/persistence/engagement, 20, 51, 100, 152, 185, 213
for concept mapping, 25, 47, 56, 70, 82, 177, 210
for cooperative learning, 25, 60, 73
for creativity, 60, 126
for deep motivation and approach, 15
for deliberate instruction, 25, 51, 83, 95, 97, 106, 116
for deliberate practice, 42, 45, 54, 147, 150, 156, 167, 178, 194, 198, 203, 205, 210, 222, 231
for elaborative interrogation, 98, 118, 131
for explicit teaching strategies, 106, 145, 153, 231
for family involvement, 29, 38, 44,48, 99, 121, 130, 155, 161, 174, 176, 184, 188, 203, 227, 233
for feedback, 20, 46, 75, 87, 106, 136, 162, 167, 202, 211, 217, 223
for goal commitment, 160, 174, 185, 225, 233
for goal difficulty, 15
for help seeking, 142, 173, 210, 217, 226
for imagery, 24, 25, 56, 66, 68, 128, 148, 185, 190, 209
for inquiry-based teaching, 45, 62, 130
for integrated curricula, 57, 130, 131, 182, 190, 196, 204
for learning intentions, 21
for manipulatives, 25, 66, 79, 128, 148, 185, 190
for mathematics, 67
for meta-cognitive strategies, 20, 24, 26, 36, 63, 77, 105, 116, 117, 126, 142, 162, 186, 190, 209, 222
for micro-teaching, 42
for mnemonics, 96
for peer- and self-feedback, 168, 195, 224
for peer- and self-grading, 89, 154
for phonics instruction, 95
for planning and predicting, 59, 79, 133, 191
for problem-solving teaching, 26, 133, 160
for providing formative evaluation, 75, 102, 145, 215, 217, 225, 232
for questioning, 25, 81, 144, 186, 201, 210, 215, 218
for rehearsal and memorization, 58, 108, 183, 188, 200
for scaffolding, 55, 72, 81, 89, 107, 193, 226
for science laboratory programs, 125
for seeking feedback about impact on student learning, 30
for seeking help from peers, 20, 46, 87
for self-concept, 99, 125, 155, 161, 176, 213, 215, 232
for self-efficacy, 69, 98, 152, 169, 208, 213, 217, 232

for self-judgment and reflection, 20, 56, 61, 97, 108, 125, 133, 154, 167, 171, 202, 211, 224, 233
for self-questioning, 24, 25, 90, 112, 209, 226, 233
for self-regulation strategies, 28, 36, 126, 161, 163, 175, 194, 224, 227, 232
for self-verbalization, 24, 90, 112, 209, 226, 233
for small group learning, 58, 106, 137, 187
for spaced practice, 41, 70, 95, 127
for strategies to integrate with prior knowledge, 38, 52, 56, 66, 108, 129, 131, 139, 163, 198, 210, 213, 214, 218
for strategy monitoring, 20, 24, 26, 75, 90, 136, 149, 153, 175, 200, 209, 224, 227
for strong classroom cohesion, 169
for student-centered teaching, 28
for success criteria, 15, 21, 73
for summarization, 114
for task value, 113, 184, 213
for teacher clarity, 21, 43, 48, 52, 72, 144, 162, 165, 193, 208, 213, 217, 226
for teacher credibility, 129
for teacher estimates of achievement, 29
for teacher expectations, 30, 78, 112, 127, 163, 214, 220
for teacher and student expectations, 15
for teacher–student relationships, 63, 108, 110, 154, 161, 215
for teaching communication skills and strategies, 35, 169
for time on task, 88, 138, 185
for transfer strategies, 26, 69, 83, 88, 135, 152, 194, 221
for vocabulary instruction, 25, 35, 38, 39, 62, 80, 127, 153, 160, 231
for working memory, 183, 186
for writing programs, 196
efficacy, 15, 30, 124, 129, 207–8, 234
elaborative interrogation, 98, 118, 131. See also effect sizes
ELDS. See Early Learning and Development Standards
elephants, 163–65, 167–68, 200–202
emotions, 36–38, 65, 114, 168, 176–79, 216
  anchor chart, 177, 179
  emotional development, 13, 33, 159–63, 165–81
  emotional skills, 2, 159–61, 169
  emotion words, 160, 177, 179, 194
empathy, 36, 40, 122, 163–65, 167–68
empty spaces, 75, 77, 89
engineering, 132–38
English language learners, 128, 214
examinations, 96, 129, 138, 185
executive processing, 36, 39, 63
exemplars, 24, 209, 212
expectations, 9–10, 15, 24, 33
experiments, 109, 127, 138, 185
explicit teaching strategies, 106, 145, 153, 231. See also effect sizes

Build your
Visible Learning®
library!

VISIBLE LEARNING

**VISIBLE LEARNING
FOR TEACHERS**

**VISIBLE LEARNING
AND THE SCIENCE OF
HOW WE LEARN**

**VISIBLE LEARNING
INTO ACTION**

**INTERNATIONAL
GUIDE TO STUDENT
ACHIEVEMENT**

**VISIBLE LEARNING
FEEDBACK**

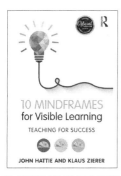

**10 MINDFRAMES FOR
VISIBLE LEARNING**

**10 MINDFRAMES
FOR LEADERS**

**GREAT TEACHING
BY DESIGN**

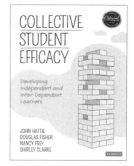

**COLLECTIVE
STUDENT EFFICACY**

**DEVELOPING
ASSESSMENT-
CAPABLE VISIBLE
LEARNERS,
Grades K–12**

**VISIBLE LEARNING
FOR LITERACY,
Grades K–12**

**TEACHING
LITERACY IN THE
VISIBLE LEARNING
CLASSROOM,
Grades K–5, 6–12**

**VISIBLE LEARNING
FOR MATHEMATICS,
Grades K–12**

**TEACHING MATHEMATICS IN THE
VISIBLE LEARNING CLASSROOM,
Grades K–2, 3–5, 6–8, & High School**

**VISIBLE LEARNING
FOR SCIENCE,
Grades K–12**

**VISIBLE LEARNING
FOR SOCIAL STUDIES,
Grades K–12**

CORWIN

CORWIN
A SAGE Publishing Company

Helping educators make the greatest impact

CORWIN HAS ONE MISSION: to enhance education through intentional professional learning.

We build long-term relationships with our authors, educators, clients, and associations who partner with us to develop and continuously improve the best evidence-based practices that establish and support lifelong learning.